COMMUNITY MUSIC IN OCEANIA

COMMUNITY MUSIC IN OCEANIA

Many Voices, One Horizon

Edited by Brydie-Leigh Bartleet,
Melissa Cain, Diana Tolmie, Anne Power,
and Mari Shiobara

University of Hawai'i Press
Honolulu

© 2018 University of Hawaiʻi Press
All rights reserved
Paperback edition 2021
Printed in the United States of America

26 25 24 23 22 21 6 5 4 3 2 1

Library of Congress Cataloging-in-Publication Data

Names: Bartleet, Brydie-Leigh, editor. | Cain, Melissa, editor. | Tolmie, Diana, editor. | Power, Anne (Professor of music education), editor. | Shiobara, Mari, editor.
Title: Community music in Oceania : many voices, one horizon / edited by Brydie-Leigh Bartleet, Melissa Cain, Diana Tolmie, Anne Power, and Mari Shiobara.
Description: Honolulu : University of Hawaiʻi Press, [2018] | Includes bibliographical references and index.
Identifiers: LCCN 2017043468 | ISBN 9780824867003 (cloth alk. paper)
Subjects: LCSH: Community music—Oceania—History and criticism. | Community music—Asia—History and criticism.
Classification: LCC ML3774 .C66 2018 | DDC 780.99—dc23
LC record available at https://lccn.loc.gov/2017043468

ISBN 978-0-8248-9256-2 (paperback)

University of Hawaiʻi Press books are printed on acid-free paper and meet the guidelines for permanence and durability of the Council on Library Resources.

Cover photograph by Diana Tolmie. Courtesy of the artist.

Contents

COMMUNITY MUSIC IN OCEANIA

CHAPTER 1

Community Music in the Asia Pacific

An Introduction

Brydie-Leigh Bartleet, Melissa Cain, Diana Tolmie, Anne Power, and Mari Shiobara

Community music as a field of practice, pedagogy, and research is continuing to come of age. Across the world, we have seen an exponential growth in projects, courses, programs, and research over the past decade. With this growth in practice and scholarship new debates about the nexus of practice, pedagogy, research, and ethics as well as new voices have emerged and begun to broaden the agenda to include settings where community music is engaging in social justice, political activism, peacemaking, health and well-being, and online engagement, among many other fields. As more and more practitioners from diverse cultural backgrounds have entered this space, we have witnessed a challenging and problematizing of accepted approaches, priorities, and ideas within the field. The increase of scholarship and academic courses have also significantly increased the number of people engaging in community music, and these new voices, agendas, and contexts indicate that the field is continuing to expand, diversify, and mature.

Practitioners of community music and scholars from the Asia Pacific region have been actively involved in these broader disciplinary developments. In 2010 a group of community musicians from the region gathered at the China National Convention Centre in Beijing during the 2010 International Society for Music Education (ISME) World Conference. Quite simply, we wanted to develop a network of community music practitioners and scholars in the Asia Pacific region. Inspired by the ISME Community Music Activity

(CMA) Commission we had just attended in Hangzhou the week before, we felt a pressing need to keep the seminar's momentum going. During the seminar we had heard many stories and examples of musical practices, community contexts, pedagogical approaches, and research ethics; however, set against the backdrop of this Chinese context, these familiar topics seemed to take on a new meaning (see Bartleet 2011). As we experienced the local culture and interacted with some of our Chinese colleagues, we were reminded that notions of what community music is and its social and educational functions are always fluid and varied depending on where you are in the world. After the seminar, our sense was that there are new voices and ideas relating to community music coming from this region that need to be heard. On the surface this goal seemed quite straightforward.

As we began conceptualizing what this network would look like and how it might function in more concrete terms this supposedly straightforward task became very complicated. We wrestled with what we meant by "Asia Pacific" and where we would draw our boundaries (if at all); we grappled with the diversity of musical practices, cultural politics, and educational systems found in this region and how we could bridge these worlds. We settled on the idea that the Asia Pacific could include, but was not limited to, East Asia, South and Southeast Asia, and Oceania and kept engagement with this network open to community music practitioners and scholars who live and work in this region or to those from other parts of the world who focus on this region in their work. We then became entangled in discussions about the intersections of traditional and contemporary musical practices in this region and the challenges of cultural sustainability and legacies of colonization still exerting impact upon the dynamics of many of these cultural practices. As our conversations went on, a range of pragmatic and logistical issues also arose in the form of difficulties in facilitating meetings across such vast geographical distances and communicating with one another and publishing our work in so many different languages. But in the spirit of many community-driven projects like this one, we decided it was worth taking up the challenge and seeing where it would lead. Since then we have produced a special issue journal of the *International Journal of Community Music* (5.1) on practices within the region and hosted an inaugural seminar in Brisbane, Australia, in 2013 in conjunction with the International Music Council's (IMC) World Forum on Music. The Asia Pacific Community Music Network (APCMN) seminar brought together community music practitioners and scholars to celebrate and explore the music-making practices, pedagogies, and cultural politics that are currently shaping community music in this region. Delegates presented work from Australia, China, Japan, Korea, Fiji, Aotearoa New Zealand, and Singapore. In 2015 we held our second seminar in Japan and brought together another group of community musicians from Australia, Aotearoa New Zealand, Malaysia, India, the United States, the United Kingdom, and Japan. This publication continues the efforts of the network to serve as a vehicle for activating relationships between these practitioners and scholars, as well as a channel for developing cross-cultural partnerships and disseminating research about community music in this region.

As editors we are committed to fostering further collaborations and knowledge sharing within our region. Collectively we have worked in a number of locations across the area including Australia, Japan, Singapore, Thailand, China, and Taiwan. Thus, although all of us find ourselves in an environment that has a long history of non-Western values and culture, we are equally mindful of the colonial influences of Europe and other Asian colonial empires in our region. Balancing the culturally diverse and complex approaches to scholarship, the construction of knowledge, the embodiment of musical practices, and the ethics of cross-cultural interactions, as well as our own agendas as community musicians and educators has not been an easy task. We have seen practices and ways of thinking about community music rub up against "interventionist" models commonly accepted by colleagues in the Northern Hemisphere, particularly in the UK. However, we have been willing to challenge our western European concepts of music making and even knowledge itself, and have worked from the premise that the way forward requires us to engage with the process of both critiquing and personalizing our cultural experiences and embodied understandings. Indigenous Australian scholar Martin Nakata calls us to act on these tensions that arise from the "interfaces" between cultures and embrace the new insights that can emerge from such spaces. As Nakata (2002, 15) suggests, "what is certain is that the intersections of different knowledges, systems, concerns and priorities will converge to inform and develop new practices in this area." What he argues is that, without a struggle, without these tensions, there is only the voice of a single dominant culture being heard. It is this struggle that we hope to represent here as an introduction to the colorful and diverse musics and practices that form this region's community music landscape.

The chapters in this volume strongly resonate with the ideas and insights we have discussed in relation to both the literature and our own work, and provide illuminating stories and analyses of the dynamics, realities, and future possibilities of community music making in this region. Perspectives are shared from Japan, Fiji, Aotearoa New Zealand, China, Australia, Taiwan, Malaysia, Singapore, and Korea. We have organized these chapters into three overarching sections that focus on musical traditions, broader social justice, and interdisciplinary intersections, and lastly music learning and teaching.

In the first introductory section, authors look at ways of maintaining and evolving musical traditions in community music making across a wide range of cultural contexts. Gillian Howell's chapter seeks to map the diversity of community music in Timor-Leste and to explore the role that community music making plays in the experience of national development, rebuilding, and future thinking there. Te Oti Rakena then describes the implementation of the *Tuvalu: Pacific Project,* a research collaboration made up of indigenous creative artists from three partner institutions in his chapter. In his chapter he discusses the challenges of establishing and sustaining research partnerships within the current tertiary sector and touches on the dynamics of indigenous researchers researching "other" indigenous populations. It also highlights the importance of diminishing an eco-colonial gaze by embodying the Māori concept of *whanaungatanga.*

Mari Shiobara's chapter looks at issues that surround the transmittal of Japanese folk song and strategies for nationalizing the local and taking it into schools. In particular, her chapter examines four main issues with the transmission of *min'yō.* These include folk songs that have been standardized but were subsequently modified from their original meaning; traditional informal community singing being replaced by performance, often in competitive situations; music teachers' lack of familiarity with this genre and who are therefore likely to rely on teachers sent by the association; and lastly, *min'yō*'s informal teaching strategies being formalized by the association before reaching students in schools. With these issues in mind, this chapter explores possible solutions concerned with how and in what ways these traditional Japanese folk songs can be taught while trying to maintain their originally intended essence.

Jennifer Cattermole's chapter then examines teaching and learning in Fijian *sigidrigi.* She discusses the varying degrees of formality in *sigidrigi* tuition (ranging from casual observation to formal apprenticeship), as well as the variety of contexts in which *sigidrigi* teaching and learning take place (e.g., during public performances, in private, in schools, during child's play). In particular, she looks at some of the factors that restrict learners' engagement with the genre and thus threaten its sustainability (e.g., their musical proficiency, gender, age and social status; the amount of free time they have available; and the availability of musical instruments).

Christian Mau's chapter focuses on the case of the Myōan *shakuhachi's benkyō-kai.* He looks at the *shakuhachi* in a "religious" context, but takes the investigation inside a temple to a more formalized or institutionalized setting. He discusses the way in which, rather than serving as peripheral accessory to a "religious" tradition, it is the *shakuhachi* itself that binds this particular community's existence. In so doing, he considers the criteria involved in forming this particular community, which includes some of the historical factors, but also other considerations, such as the repertoire itself and how studying it as a group not only contributes to defining the community but also reinforces and sustains it.

Lastly, Karyn Paringatai's chapter investigates *Hei te pō, hei te ao* (singing in the dark) through the lens of the revival of an indigenous teaching methodology. In this chapter she discusses the origins of Māori thought, and the use of *waiata* (songs) and *haka* (chanted forms of performance) to transmit this knowledge in its entirety. She describes how this particular method involves immersing students in darkness in order for them to learn the words and tunes to various *haka* and *waiata.* The emphasis is then placed on oral communication and the enhancement of aural receptive skills; both of which suffered upon European arrival to New Zealand. Karyn then discusses the implications of including this particular methodology in a university classroom.

The Part II examines community music and broader social justice considerations and interdisciplinary intersections in the Asia Pacific. Phil Mullen's chapter explores the development of a performance with people with intellectual challenges during the 2012 Beijing Traditional Music Festival. In particular his chapter looks at community music processes underlying the project such as inclusion, differentiation, and empowerment and giving a voice to those who may in the past not have had regular access to music performance and development. He discusses the ways in which the performance addressed issues of social justice and well-being in terms of the participants' acceptance and reception by a public audience in a prestigious venue. Kirstin Robertson-Gillam's chapter then touches on community music therapy and offers examples from Australia to discuss how this is a viable approach for working musically with socially disadvantaged and isolated people living in the community. She gives examples and vignettes of community music therapy in action, ranging from treating disabilities, mental health, care of the aged, and palliative care, and discusses how this approach builds collaborative health communal activities, thus contributing to the ecological balance of culture and society.

Julie Rickwood's chapter discusses the "Big Sing in the Desert" program, which is run in central Australia. In particular her chapter looks at the ways in which many community choirs have sought to find ways to capture and reflect reconciliation and national identity through singing these songs, even though most are dislocated from the indigenous musics they sing. She also examines how other choirs or choral events bring indigenous and nonindigenous singers together into a cross-cultural exchange or collaboration, which can result in very different musical practices. Her chapter looks at the ways in which these musical encounters can introduce songs that unsettle nonindigenous assumptions regarding indigenous musics and explores the various ways in which "traditional" and "contemporary" indigenous musics are introduced and circulated in community choral networks. Continuing with the theme work community music practices within indigenous contexts, Anne Power, Brydie-Leigh Bartleet, and Dawn Bennett's chapter explores the experiences and reflections of groups of university students who have engaged in arts-based service learning with Australian Aboriginal students and communities over the past six years. Using Yunkaporta's (2009) "8 Ways Framework." their chapter touches on some of the key transformative learning experiences shared by these arts students and pre-service teachers, and discusses broader implications of this framework for arts-based service-learning programs with First Peoples.

Lastly, David Lines' chapter looks at the themes of emergence, care, and sustainability through the lens of a community arts project in early childhood. His chapter examines a project that involved community artists (music, dance drama) working with teachers and young children in Auckland, New Zealand. In his chapter David shares how these themes developed, using examples of multiple voices of involved artists, teachers, children, parents, and researchers, and discusses some of the preliminary findings and what they mean for community music and early childhood programs in the New Zealand context.

In the third part authors reflect on a range of learning and teaching dynamics that can be found in community music contexts in the Asia Pacific region. Jennifer Walden's chapter opens with the idea of stepping outside the classroom and exploring the wealth of community musics at your doorstep. As she explains, many music programs in international schools proceed through a fairly predictable program of study, following a guided curriculum that is often based on Western music, and points out that what tends to get overlooked is the wealth of cultural resources existing in surrounding communities, and often even within the school itself. Ironically, many of the musical concepts and sociocultural issues covered in international school curricula can be supplemented and enhanced through connections with community musicians in the host country. Walden's chapter takes a journey through three Asian countries (Taiwan, Malaysia, and Singapore) from her perspective as an international school music teacher and examines steps involved in building school–community relations and the lessons learned through making connections with community musicians.

Eugene Dairianathan and Lum Che Hoo's chapter looks at Shuo Chang as burden in song and *Xinyao* and education communities of practice in Singapore. Their chapter reflects on enactments by various agencies in their negotiation and navigation of *Xinyao:* as language of choice; of language in songs associated with music of adolescence; as language connoted with local popular culture; and eventually on language as political marker, namely national identity. In their chapter they draw on *Xinyao* songs, recalling Gayatri Spivak's (1993) articulation of the concept of "burden" of the teaching of English in India but also its special relevance in musical practice as well as continuities of such practices. This chapter hopes to explore how *Xinyao* is continued and sustained as a venue through communities in education. Continuing with the focus on Singapore, Leonard Tan and Melissa Cain then focus on the community band experience in Singapore through two lenses: the local and the expatriate. Leonard and Melissa recount their experiences with community bands in Singapore via two separate autobiographical accounts written independently and explore four distinct but interrelated themes: continuity, community, glocality, and identity. Their chapter then outlines the implications for community music and music education.

Joanne Ruksenas' chapter looks at how a music program can build and sustain a community. It discusses the role and influence of "Aria Angels," an early childhood music program in Brisbane, Australia, focusing in particular on how active engagement with this kind of music making can influence the development of resilience in preschool-aged children. The final two chapters focus on pedagogy and engagement within community and education contexts. Naomi Cooper looks at techniques and tools for music learning in Australian community choirs. This chapter examines the teaching and learning practices occurring in Australian community choirs, including aural, visual, and physical transmission approaches that are used for teaching parts, rhythm, groove, pitch, expression, keeping a song going, vocal technique, memory devices, ensemble technique, and embodied singing. Diana Tolmie's chapter then looks at engaging with sax beyond the conservatorium walls and documents the community engagement activities of the Queensland Conservatorium Saxophone Orchestra (QCSO). Her chapter explores the QCSO student perspectives of music education (tertiary, secondary, and primary), focusing in particular on strengthening community engagement, enterprise, and networking, plus their regard for creating meaningful music within and beyond their degree. Diana's chapter offers an outline of the resultant implications and recommendations for this model that may serve as a guide for other tertiary music institutions wishing to integrate similar programs.

This arrangement of chapters offers a diverse range of perspectives and practices relating to community music in this region, hence our subtitle "Many Voices." While these chapters stand independently as musical lines in themselves, they also come together to paint an insightful picture of the ways in which practitioners and scholars are conceptualizing community music in this region. And although the perspectives given in these chapters share many common themes and contours in terms of the pedagogies and practices used and the values surrounding accessibility and community engagement, thus pointing us all towards "one horizon," they also provide contrasting realities when it comes to the specifics of how community musicians fit into the musical ecosystems of their respective cultural contexts.

Moreover, taken together, the chapters also bring to view perspectives on the development and delivery of community music practices that are quite specific to this region. As we have already mentioned, in some respects this is in contrast to the "interventionist" methods so commonly used in the Northern Hemisphere. The Asia Pacific covers a large area, and its inhabitants face not only difficulties in sustaining their music cultures but also unique challenges in their physical environments and political contexts. All these factors have a bearing on the ways in which community music operates in such locales. In this region there is also much greater predominance of what might be called "organic" approaches to community music, whereby community music practices are frequently connected to long-standing cultural traditions. Collectively, the chapters illuminate these points through discussions about the maintenance and recontextualization of musical traditions, the lingering impact of colonization, the growing demands for professionalization of community music, the implications of government policies, tensions among various ethnic groups within countries, and the role of institutions such as universities in community music across the region. Likewise, they also highlight the transformative nature of community music in terms of providing activities, opportunities, and outcomes for intellectually challenged, marginalized, disadvantaged, plus socially and/or geographically isolated music participants in this region. This edited volume does not seek to engage in the problematic task of synthesizing these themes in a reductionist manner, but rather aims to produce an intricate and illuminating picture that collectively highlights the diversity of practices, pedagogies, and research currently shaping community music in the Asia Pacific.

References

Bartleet, B.-L. 2011. "Connections in China: Harmonizing Stories of Community Music from around the World." *International Journal of Community Music* 4 (1): 7–14.

Nakata, Martin. 2002. "Indigenous Knowledge and the Cultural Interface: Underlying Issues at the Intersection of Knowledge and Information Systems." *IFLA Journal* 28 (5–6): 280–291. doi:10.1177/034003520202800513.

Yunkaporta, T. 2009. "Aboriginal Pedagogies at the Cultural Interface." PhD diss., James Cook University, Townsville. Retrieved from http://eprints.jcu.edu.au/10974/4/04Bookchapter.pdf.

PART I

Maintaining and Evolving Traditions in Community Music Making

CHAPTER 2

Mapping Community Music Development in Timor-Leste

Gillian Howell

It was 5 a.m. when the little wooden fishing boat pulled away from the shore and began to cross the straits that separated the island of Atauro from mainland Timor-Leste and the port of Dili. My travel companions were sleeping on the deck in the dawn's damp half-light, but the noise and vibrations of the boat's engine were too vigorous for me, and so I sat up and shakily made my way forward to join the ship's captain at the bow of the boat. He was singing out to sea at the top of his voice. I asked in my halting beginner's Tetun if he would mind if I filmed him. He didn't mind, in fact, he enjoyed the attention. "I know lots of songs, all sorts of songs" he told me. At least, that was what I thought he said. I'd only been learning Tetun for two weeks at that time. His songs praised God and Jesus, but they did not sound like transplanted Christian songs composed elsewhere and translated into Tetun. The melodic lines had a free, unfettered quality to them, a full-voiced, declamatory boldness with audacious swoops from the top of the voice to the lowest range, as if written to be sung from a mountaintop, or to gather the masses. The singer moved fluidly through the notes of a pentatonic scale, leaping octaves with ease. "I love to sing" he told me at the end of one song. "I sing everyday—to the water, to the fish, to whoever." His crewmate, curled on the deck right at the boat's prow, started to laugh at this, but then seemed to find it less remarkable, and took himself off to the back of the boat so that the captain could keep singing and I could keep filming, while the sun rose and Dili Harbour came slowly into view.

—Vignette drawn from Gillian Howell, "Dawn Songs"

The opening vignette offers an idea of the ease and ubiquity of music making and music sharing in Timor-Leste. Particularly in rural areas, people often burst into song. Such casualness marks it as both a remarkable (in contrast to the uneasy engagement with music among the general public in my own context, Australia) and an unremarkable (in being barely worthy of remark among Timorese people) phenomenon for me.

My first visit to the tiny half-island of East Timor, or Timor-Leste as it is officially named, took place in 2010. I travelled there from Australia to work as a visiting musician in a rural town for four months, engaging with local children, instrument makers, and educational programs to develop a community music project on behalf of a culture-focused nongovernment organization (NGO). During that project, I observed many aspects of people's engagement with music, such as the strong desire of many people—particularly children—to learn more and have new experiences in music. They were filled with curiosity and eager to participate and interact.

There were few formal opportunities for them to do this, for in poverty-ridden, newly independent Timor-Leste, education infrastructure and curricula were at that time, and still are, evolving, with the requirements for large-scale physical infrastructure preoccupying most government decisions and spending. Nevertheless, music was important to the people, and music-making opportunities were "[taken] with both hands" (Howell and Dunphy 2012) and seen as opportunities for personal development, which in turn could help their country grow and prosper.

This chapter seeks to map the diversity of community music in Timor-Leste and to explore the role that community music making plays in the experience of national development, rebuilding, and future thinking in Timor-Leste. It builds on my first experiences of Timorese community music (see Howell 2012a; Howell 2012b, 2013; Howell and Dunphy 2012) along with more recent data gathered during five weeks of fieldwork done in 2014. The ethnographic data draws upon observation of music activities and interviews with numerous musicians, community music project leaders, and government representatives.

The researcher-practitioner perspective with which I write has some limitations: for example, my rudimentary local language skills and the brevity of time I spent in-country mean that there may be nuances that I have missed in my interpretation. I foreground the voices of the research participants in an effort to counteract this. Furthermore, Timor-Leste's music scene and the different activities on offer are highly mutable, a reflection of the challenges of sustaining community music activities in developing country contexts. Programs that were thriving at the time of fieldwork may have begun to flounder a year or several years later. Therefore, this chapter offers a snapshot in time of the diversity of activities under way.

A key finding of this research has been to identify the multiple roles played by the Catholic Church and its representatives in enabling and supporting community music in Timor-Leste. For this reason, I consider the historical development of the Timorese Catholic Church in the overview of the events that have informed Timor-Leste's current sociocultural-political environment. Following this, I identify and map the approaches to community music making in Timor-Leste that I found. From there, I discuss a recurrent theme that wove its way into many of the research participants' narratives—that of the central role being played by the Catholic Church and its clergy in Timor-Leste's community music. In sum, I show how community music is an important tool for realizing people's personal development goals, as well as a vehicle through which individuals can contribute to national development goals, findings that have relevance to other developing nations and economies elsewhere in the Asia-Pacific region.

Colonization, Conflict, and Catholicism in Timor-Leste

The recent history of Timor-Leste is one of occupation, conflict, and rebuilding. Mapped upon this is a parallel narrative of national identity, and the role and place of religious faith in the development of nationhood. As a far-flung outpost of the Portuguese colonial empire, the half-island of East Timor was plundered for its sandalwood and utilized as a convenient place of exile for dissidents and delinquents but scarcely developed by its colonial rulers. Catholic missionaries arrived as part of the Portuguese colonial apparatus. Initially, like the ruling elite, they were based largely in coastal areas, although during the early twentieth century they moved into the mountainous interior and over the centuries provided basic health and education services throughout the country (McGregor, Skeaff, and Bevan 2012).

Then, after five hundred years of Portuguese colonization and a short-lived and violently contested period of independence, Indonesia invaded and annexed the half-island in December 1975. The invasion was forcible, and executed with considerable violence. It subjected the Timorese people to twenty-four years of punitive military occupation, during which the occupiers engaged in tactics of coercion and control including constant human rights violations, starvation, massacres, "disappearances," and the proscription of any markers of Timorese culture and national identity (Post-CAVR Technical Secretariat 2013).

The invasion was strongly resisted by the Timorese people. An armed resistance, supported by civilian clandestine networks, worked to disrupt and damage the occupier's military apparatus. Resistance was also expressed in more subtle ways. For example, at the time of the Indonesian invasion, only 30 percent of the population identified as Catholic (Cristalis 2009, 61). Imposition of the Indonesian national development ideology of Pancasila, which required all citizens to identify as following one of six recognized world religions, saw Catholicism in East Timor rise dramatically. The people turned to Catholicism as an affirmation of Timorese identity and way of asserting that they were *not* Indonesians, even if their religious conviction remained only a tenuous veneer over centuries of animism (Cristalis 2009; McGregor, Skeaff, and Bevan 2012). By 1994, 90 percent of the population had embraced Catholicism, making it the largest per-capita Catholic population in Asia (McGregor, Skeaff, and Bevan 2012). During this period, Catholicism and Timorese national identity became inextricably bound.

Unlike during the colonial era, when the Catholic Church and its missions were clearly aligned with the Portuguese state, the Catholic Church during Indonesian times was an outspoken and courageous defender of the Timorese people and a critic of the Indonesian government. As one of the only international organizations permitted to work in Timor throughout the occupation, the Church provided a safe haven to the Timorese people in material ways, sheltering vulnerable people—the displaced, those fearing military violence, resistance fighters, members of the clandestine support network, orphans, and others—and providing food, education, and basic medical care for the neediest of the population. During times of crisis, Church personnel and facilities sheltered thousands of refugees (McGregor, Skeaff, and Bevan 2012; Silva 2008).

The Church also provided deep spiritual and cultural support for the Timorese people, acting to protect and cherish Timorese culture, offering a space for people to gather in their shared opposition to the occupation, and "providing a discourse of martyrdom to understand the death and sacrifice of the Timorese victims of the regime" (Hodge 2012, 327). The liturgy was presented in the local language of Tetun, further "strengthening the cultural identity of the Timorese while ostracising the occupier" (McGregor, Skeaff, and Bevan 2012, 1135). Church personnel documented and spoke out internationally against human rights abuses in Timor-Leste and advocated vociferously for Timorese self-determination.

In 1999, a UN-sponsored popular referendum declared the Timorese people's collective desire for independence. The Indonesian military and their proxy militias retaliated with vengeful acts of extreme brutality that inflicted yet more violence upon the population and destroyed more than 70 percent of the country's infrastructure—roads, public and private buildings, essential services, telecommunications, and more (Chomsky 2003; East Timor Government 2008; Kingsbury and Leach 2007). The newly independent Democratic Republic of Timor-Leste needed to rebuild its country and institutions of state and civil society literally from the ground up.

A large-scale international project of stabilization, state-building, and reconstruction ensued, led by the United Nations. Multiple UN agencies, other government and development bank agencies, NGOs, and faith-based agencies have been active and ubiquitous participants in Timor-Leste since the 1999 referendum. Some scholars have argued that the secular mindsets of the major donor agencies did not recognize the tremendous reach and social trust the Catholic Church enjoyed throughout the country, nor its political influence. It was frequently sidelined as a contributor to the large-scale nation-building and state-building endeavor (McGregor, Skeaff, and Bevan 2012).

Six Constitutional Governments of the Democratic Republic of Timor-Leste (at time of writing) have been convened. Although the United Nations' political mission ended in 2012, there remains a considerable international aid agency presence across the country. Timor-Leste's complex raft of human development needs—low rates of education, high child mortality, poor access to essential services, high unemployment—and the corresponding need for external assistance to address these has ensured that these agencies remain a pervasive influence and provider of opportunities for the Timorese people. At the same time, much development progress has been made in little more than a decade of independence, and the Timorese people are strongly invested in the future prosperity and stability of their country. National narratives recall the long collective struggle for independence, and posit that the future development of the country will be a similarly collective endeavor. In this framing, development is very much a shared project in which every person has a part to play.

Community Music as Music Development

What should be included in the scope of a survey of community music in Timor-Leste? Without a clearly delineated professional class of musicians, and no provision for music in the national school curriculum, it could be argued that *all* music-making activity in Timor-Leste is in fact community music, grounded as it is in local communities of shared geography, faith, and interest. However, such a broadly sweeping and inclusive definition is not particularly helpful in a complex post-conflict, intercultural environment, as it sheds limited light on epistemologies of community music—the *how* and *why* of opportunities for music participation and learning, and the structures that sustain them.

Taking my lead from the many research participants that spoke of their music activities in terms of impacting both personal and national development needs, I focus on community music activities where the endeavor had a development or change intention. In other words, the community music projects examined in this chapter are those in which participants and organizers understand their efforts in the present as influencing or contributing to a desired future development outcome. These are frequently expressed in terms of people's personal goals of development (towards education, livelihoods, personal growth, and new opportunities). For many this is also understood as progress for their nation, in that the national agenda will benefit. Such a mindset is not exclusive to Timor-Leste, nor to developing country contexts; however, the frequent evoking of national progress or developmental needs when discussing music activities is certainly less prevalent in high-income countries like Australia.

I therefore use the terms "community music" and "music development" interchangeably throughout this chapter. The following examples of community music activity are by no means exhaustive; however, they demonstrate a range of music-making opportunities that encourage individuals or groups to develop new skills and improve their musicianship or performance work, to connect with others, and to draw comfort, healing, and meaning from the experiences. Research informants frequently cited the social outcomes as contributing to the national interest.

Social Music-Skills Development through Interaction with More Learned Others

One of the key ingredients of community music making in Timor-Leste is the prevalence of unstructured, informal learning, where a person with greater knowledge helps another person—a learner—to get started or improve. This "more learned other" is not necessarily an expert, and the context in which the learning happens is primarily social and serendipitous, rather than scheduled and planned.

Learning music in this way in Timor-Leste, given the limited access to instruments, limited formal pedagogical knowledge and even more limited direct experience of sound pedagogical techniques, demands considerable perseverance on the part of the learner. Etson (bass guitarist and songwriter with popular band Galaxy, and a highly regarded local music expert and teacher) described the way he hung around the older boys in his town who knew how to play guitar:

> I started by watching the guitarists that I thought played really well, and tried to copy what they did. Then, there was a friend, Jario, who would come to my house in the evening. He was teaching my older brother to play guitar and he asked me if I wanted to learn too. At first he started teaching me the very basic chords, and then some others. At that time I didn't have a guitar so I had to borrow friends' guitars. Starting from learning that way I was able to learn to sing and play chords on my own.
>
> So I kept learning, little bit by little bit. Sometimes when older guys in the community took part in festivals, everyone would get into the circle and play together and if there were chords that I didn't know I would watch their hands closely and then when I got home I would practice those new chords on my friend's guitar. (Etson, bass guitarist and music teacher, interview, May 26, 2014)

For some, their participation in religious worship led to opportunities to join choirs or contribute in some way to the music required for mass and other services that required only basic musical skills. For example, António described how, as a regular attendee at the Balide Church in Dili, he "started being an acolyte, serving the priest, and then after that they said, you can join the choir, feel free—so I did. And I started to play the organ, slowly. . . . I was taught by one fellow there, just the chords. And I started to accompany the choir then" (António, May 27, 2014).

Others began their learning in similarly informal ways, guided by a more learned other, but later had opportunities to take part in a structured program: "In 2006 I started doing music by joining a band. I learned how to play guitar from my friends, in that group. . . . But then, my friend asked me to play the bass guitar so that we would have all the instruments. And we helped each other in the group, so I decided to play bass guitar at that time. Then in 2009 I went to Arte Moris when they started the music program" (Nelson, bass guitarist and tutor at Arte Moris, interview, June 5, 2014).

These informal and social exchanges of knowledge take place with "more learned" Timorese people, and also with foreigners. As a result of the large-scale international aid effort, many foreigners ("international people") have come to Timor-Leste for short and longer periods of time, and some of them have "shared skills and experiences with staff and some of the artists here [at Arte Moris], and that's a good thing that's happened" (Etson, interview, May 26, 2014).

Many of the musicians that learned in these social and informal ways described themselves as "self-taught," even though their descriptions included influential people in teaching roles. However, the "self-taught" descriptor is apt, because the learner's motivation and determination remain the critical factors for success in music learning and development. These examples demonstrate the way that social, informal music making is an important site for individual music development in communities across Timor-Leste.

Informal Learning in Non-formal Settings

In addition, some young people in Timor-Leste take up opportunities to learn music in *non-formal* environments—here, the word "non-formal" is used to refer to community contexts that are outside formal schooling and other educational institutions yet where the music making is led by adults (D'Amore 2014). I visited three sites where "non-formal" music learning was taking place, focused primarily on guitar, keyboard, and rock band instruments.

At Arte Moris (the school mentioned by Nelson and Etson in the previous section), a six-month Rock School program was under way during the fieldwork period. Students paid a US$5 registration fee to access the program, and could learn rock band instruments (guitar, bass, drums, and vocals) from established local rock bands, form their own bands, perform in a showcase concert, and have the opportunity to record their work in the Arte Moris studio. They also took part in "Stomp," a dynamic percussion ensemble featuring "junk percussion" instruments and many "found object" sounds, performing on occasion in local festivals and community events. After attending five days a week (in the mornings or afternoons) for six months, the students received a certificate acknowledging their participation and achievement, and were encouraged to continue accessing Arte Moris facilities and equipment if they wanted to keep rehearsing as a band after completing their course.

The Rock School program was not receiving any outside funding. The teaching staff was not paid for their time, describing their work as part of their contribution to Arte Moris (which runs as an artist collective with many of its artists living on site) and acknowledging a sense of obligation to "give back" and "pass on" knowledge about music that they felt fortunate to have been able to develop over the previous years at Arte Moris. The school included alumni among its teaching staff, like Nelson, a former student of Etson's and participant in the first Rock School music course, who "feels really proud to have been involved and that he can now be here teaching as well" (Etson, interview, May 26, 2014).

Ba Futuru's After-school Music Club was a shorter-term, more informal program. Ba Futuru (For the Future) is a local NGO offering a range of learning and participation programs for young people focused on conflict resolution and human rights education. Led by a local multi-instrumentalist, the Music Club gathered a group of teenage boys and girls three times a week to learn the basics of guitar, ukulele, or mandolin. Over the twelve-week course, they learned to sing and play a number of popular songs and presented them in a showcase concert in the final week.

> An important thing that we are more focused on is the community songs. That means those songs that, when you sing, the community also can sing with you . . . an important thing is to sing the song that the audience all understand about [recognize] the song, so everyone will sing together with you and then they will say, "Ah! He's great! He's a great one! He's a great singer! Because he knows what we want, he knows what songs we want!" (Vincent, Ba Futuru Music Club co-tutor and coordinator, June 11, 2014).

The community songs to which Vincent refers are a collection with considerable social and emotional power that play a tangible role in reinforcing feelings of national identity, pride, and shared history. Because of this, there is considerable social status associated with knowing how to play and lead these songs.

A third non-formal music development program on offer in Dili during the fieldwork period was a program of the diocese of Dili, known as "Sunday school," or *Dejukdldil* (an anagram of Department of Youth Catholic Diocese of Dili). The program was open to young people aged nine to twenty years of age and operated every Sunday afternoon in a cluster of buildings on the grounds of the Dili Cathedral. Music has been a mainstay of *Dejukddil*'s program since it first began in the aftermath of the 2006 civil crisis.

On the day that I visited, Sunday school was a hive of activity. A group of children were clustered around a keyboard in front of the main building. One person demonstrated, and others waited their turn to have a try. A similar arrangement was in place for learning to play drums—a single kit was set up (in a state of some disrepair) and children took turns having a try, watching those more experienced in order to learn what to do. Inside, a guitar class attracted one of the largest groups, with several young women teaching groups of eight to ten children how to play different chords. Again, watching and waiting was an essential skill for the young learners.

Although it is difficult to gauge how much music learning could realistically take place in such large groups and with such limited equipment, the program nevertheless had its success stories. One group of "graduates" is an all-girl rock band, Putri Band, who performed at a popular local bar during the fieldwork period. The learning process at *Dejukddil*—one of careful watching, and patiently awaiting one's turn to have a try—was identical to the informal learning described by the self-taught musicians in the above section, but here it was taking place within a supported, structured environment. Both the links to the diocese and the weekly program structure offered possible transitions to performance and leadership opportunities for the keenest and most skilled individuals.

Lastly, non-formal, organized music participation activities also take place from time to time under the auspices of locally based NGOs. Across a five-year period, Plan International offered a rock-band development program in two rural areas, creating opportunities for young musicians to form bands, write songs, and record CDs as part their youth engagement program. The community arts center Afalyca, in the coastal city of Baucau, has hosted numerous music projects with visiting and local artists, including one that I led for Human Rights Week in December 2010 (Howell 2012b). And during the fieldwork period, cultural development NGO Many Hands International commissioned Etson, the director of the Arte Moris music program, to create and lead a "Stomp" ensemble percussion piece with local youths for the opening festivities of its regional arts and cultural center in the rural town of Lospalos.

These examples demonstrate ways in which music participation may be employed in non-formal settings as a vehicle for developing music skills as well as realizing other development goals, such as positive diversion and conflict resolution. The activities make an important contribution to provision of inclusive music opportunities in a constrained education environment and to the overall music development of individuals and their communities.

Music Development with Industrial Goals

The development of the country's "cultural and creative industries" has been a project of Timor-Leste's State Secretariat for Art and Culture for more than half a decade now (East Timor Government 2008). However, in a context with so many competing needs and priorities, and with insufficient infrastructure and few mechanisms in place to support cultural-industrial growth, sustained support for music industry development has been slow. In terms of rock, metal, and popular music, this has created a large chasm of knowledge between fledgling musicians and bands taking part in non-formal development opportunities and local festivals, and the requisite knowledge to be a successful "professional" musician, able to deliver the performance skills, and knowledge that the role of gigging musician demands.

The "Rock Band Community" was formed to address this gap, as its founder Kiera explained:

> It basically came out of the situation where it is very difficult to have music live in this country, and to have people value it as a production of an intellectual work. . . . Culturally, people are very musical, but to take it from there is not one of the priorities. The priorities for this country are infrastructure, and political sort of priorities, rather than music. . . . So we thought that this [Rock Band] community can be a way of gathering all these bands who are striving themselves to be learning and growing and be professional. This community is looking at these ways of organising the band itself, supporting the band members but at the same time strengthening the organisation side of it, and hopefully people will see the community as a way of linking with activities abroad. (Kiera, founder of Rock Band Community, interview, June 5, 2014)

The Rock Band Community functions *as* a community, and also works *within* communities, and thus facilitates community music making on multiple levels. Its existence responds to a perceived development need within the country, not just in terms of musicians' development, but also in building a more self-sufficient sector that is less dependent on importing overseas artists for local celebrations, and it hopes to bring greater recognition to local musicians by increasing their professionalism. Its growing reach and networks have seen it engaged as a partner by different government ministries to produce concerts, workshops, and other youth-focused community music events.

Preserving and Celebrating Traditional Music Knowledge

Successive governments of independent Timor-Leste have explicitly recognized the urgency of preserving the diverse cultural traditions of the country and their role in building a shared sense of national identity (East Timor Government 2008). There are frequent government initiatives to celebrate and promote the indigenous music traditions, customs, and rituals through festivals and media promotions. Many of Timor-Leste's music and dance traditions take place organically as an expected part of community life, without the need for strong external drivers. Others are more fragile due to their proscription during the years of Indonesian occupation that disrupted the traditional transmission patterns, or to the pervasive dominance of contemporary music that seems more "modern" and therefore of the future, or because their grandness of scale requires financial resources that are prohibitive in the current economic environment (Dunlop 2013, 2015).

Stemming from a concern for the fragility and importance of their traditions, groups or programs exist that encourage young people to engage proactively with the music and dance traditions of their district. These groups represent their locality in district and national competitions and festivals and generally work to promote and celebrate local cultural traditions and ensure their preservation. One such group is Lian Babado'ok (Voice of the Drum). This small traditional arts organization is based in the district of Aileu, a mountainous region several hours drive from the capital, Dili. The organization's central year-round activity is a music and dance group for local children in which a group of girls and boys aged ten to fourteen meet weekly to learn traditional songs, dances, and instrumental accompaniments. The group sees their work as essential and urgent, as they feel that the world of modern technology is eroding knowledge of traditional cultural practices and endangering its preservation.

In addition, Lian Babado'ok runs an annual festival of traditional culture, in which schools throughout Aileu district are encouraged to prepare performance items of traditional music and dance and "revolutionary songs" from the resistance period, competing against each other for prizes in a one-day festival event. The young members of Lian Babado'ok were quick to state the importance of maintaining and celebrating Timor-Leste's unique cultural traditions, seeing this knowledge as "a gift from the ancestors" to them (Lian Babado'ok focus group, June 7, 2014). However, they also wanted to play their part in transforming international perceptions of Timor from a place of war and conflict to a place of culture: "We do it to help rise up Timor's name. We want to take Timor's name and culture to Australia, and to any other culture. And we want to show to other countries that Timor also can do this culture. We want to promote Aileu district as well" (Lian Babado'ok children's focus group, June 7, 2014). Thus, their motivations for being part of this group are strongly linked to their understanding of their country's development needs. They want to celebrate and share their distinctive culture, but also see this as a vehicle for cultural exchange, helping their country and local district achieve greater international recognition.

Music Development as an Active Intervention

As is the case in many developing countries, people living with a disability in Timor-Leste often face considerable discrimination in their access to education and have even fewer opportunities for their development and to earn livelihoods than the general population (UNHR 2011). One organization working with blind people has undertaken to address both these areas of concern by including a music program in its provision of education and vocational training for the blind.

Fuan Nabilan is a nongovernmental organization based in the rural town of Same, many hours' drive across difficult terrain from the Timor-Leste capital of Dili. Established by a husband-and-wife team, Joaquim and Joana, Fuan Nabilan works to support and advocate for blind and vision-impaired people, running a school and vocational training program that teaches Braille, handicrafts, music, and massage. The intention is to provide their students with skills that will allow them to integrate into mainstream schools, help them lead more independent lives, and build livelihoods.

Music is a favorite activity at Fuan Nabilan, and the school has formed a music ensemble, performing at community events and on national television. They have recorded three CDs, an important promotion for their work, and the music program has led to some students gaining paid work as musicians and music teachers in their communities.

The Fuan Nabilan musicians perform original songs written by Joaquim that are intended to "educate and motivate the students" (Joaquim, Fuan Nabilan codirector, interview, June 7, 2014) and inspire their audiences to recognize and celebrate the students' skills and ways of contributing to their community, thus addressing the ongoing issue of discrimination and stigma towards people with disabilities. The original songs they perform are important to the students and a source of pride for them: "Our director always advised us to be patient in order to learn. He says to us we shouldn't play other people's songs, but our own songs. This made us excited and was a big motivation. It meant we could show to other people that disabled people can do something that other people can't do" (Julio, Fuan Nabilan student, interview, May 30, 2014).

Fuan Nabilan's music program thus serves a number of purposes. It has been an important tool for student engagement and enabled a higher level of visibility for the students through their community performances, which in turn raises their social status and challenges negative perceptions of vision-impaired people. It has also provided an additional source of income for some of the students, equipping them to take on roles as musicians for community events, or work as music teachers. It is an example of what Higgins (2012) describes as an "active intervention" led by a skilled music leader that aims to address areas of identified social need through music participation. At the same time, the ubiquity of such participation in Timorese culture means that Fuan Nabilan's music program is enabling a marginalized group to "show what they can do" and to play an active role in the musical life of their community, thus asserting their right to inclusion and recognition in that space.

Community Music as Creative Agency and Self-expression

During my fieldwork I learned that many Timorese people use songwriting as a way to express and process their responses to traumatic events or to call for social change. This group includes people that do not necessarily identify as musicians or songwriters. Their songs follow different narratives. Some people, like Joaquim quoted in the previous section, write "educative music" that advocates for a particular change, or songs that express their concerns and hopes for their country. These songs are performed in their local communities, often to great public interest: "Music that is about the many tragedies of Timor Leste—people like it, because they like to sing [it]. . . . For example, Joaquim writes songs about refugees [Timorese diaspora] in other people's countries [*tasi sorin*], and he calls the refugees to come back here and to help build the new Timor-Leste. I think that people really appreciate that song" (Joana, Fuan Nabilan codirector, interview, June 7, 2014).

Songwriters also write songs to express their responses to traumatic events. Mana Lu Lourdes, a Timorese activist, community leader, and deeply trusted religious sister, reportedly wrote more than three hundred songs during the years of Indonesian occupation: "every time she would get outraged with scenes she had witnessed or the latest crime to ripple through Timor, she would write a song!" (Dunlop 2009).

Channelling grief and despair into musical creativity has provided comfort not merely for the individual songwriter but for their communities. Veteran journalist Max Stahl travelled to the town of Suai in the aftermath of a brutal massacre there in 1999 and described how, within a year of the massacre:

> A hundred songs had been written about that massacre. . . . And people in all sorts of places would play you a song that they'd written. Small villages, and so on. Radio was barely functioning at that point. Television just wasn't happening at all. So people would use this kind of creativity, this strong tradition of music in Timor-Leste. Part of it is variations on popular music of one kind or another. Part of it comes from Timor's older tradition of music. And part of it comes from Indonesian music. But it's very creative and it's full of very powerful stuff if you pay attention. And it's not easy for some observers, foreigners, to understand, because it's obviously in local language and it's also not played in public. It's played to each other, it's played in communities. (Max Stahl, journalist, interview, June 16, 2015)

Community music that uses lyrics to reflect upon shared experiences may be a contemporary incarnation of the indigenous Timorese tradition of daily work songs, where the words of a song that accompanied a daily task would comment on local events or offer a perspective on an issue pertinent to that community, with new lyrics improvised afresh each day (Dunlop 2013; King 1963). However, the examples shared here add a further dimension to the "work song" tradition, with music fulfilling an important social function of relieving suffering and enabling healing, according to the songwriting stories that people told.

The Catholic Church as a Central Player in Community Music Development

Woven throughout the community music narratives of the research participants is the presence of the Catholic Church, which supports different aspects of community music and individual music development in both rural and urban Timor-Leste. In the absence of formal governmental provision through community initiatives or the education system, churches, local parish priests, and faith-based organizations perform many essential services in enabling both music participation and music development opportunities throughout the country.

The role of the Church in nurturing music learning and participation can be seen in several ways: through verbal encouragement and endorsement of young music enthusiasts; through providing access to musical equipment and rehearsal space; through the establishment of church choirs that offer an important emotional outlet for many people; and in the strategic use of music to foster collective emotional and spiritual healing after traumatic events.

Many participants recalled clergy that had played supportive and practical roles in their personal music development. For example, members of the Catholic clergy provided encouragement, knowledge, and practical guidance for many music learners I interviewed. Classical guitarist Aurelio described the importance of his parish priest in rural Ermera in encouraging his interest in classical (rather than popular) music by lending him cassette tapes of classical guitar recordings and urging him to persevere and be ambitious for himself. This priest attributed universal status to classical music, declaring it as "good music [and] eternal music that will not die," and described the classical guitar as "like a miniature orchestra—you can play the bass, the rhythm, and the melody all at once" (Aurelio, interview, June 17, 2014), ideas that made a strong impression on the young boy in a isolated rural location at that time. The priest did not know how to play guitar himself, but he understood enough about the process to provide Aurelio with enthusiastic guidance, encouragement, and motivation.

Many research participants recalled church facilities being critical to their music development. Several musicians described receiving their first opportunities to rehearse and to play through their local parish church. Churches had musical equipment—guitars, keyboards, amplifiers—that the majority of young people were in no position to own themselves or access in other ways, given the lack of formal music education in schools. Churches also had space suitable for rehearsal. Etson recalled how he moved from being a social guitarist to being a performer with the celebrated band Galaxy. The transition began with the suggestion that he and a friend could practice together in the local church; even though they "just used the church for rehearsal, we weren't preparing [music] for the mass" (Etson, interview, May 26, 2014). Later, they were invited by the priest to augment their group with some more players and perform in a community celebration at the church. More opportunities followed that first performance experience, and in time he was invited to join Galaxy as their bass player: "Then the Galaxy band started practising at the church and became the main church band, playing for parties and events, and so it took over from the other band. And whenever there was a celebration at the church then we would play" (Etson, interview, May 26, 2014). This was by no means an unusual musical development pathway. What is more, these bands did not necessarily conform to Catholic doctrine; the opportunities came about because of their musical interests and growing skills. This points to the way that churches function as shared community spaces in addition to being sites for religious devotion.

Beyond this direct encouragement of young musicians, Catholic churches and people's religious faith have always been sites for many community music-making events. Singing is an important element in traditional Timorese culture (Dunlop 2013), and the early Catholic missionaries connected with and utilized this tradition in attracting people to their mission. In contemporary Timor-Leste, churches throughout the country have choirs, and the people are proud of their singing skills and beautiful harmonies. Church choirs offer music participation opportunities that are meaningful on two levels: for the opportunity to participate in a musical ensemble and develop skills and talents; and for the connection between the choral singing, worship, and faith.

The choirs augment the congregations' own music-making as part of worship and ritual. For the schoolchildren I interviewed in the rural village of Bessilau, the participatory music that accompanied religious worship best typified communal music making in their communities. One stated, "When we pray together in the community we use music to accompany the Mary and Jesus statues from one house to another house" (Bessilau children's focus group, June 6, 2014).

A final illustration of the centrality of the Catholic Church to community music development in Timor-Leste involves the facilitation of music in the community as a healing and nurturing force and has its foundation in the protective role the Catholic Church played for the Timorese people during the years of Indonesian occupation.

McGregor, Skeaff, and Bevan (2012) have described the way that "at a local scale Catholic churches were considered sacred and largely immune from Indonesian influence" and offered a safe space where people could speak freely in their own language and share their experiences. Music and songs were some of the ways the people used this safe space—"people would sing their opposition to the occupation during Church services and pray for salvation" (1135). In the churches, music helped to fuse and integrate national identity and a common cultural history with Catholicism and faith.

Following the Indonesian departure, the traumatized population again turned to the church for spiritual and emotional support. Shared music making was an important part of the healing processes in many parishes. For example, during the period of recovery that followed the Suai Church massacre in 1999, Max Stahl observed what he felt to be a very powerful use of music to help the local children heal.

> One priest, a Filipino, became extraordinarily dynamic and creative in the use of music in what seemed to me to be a way of making sure that the community didn't *get stuck*. The music wasn't distracting music, it wasn't about making people forget. Quite the opposite, it was stories about the killings. It was celebrating the lives and the martyrdom of the priests, and of all the people. It was songs which the children, the little children learned by heart. . . . In the church, in the same rooms where it happened! . . . The genius of this priest was that he understood how this stuff works in the community in Timor. (Max Stahl, journalist, interview, June 16, 2015)

Churches were important sites of regathering, and of sharing and expressing collective suffering. Music was one of the ways this could be expressed, and songs were chosen for the way they could reinforce the sense of shared meaning and emotion.

> After that Indonesians had gone, we all go and looking for each other to continue the [St. Cecilia's] choir. At that time we are very stressed, traumatised. So the things that we have to do is gather together and get some ideas and then work together or *do something,* through music. So we just throw our stress to music. We are singing, and not just in the singing to take out our stress, but singing to help us show others. So we do our performances in the church, and we have concert, and then we ask everyone to watch, to see, so as not to feel afraid or not to be traumatised [any] more. . . . When we sing, all the music is related to those trauma things, through the words, so [the songs] make us feel maybe less stressed (Milka, choir member, interview, May 27, 2014).

Each of these examples illustrates the interwoven nature of music, faith, social care, and development as a personal and community endeavor in Timor-Leste. The Catholic Church's dominance in community music activities across Timor-Leste is not surprising when we consider the scope of the institution's work across the country. Its remit extends beyond guiding people's religious faith; rather, it concerns itself with the needs of the whole person, and the whole of community life, running schools, orphanages, hospices, healthcare facilities, and social enterprises that support community livelihoods. This inseparability from the patterns of daily life gives the Church considerable social and political power.

It is beyond the scope of this chapter to more critically analyze the extent of Catholic Church influence in music (and social) development and how this has evolved in the years since independence. The key point I wish to emphasize is that the Catholic Church functions much like a community development organization, particularly in the absence of any systematic state support for musical participation and education, and it has therefore been a key influence in the musical lives of the Timorese people. Just as societies are dynamic, so too are the institutions embedded within them. Given this, it is useful to consider the Catholic Church's multiple roles as an institution, as a political entity, and as a "People's Church" if we are to understand community music in Timor-Leste.

Music Making as an Act of Development

At the beginning of this chapter, I suggested that a lack of any kind of music or cultural *industry* in Timor-Leste rendered *all* music-making activity community music. Following the findings presented in this chapter, a more nuanced perspective is to observe that through these various acts of music making, organizers and participants alike are actively engaged in *rebuilding community,* a community that has been damaged and divided through successive decades (even centuries) of occupation and violent social conflict. Music has always been a part of the social fabric, and when that social fabric was profoundly damaged through the violence, destruction, and traumata of occupation and war, music was employed as a natural counteraction and tool for rebuilding.

The examples I have shared find community music activities in Timor-Leste located at an intersection of arts and culture, religion and worship, community education, informal learning, and traditional and contemporary cultural knowledge. What is more, many practitioners understand their music making to be a vehicle for personal and national development, alongside its value as an expressive and aesthetic act. Even when it invokes the past, through traditions passed down by ancestors or as an expression of past suffering, it remains a strongly future-oriented act.

Unlike in many high-income countries, where any inherent value of the arts has been undermined through decades of economic rationalism, resulting in a corresponding tendency towards instrumentalization of arts and music (Stupples 2014), the Timorese use of music as a vehicle for development, rebuilding, and healing is instinctive and holistic. Paradoxically, this may be because in Timorese culture music is not "an entity on its own, it's not what's important on its own. It's like the knife to eat the meal with, you know. It's part of the meal. It's not something that's stuck on the stage or separate or anything. Music and stories and all of that stuff is [about] love really, and nurturing, and making people feel safe and included. And that's not the way we perceive music in [Western] society" (Ros Dunlop, ethnomusicologist, interview, April 21, 2014). Dunlop is describing here an indigenous epistemology of music as defined by its social and spiritual functions, and this distinction is an important one to consider when exploring what community music is across the Asia-Pacific region. It may be a vehicle for local-level political action, or to educate and impart messages of importance to the community. It is often employed to both celebrate and build community. What is more, the organic and community-led nature of community music demonstrates the capacity for these kinds of projects to be highly self-sustaining in environments with limited material resources. From an international development perspective, such projects need to be recognized for the value and social significance they offer and their capacity to be sustained without need for external drivers.

The centrality of the Catholic Church and faith to many music activities in Timor-Leste is a reminder that Western norms of secularity are often contested in modern Asian nation-states, particularly in those countries with developing economies, or where indigenous traditions are still maintained by a majority of the population while simultaneously they navigate the considerable cultural and economic transitions demanded by modernity and globalization. Similarly to the way in which the Catholic Church was arguably overlooked as a principal development actor in the secular UN-led rebuilding of Timor-Leste (McGregor, Skeaff, and Bevan 2012), the secular sensibilities of many researchers coming from outside the region may mean that a symbiotic relationship between faith and music making could be overlooked or downplayed in Asia-Pacific contexts.

Ultimately, the ubiquity of music making in Timor-Leste is inextricably tied to the East Timorese people's sense of personal identity and expression, and to national identity and future goals. Timor-Leste is a country where everyone holds a stake in their country's future growth and a commitment to playing a role in realizing its potential. For many people, community music is one of the ways this stake and commitment are expressed, explored, and frequently asserted as a meaningful and powerful tool for personal and national development.

References

Chomsky, Noam. 2003. *Radical Priorities.* 3rd ed. Chico, CA: AK Press.

Cristalis, Irena. 2009. *East Timor: A Nation's Bitter Dawn.* 2nd ed. New York: Zed Books.

D'Amore, Abigail, ed. 2014. *Musical Futures: An Approach to Teaching and Learning.* 2nd ed. London: Paul Hamlyn Foundation.

Dunlop, Ros. 2009. "Timor Trip November 2008." January 16, 2009. Retrieved from http://tekeemedia.com/timor-trip-november-2008.

———. 2013. *Lian Husi Klamar* [Sounds of the Soul]. Dili, Timor-Leste: Tekee Media Inc.

———. 2015. "Maulelo, a Multimedia Ritual Performance from East Timor and Its Relevance to the Society It Originated from Today." Paper presented at the 43rd World Conference of the International Council for Traditional Music, Astana, Kazakhstan, July 16–22.

East Timor Government. 2008. "History." Retrieved December 22, 2011, from http://www.easttimorgovernment.com/history.htm.

Government of Timor-Leste. 2009. "National Cultural Policy." Retrieved from http://www.cultura.gov.tl/sites/default/files/National_policy_culture_english.pdf.

Higgins, Lee. 2012. *Community Music: In Theory and in Practice.* Oxford: Oxford University Press.

Hodge, Joel. 2012. "Church, State and Secularism in Asia: The Public Nature of the Church in Timor-Leste." *International Journal of Political Theology* 16 (2): 323–348. doi:10.1515/ijpt-2012–0020.

Howell, Gillian. 2010. "Dawn Songs." October 20. Retrieved from http://musicwork.wordpress.com/2010/10/20/dawn-songs.

———. 2012a. "The Practitioner as Foreigner: Challenges and Dilemmas in Cross-cultural Music Projects." Paper presented at the *Eleventh International Conference on Cultural Diversity in Music Education, Singapore, 4–6 January 2012.*

———. 2012b. "The Right to Play: A Children's Composition Project in Timor-Leste (East Timor)." Paper presented at *30th International Society for Music Education, Thessaloniki, Greece, 15–20 July 2012.*

———. 2013. "Finding my Place: Examining Concepts of Community Music as a Visiting Artist in Rural East Timor." *International Journal of Community Music* 6 (1): 65–78. doi:10.1386/ijcm.6.1.65_1.

Howell, Gillian, and Kim Dunphy. 2012. "Toka Boot/The Big Jam: Making Music in Rural East Timor." *International Journal of Community Music* 5 (1): 27–44. doi:0.1386/ijcm.5.1.27_1.

King, Margaret. 1963. *Eden to Paradise.* London: Hodder and Stoughton.

Kingsbury, Damien, and Michael Leach. 2007. "Introduction." In *East Timor: Beyond Independence,* edited by D. Kingsbury and M. Leach, 1–16. Melbourne: Monash University Press.

McGregor, Andrew, Laura Skeaff, and Marianne Bevan. 2012. "Overcoming Secularism? Catholic Development Geographies in Timor-Leste." *Third World Quarterly* 33 (6): 1129–1146. doi:10.1080/01436597.2012.681497.

Post-CAVR Technical Secretariat. 2013. *Chega!: The Final Report of the Timor-Leste Commission for Reception, Truth and Reconciliation (CAVR). A Plain Guide.* Jakarta, Indonesia: KPG in cooperation with STP-CAVR.

Silva, Kelly Cristiane da. 2007. "The Bible as Constitution, or the Consitution as Bible?: Nation-state Building Projects in East Timor." *Horizontes Antropológicos* 13 (27): 213–235. doi:10.1590/s0104-71832007000100010.

Stupples, Polly. 2014. "Creative Contributions: The Role of the Arts and the Cultural Sector in Development." *Progress in Development Studies* 14 (2): 115–130. doi:10.1177/1464993413517779.

United Nations Integrated Mission in Timor-Leste (UNHR). 2011. "Of Course We Can: Report on the Rights of Persons with Disabilities in Timor-Leste." Retrieved from http://unmit.unmissions.org/Default.aspx?tabid=156&andctl=Details&andmid=456&andItemID=15055.

CHAPTER 3

Conserving Knowledge and Language Practices of Singing Cultures in Low-lying Pacific Islands

Te Oti Rakena

I sit jet-lagged in a European hotel with the air-conditioning turned up to maximum. I have flown twenty-eight hours to get here and the temperature is an unusually humid thirty degrees Celsius. I turn on the television. I am greeted by a CNN special report with the dramatic title *You're Making This Island Disappear*. It is another environmental story describing industrial society's impact on small Pacific Island nations, in this case the Marshall Islands. The irony is not lost on me, as I calculate my carbon footprint and turn off the air-conditioning. The news event targets the first world CNN audience. It is already a familiar story for those residing in low-lying Pacific Island atolls. The current climate change discourse has been reignited by the scientific "news" that the warming of the atmosphere by even two degrees, something that could happen by the end of the century, will commit some coastal cities and island nations to drowning (Sutter 2015).

The special report describes the impact of climate change through the eyes of a journalist and discusses the decision of some Marshallese families to leave the Islands. Many Islanders, ten thousand in fact, have relocated to Northwest Arkansas thanks to the 1986 Compact of Free Association with the United States of America, an agreement that allows the Marshallese to live and work in the United States. For other Pacific nations the option for relocation is severely limited, adding potency to the term "climate refugees," a category first used by a Washington-based nongovernment organization

(NGO), Worldwatch Institute, in 1988 (McNamara and Gibson 2009). This geopolitically aligned label has facilitated an NGO agenda that in some documents portrays whole populations of Pacific Island people as helpless, passive victims (Farbotko and Lazrus 2012; McNamara and Gibson 2009; Mortreux and Barnett 2009). This discourse of victimhood and the notion of migration versus mitigation, has contributed to the resistance by Pacific Island nations to this label (Farbotko and Lazrus 2012; McNamara and Gibson 2009; Warne 2008). Pacific leaders have stated that focusing on migration is "defeatist and a globally irresponsible vision for the future" (McNamara and Gibson 2009, 480). For Pacific peoples, sovereignty remains paramount, invoking nationalistic reactions like "We do not want to leave our land" (McNamara and Gibson 2009), and "We are not drowning we are fighting" (Butler 2014).

Representatives of Pacific Island nations, led by Tuvalu, have managed to sustain a constant presence at key international gatherings dealing with environment and climate change. Their message is clear; mitigating the future impacts of climate change should be industrial society's highest priority (McNamara and Gibson 2009, 480). Though not all scientists agree about the future of low-lying Pacific Island atolls (Allen 2004), most environmental scientists agree that warmer water will mean stronger cyclones and that, with the additional effect of the polar ice melt due to global warming, a doomsday scenario is possible. Considering the information gathered and reported over the past twenty-five years, we can agree that "climate change is a narrative and a material phenomenon" (Farbotko and Lazrus 2012, 382).

The environmental impact on island nations such as Tuvalu, the Marshall Islands, Tonga, Fiji, and Kiribati has brought to the surface the by-products of globalization and revealed to an international audience "how the predicaments of the local Self and the global Other are intertwined" (Cameron 2011, 883). These islands have established, over generations, sustainable environments built within collective societies (Pollack 2006; Bayer and Salzman 2005). When relocation to another country was suggested as a solution to the rising seas a Kiribati citizen responded: "We might lose our identity. We have so many unique things, the way we dress, the way we eat, and the way we speak. I don't believe we will disappear soon, but as more people move away we will lose our identity, and then Kiribati will be nothing and we will never be known again in the history of the world" (Williams 2001, 28).

A thread running parallel to the environmental discourse is that of cultural maintenance and sustainability and the notion that music and music traditions, although not a finite resource, are potentially endangered when too few people are left to support that tradition (Titon 2009a). Ethnomusicologist Titon suggests we think of music, a product of human life, as a biocultural resource, aligning the potential loss of musical traditions with environmentalists' concerns about the depletion of natural resources: "squandering resources diminishes the quality of life in the present and impoverishes life in the future" (2009a, 5). He adds that "each music-culture is a particular adaptation to a particular circumstance . . . each world [of music] can be regarded as an ecological system . . . a change in any part of the ecosystem affects the whole of it" (as cited in Titon 2009b, 123).

Allen reports that it is surprisingly difficult to see through the fog of rhetoric and conflicting scientific views to where global climate theory might or might not intersect with Tuvalu's people (2004, 45). Speaking from the Pacific Islander's perspective, Hau'ofa states, "Views of the Pacific from the level of macroeconomics and macropolitics often differ markedly from those from the level of ordinary people" (1994, 148). Whatever factors have contributed to the current dilemma in Tuvalu, it is a vulnerable island state. Central to the discussion in this chapter is how to safeguard the conditions that Tuvaluans have already created to sustain their musical traditions as a response to their changing ecosystem. Presumably, these are what Hau'ofa referred to as "grass root activities" (1994, 148).

Reframing the Dilemma

While the focus in this chapter is the potential loss of performance traditions, the project also presents the opportunity to examine a research procedure that diminishes the "eco-colonial gaze" (Farbotko 2010, 47) by enveloping the whole process in the Māori concept of *whanaungatanga*. This term is understood across the indigenous cultures of the Pacific Islands, but here it is expressed with the indigenous Māori term. McNatty comments that "attempts to define Māori words using English are doomed to failure: such definitions imply a type of cultural congruity that simply does not exist" (2002, 94). In order to avoid a shallow understanding of the concept, a problem sometimes associated with the Western misrepresentation of Māori and Pacific words and concepts when attempted to be captured by European researchers (McNatty 2002), this project uses *whanaungatanga* as an intervention, but recognizes that this model must include the spiritual dimension, understand the relationship of Māori—and in this case Pacific—cosmology, and acknowledge the responsibilities and duties of reciprocity expressed within *whanau/fanau*[1] relationships.

One of the ways of expressing responsibility and duty of reciprocity is through the relationship *tuakana/teina,* or loosely translated, elder sibling-younger sibling (McNatty 2002). For Māori who come from the Pacific but have been assigned the indigenous label in Aotearoa[2]/New Zealand, we see the Pacific nation migrants as our *teina,* younger siblings, and therefore our responsibility and duty to these communities through *whanaungatanga* is to care for and protect them. In the wider Pacific context, however, we are often the *teina,* and the older, more established Pacific cultures are our *tuakana* (older siblings), from whom we gain insight and wisdom.

For fear of colonizing a Pacific Island project with a Māori paradigm, the "*fanau* concept" also underpins the function and operation of Pacific Island communities (Mataia et al. 2011): "Despite great distances and centuries of isolation, the various peoples of Polynesia have maintained close cultural similarities that are rooted in a parental culture of some two thousand years ago. They share similar myths, ancient religions, languages, and physical appearances" (Hau'ofa 1985, 168). We have shared stories and traditions, and have voyaged together across the Pacific, intermarrying and trading across the millennia. Our understanding of this world, the spiritual realm, and our relationship to the sea has largely been shaped by these activities, which all descend from a similar cosmological view of the world. In this case, operating from a New Zealand context, and with the experience already gained from archiving and conserving Māori and other Pacific peoples' music, we saw ourselves in the *tuākana* role. While this was a community-music-based intervention, successful completion of the project was more accurately akin to that of a familial obligation.

Conversations between Institutions

This chapter describes the implementation of the Tuvalu: Pacific Project, a research collaboration made up of indigenous creative artists from three partner institutions. Located in Australia, New Zealand and Canada this project illuminated the challenges of establishing and sustaining research partnerships within the current fluid tertiary sector. It presents an example of indigenous researchers researching "other" indigenous populations. Finally, it describes a significant research outcome, a joint music conservation project with Tuvalu Media Corporation (TMC) a broadcasting enterprise sponsored by the Japanese NGO Tuvalu Overview.

The Pacific project was initiated by the President of Emily Carr University, in Vancouver, Canada; the Dean of the National Institute of

Creative Arts Industries at the University of Auckland, New Zealand; and the Dean of the Victorian College of the Arts, Melbourne, Australia. During a meeting of University leaders from around the Pacific Rim, the group noticed the increasing regional focus on the Pacific Rim countries and tertiary institutions, many with wealth and plentiful resources. The three university leaders had a mutual interest in turning the focus inward to the middle of the Pacific where they saw a real need for support from first world institutions. In September 2007, a meeting was held in Auckland the largest Polynesian city in the world and the city with the most diverse representation of Pacific Island nations. The partners from the three institutions met leaders from Pacific Island communities, which included the Auckland Tuvaluan community. At the end of the gathering they had forged an agreement to visit Tuvalu.

The purpose of the project was to explore, through consultation, an intellectual, artistic and social/cultural engagement with Tuvalu, and the Tuvaluan communities in each of the partner countries. The broad areas of interest included cultural resilience and irreversible loss, sovereignty/self-determination, and the challenges of globalization.[3]

An initial scoping visit occurred in 2008 and was a collaborative venture between indigenous researchers situated at the three universities, all with a common interest in indigenous research themes and various aspects of the fine arts and performing arts. The Australian participant created this small memorandum of understanding:

> To engage with the art of another culture is to engage with the culture itself. This project will avoid the subordinate position from which western philosophies have often viewed non-western practices, applying Pacific Island methodology to all research projects attached to this proposal. The research project outcomes will be expressed in a variety of artistic modes including performing arts, visual arts, architecture, and planning. The use of traditional or contemporary as artistic labels will be limited, defining artistic practice as including that, that has been developed over generations and still widely practiced and continuing to develop.[4]

Because of institutional changes in one of the universities, and conflicting research activities in the other, only one of the institutions that participated in the 2008 scoping trip was able to revisit Tuvalu in 2010 with a specific project. The project took place at the New Zealand institution in Auckland.

Conversations in Tuvalu

This project was not a top-down validation of tradition or tradition bearers (Titon 2009b, 120) by university experts but an intervention that emerged as an organic process from discussions with the local experts in cultural management.[5] A key figure in the development of this project was the Cultural Officer based in the Ministry of Home Affairs and Rural Development. The government official met with the team twice during the 2008 visit and then again during the 2010 visit. Her interests included archival documenting that sustains traditional music practices. We were somewhat hesitant to embark on a conservation project, mindful that the archiving of indigenous peoples' intangible performance traditions has a difficult history (Treloyn and Emberly 2013; Titon 2009); however, the Cultural Officer emphasized the urgent need to conserve archived traditional music practices. In particular, she expressed her concern over a large collection of historically important archival recordings housed in the buildings of the Tuvalu Media Corporation (TMC).

The recordings housed by TMC were on tape and were rapidly reaching, and in some cases had exceeded, their usability. In 2008, a PhD student[6] from the University of New England, Australia, with approval and assistance from TMC technicians, attempted to capture the audio from over one hundred of these archive tapes. Although this was a useful exercise, it did not produce recordings of good archival standards. After discussions with the director of the TMC, the remaining members of the team decided it was essential that these tapes be re-digitized. The Archive of Maori and Pacific Music at the University of Auckland had the necessary experience and technical skill to complete this task. The project's specific aim was to digitize and preserve all remaining tapes stored in the TMC building in Funafuti, Tuvalu, and to bring a technician from Tuvalu to Auckland, where they would advise and assist in the digitization.

Intangible Cultural Heritage

The tapes stored in the archive included examples of precolonial songs called Old Songs, a genre of Tuvaluan music that is being lost as elders knowledgeable in the performance of this song form die off or migrate. There are broadcasts by Radio Tuvalu across the Tuvalu Islands and around the Pacific, including Australia and New Zealand.

Since Christianity came to Tuvalu in the mid-1800s, songs from pre-European contact have fallen into disuse. They differ from the European-influenced contemporary Tuvaluan music. They are composed in a very old poetic style and discuss themes of land, sea, fishing, and the environment in the context of over one hundred years ago. Gerd Koch mentioned in his book *Songs of Tuvalu,* published in 2000, that when he returned to Tuvalu after a thirty-six-year absence many of the traditional songs he had recorded and given to the radio station were still being sung in the community relatively unchanged, still highly regarded, and not forgotten. He believes this is because Radio Tuvalu broadcasts Old Songs from the archive almost daily, inserting them among all the contemporary pop songs (Koch 2000, 8).

It was clear from conversations with local Tuvaluans that these tapes should be preserved. They saw the archive as having contemporary relevance as well as historical importance, and the collection as a crucial resource for retaining knowledge of this type of indigenous music. The collection of tapes is arguably one of Tuvalu's most valuable repositories of indigenous knowledge, making this type of community music a vital biocultural resource. The transmission of these songs on Radio Tuvalu has created a heritage space that is helping to counter the effects of diaspora, the associated patterns of language loss and loss of cultural knowledge, by providing a musical resource that makes it possible for the community to reconnect with traditional and contemporary Tuvaluan culture.

The Conservation Process

TMC freighted all the remaining tapes, a total of 540, to New Zealand for digitization and preservation. Many tapes were in a seriously compromised state due to inadequate storage conditions. Many had failed splices, broken spools, and missing or damaged boxes. However, the worst problem was that many of the tapes, spools, and boxes were severely infested with mold. Initially, there was concern about our ability to play them successfully and achieve a satisfactory digital capture without catastrophic damage to the tapes. Considerable care was taken to ameliorate their condition using available conservation techniques. About a dozen tapes demanded extra-special care to nurse them through playback, but overall the results were surprisingly good.[7]

A TMC technician[8] travelled to New Zealand to assist with cleaning and categorizing the tapes. The technician was also trained to use new software that would help in the labelling of the digital copies. The technician returned to Tuvalu with the completed archival recordings and the software. The viable tapes remaining in the collection were captured to a good archival standard. The project partners were aware of the ephemeral nature of digital data and the possibility of digital copies being lost, and so the University of Auckland agreed to securely store the original tapes and has preserved the digital data in multiple ways. Now that the digital copies have been repatriated, access to such significant content is assured.

There were many challenges associated with the planning and completion of this project. We were fortunate to have knowledge of Tuvalu and the people's cultural perspectives from visits to the Islands and contact with the local Tuvaluan population living and studying in New Zealand. During the project, e-mail and phone coverage often went down and we would have weeks, sometimes months, of noncontact. This knowledge and the Tuvalu community in Auckland who travel backwards and forwards to the Islands helped us maintain contact and ensured that deadlines were met.

Travel in the Pacific is an ongoing issue; planning in advance was crucial, as flights to Tuvalu are infrequent and go through Fiji. Seats are often unavailable at key moments in the year. It was difficult to evaluate the quality of the tapes from a distance, and the variety of brands. We were aware of previous projects failing to capture all the archival recordings, so we made the choice of bringing all the tapes to New Zealand from Tuvalu, and that flexibility allowed us to complete the project as originally planned.

Titon (2009b, 6) notes that the ethical question "that all peoples and their cultures have a right to survive, even flourish" was the basis of Lomax's "appeal to cultural equity" and the premise on which international institutions such as UNESCO are based. In this case we were in a position to ask what cultural activities were at risk because of external influences, and how we could help sustain these practices. While there was some tension around this process due to the external research expectations of the tertiary sector and the innovative and normative outcomes expected of a "research project," the positioning of the project members within "other" indigenous collectives ensured that this project aligned with the specific needs of the community.

With regard to the Old Songs, sadly, there are only approximately twenty elderly musicians who are knowledgeable in this style of music; they are the last stewards of the genre, and when they pass away the knowledge behind these songs and their performance practices will be lost forever. Now that the digital copies have been repatriated, access to such significant content is assured. Due to the skill of the technician at the Archive of Pacific and Maori music, all the vulnerable tapes were saved and Radio Tuvalu has access to a wider range of archival recordings, ensuring that the airways remain a heritage space for the sustaining of traditions and the transmission of knowledge.

A community displaced from their land may see a gradual erosion of traditional practices and the loss of the collective. In Tuvalu the loss of these practices, symbiotic relationships with the environment, and a communal existence are seen by some to be a real risk (Bayer and Salzman 2005). However, for Tuvaluans migration is a familiar process. They have a history of mobility moving from island to island (Farbotko and Lazrus 2012), a history they share with other Pacific peoples (Kanemasu and Molnar 2013; Barcham, Scheyvens, and Overton 2009; Connell 2003; Underhill-Sem 2001; Hayes 1991). Farbotko and Lazrus note that there is cultural strength in the semi-rooted, semi-moving ways of small island nations, and "migration in Tuvalu does not stand in opposition to place based cultures" (2012, 388). Emigration is an everyday practice, now juxtaposed with a climate-change refugee status.

In 1984, Epeli Hau'ofa presented a paper, "The Future of Our Past," one of six delivered as public lectures at the University of Hawai'i titled "The Pacific Islands in the Year 2000." In it he stated:

> Although the past two hundred years have done much to destroy or change indigenous cultures, the experiences of the late twentieth century have brought about an awareness of broad cultural similarities among the peoples of the Pacific Islands. . . . It is perhaps the old gods themselves, Maui, Tangaroa, Kane and others, who have drawn Polynesians from their far flung islands to flock to Aotearoa and Hawaii in order to help keep their ancient imprints alive. An increasing number of those who have not emigrated are establishing links that will help to keep the old spirit of Polynesians alive, well into the Twenty-First Century. (169)

Pacific Islanders have forged alliances with the indigenous Māori of Aotearoa/New Zealand (Hau'ofa 1994), and Tuvalu in particular has developed strong relationships with New Zealand. Farbotko notes, "there are no large migrant groups of Tuvaluans anywhere, except in New Zealand" (2010, 51). With a deeper understanding of the term *whanau/fanau*, in this project we have located the Tuvaluan community resident in New Zealand and in the Pacific Islands within the familial *fanau* concept, or *whanaungatanga*. It is in this understanding of the concept that this particular project finds its rationale and strength. It is also through this concept that we have reframed the dilemma associated with climate change and globalization, using the *fanau* concept/*whanaungatanga* as a Pacific example of global citizenship operating at a local Pacific level and within our Pacific understanding of the world.

Notes

1 I use the Māori and the common Pacific Island spelling for the word, which has a variety of meanings, including "family" (extended and nuclear) and "community." The use of the two words acknowledges that across the Pacific peoples' oral cultures the word is and has been pronounced the same and understood in the same way. It has, however, developed multiple spellings, depending on the colonizing power that committed the language to script.

2 Aotearoa is the most commonly used Māori name for New Zealand.

3 The agreement was part of the original unpublished planning document created by Michelle Evans, the former head of the Wilin Centre for Indigenous Arts and Cultural Development at the Victoria College of arts, in consultation with Brenda Crabtree, the Aboriginal program manager at Emily Carr University, Vancouver, Canada.

4 This memorandum of understanding was agreed to by all three institutions and drafted by Michelle Evans of the Wilin Centre for Indigenous Arts and Cultural Development, but is unpublished.

5 I would like to acknowledge the Tuvalu-based team that advised us on the importance of this music archive. They included the Cultural Officer, Alamai Sioni; the coordinator of the University of South Pacific Tuvalu Campus, David Manuella; and head of the Tuvalu Media Corporation, Melali Taape.

6 The project benefited from the information provided by PhD student Marc Beaulieu. His knowledge of operating as an outsider in Tuvalu, and his passion for this musical practice, were important in shaping this project.

7 This is extracted from the final report to the funding body The Pacific Development and Conservation Trust, written by the technical project manager, Nigel Champion, from the Archive of Māori and Pacific Music at the University of Auckland. He was responsible for advising on all technical aspects of this project, the training of the technician, and the conservation and re-digitizing of the material.

8 The logistical aspects of this project were handled by the acting head of TMC, Stanley Manao, and the TMC technician sent to assist with the project in New Zealand was Afasene Kaitu.

References

Allen, Leslie. 2004. "Will Tuvalu disappear beneath the sea? Global warming threatens to swamp a small island nation." *Smithsonian* 35 (5): 44–52.

Barcham, Manuhuia, Regina Scheyvens, and John Overton. 2009. "New Polynesian Triangle: Rethinking Polynesian migration and development in the Pacific." *Asia Pacific Viewpoint* 50 (3): 322–337. doi:10.1111/j.1467-8373.2009.01404.x

Bayer, Julie, and Josh Salzman. 2005. *Time and Tide.* Film. Directed by Josh Salzman. USA: Wavecrest films.

Butler, Simon. 2014. "Pacific Climate Warriors: 'We are not drowning we are fighting.'" *Climate and Capitalism,* August 27, 2014. http://climateandcapitalism.com/2014/08/27/pacific-climate-warriors-we-are-not-drowning-we-are-fighting.

Cameron, F. R. 2011. "Saving the 'disappearing islands': Climate change governance, Pacific island states and cosmopolitan dispositions." *Continuum* 25 (6): 873–886. doi:10.1080/10304312.2011.617879.

Connell, John. 2003. "Migration in Pacific Island Countries and Territories." In *Migration Patterns and Policies in the Asian and Pacific Region.* Asian Population Studies Series No. 160, 35–65. New York: United Nations.

Corn, Aaron. (2013). "Sustaining Australia's indigenous music and dance traditions: The role of the national recording project for indigenous performance in Australia." *Musicology Australia* 35 (2): 268–284. doi:10.1080/08145857.2013.844526.

Farbotko, Carol. 2010. "Wishful sinking: Disappearing islands, climate refugees and cosmopolitan experimentation." *Asia Pacific Viewpoint* 51 (1): 47–60. doi:10.1111/j.1467–8373.2010.001413.x.

Farbotko, Carol, and Heather Lazrus. 2012. "The first climate refugees? Contesting global narratives of climate change in Tuvalu." *Global Environmental Change* 22 (2): 382–390. doi:10.1016/j.gloenvcha.2011.11.014.

Hau'ofa, Epeli. 1985. "The Future of Our Past." In *The Pacific Islands in the Year 2000,* edited by R. Kiste and R. Heur, 151–170. Honolulu: East–West Center.

———. 1994. "Our sea of islands." *The Contemporary Pacific* 6 (1): 147–161.

Hayes, Geoffrey. 1991. "Migration, metascience, and development policy in Island Polynesia." *The Contemporary Pacific* 3 (1): 1–58. http://www.jstor.org/stable/23701487.

Kanemasu, Yoko, and Gyozo Molnar. 2013. "Collective identity and contested allegiance: A case of migrant professional Fijian rugby players." *Sport in Society* 16 (7): 863–882. doi:10.1080/17430437.2013.791158.

Koch, Gerd. 2000. *Songs of Tuvalu.* Translated by Guy Slatter. South Pacific: Institute of Pacific Studies, University of the South Pacific.

Lomax, Alan. 1977. "Appeal for cultural equity." *Journal of Communication* 27 (2): 125–138. doi:10.1111/j.1460–2466.1977.tb01838.x.

Marett, Allan. 2010. "Vanishing songs: How musical extinctions threaten the planet: The Laurence Picken Memorial Lecture 2009." *Ethnomusicology Forum* 19 (2): 249–262. doi:10.1080/17411912.2010.508238.

Mataia, Stephen, Deborah Faaiuaso, Venusi Taumoepeau, and Malia Talakai. 2011. "A Pacific based approach to supporting the wider participation of Pacific

peoples in higher education." Unpublished paper. http://fyhe.com.au/past_papers/papers11/FYHE-2011/content/pdf/4B.pdf.
McNamara, Karen Elizabeth, and Chris Gibson. 2009. "'We do not want to leave our land': Pacific ambassadors at the United Nations resist the category of 'climate refugees.'" *Geoforum* 40 (3): 475–483. doi:10.1016/j.geoforum.2009.03.006.
McNatty, William, and Tom Roa. 2002. "Whanaungatanga: An illustration of the importance of cultural context." *He Puna Korero: Journal of Maori and Pacific Development* 3 (1): 88–96. http://search.informit.com.au/documentSummary;dn=884027781311679;res=IELIND.
Mortreux, Colette, and Jon Barnett. 2009. "Climate change, migration and adaptation in Funafuti, Tuvalu." *Global Environmental Change* 19 (1): 105–112. doi:10.1016/j.gloenvcha.2008.09.006.
Pollock, Elizabeth. 2006. *Atlantis Approaching*. Film. USA: Blue Marble Productions.
Titon, Jeff Todd. 2009a. "Economy, ecology, and music: An introduction." *The World of Music* 51 (1): 5–15. http://www.jstor.org/stable/41699860.
———. 2009b. "Music and sustainability: An ecological viewpoint." *The World of Music* 51 (1): 119–137. http://www.jstor.org/stable/41699860.
Treloyn, Sally, and Andrea Emberly. 2013. "Sustaining traditions: Ethnomusicological collections, access and sustainability in Australia." *Musicology Australia* 35 (2): 159–177. doi:10.1080/08145857.2013.844473.
Underhill-Sem, Y. 2001. "Flowering Identities in Samoa and the Cook Islands: Population Mobility and Environmental Transformation in the Eastern Pacific. Flowers, Fale, Fanua and Fa 'a Polynesia." *Asia Pacific Research Network Working Paper Series,* Working Paper No. 8, pp. 26–33. Wollongong: APMRN Secretariat Centre for Asia Pacific Social Transformation Series, University of Wollongong, Australia.
Warne, K. (2008). "Tuvalu: Drowning or waving." *Geographical* 80 (10) 52–62.
Williams, David. 2001. "Sinking feeling." *Time Australia* 33 (34): 26–40.
Sutter, John D. 2015. "You're making this island disappear." *CNN.* Video recording. http://edition.cnn.com/interactive/2015/06/opinions/sutter-two-degrees-marshall-islands.

CHAPTER 4

Transmitting Japanese Folk Song

Strategies for Nationalizing the Local and Taking It into Schools

Mari Shiobara

Min'yō, the term used to designate "folk song" in Japan, is linked to local places, specific locations, landscapes, and local histories. It is defined as songs that were born naturally, without lyricists or composers, within local folk communities and then transmitted aurally. They have undergone unintentional alterations and have become songs that reflect the sentiments and feelings of the common people in the region where they originated. In 1950, the Japan Folk Song Association (Nihon Minyo Kyokai) was formed by scholars and dilettantes of *min'yō.* Since then it has assumed the role of preserving and transmitting this particular musical tradition. It organizes competitions in which techniques and expressions are defined for each song and competitors often have formal lessons from professional singers and teachers, who have been certified by the association. Under its influence, the 2008 *Course of Studies for Music in Lower Secondary Schools* specifies that teaching materials should include *min'yō,* which prompted the association to produce a textbook and also to send certified *min'yō* teachers into schools.

This chapter examines four main issues in the transmission of *min'yō:* (1) folk songs that have been standardized and then subsequently modified from their original form; (2) traditional informal community singing being replaced by performance—often in competitive situations; (3) music teachers' lack of familiarity with this genre; and (4) *min'yō*'s informal teaching strategies being formalized before reaching students in schools. With these issues in mind, this chapter explores possible solutions concerned with how and in what ways these traditional Japanese folk songs can be taught while trying to maintain their originally intended essence.

Min'yō as Community Music

The term *min'yō* was coined in the late nineteenth century in order to distinguish a singing tradition among common people in Japan from other popular song traditions. It is a direct translation of the German *volkslied* (Malm 2000), with *min* translated as "people" and *yō* meaning "song." According to Scholes, one of the theories about the origin of a folk song is communal composition, "which does not preclude the fact that any individual specimen . . . must necessarily have been originally launched into use by some individual" (Scholes 1970, 366). In this vein, he goes on to say that "folk music is the composition of the race that produces it; it commonly expresses racial characteristics in a very definite way" (1970, 366). Japanese folklorist Yanagida Kunio (1875–1962) and ethnomusicologist Machida Kasho (1888–1981) contributed to establishing formal studies of *min'yō*. The former presented a detailed categorization of the songs that included their cultural and historical background (Yanagida 1929). Machida collected 2,751 songs from all over Japan with sound recordings that were eventually published in nine volumes by the Japan Broadcasting Corporation (NHK) as *Survey of Japanese min'yō*. It took thirty-six years to complete before being released in 1944.

Takeuchi states that the common use of the term *min'yō* for people's songs is a relatively new phenomenon in Japan that came into use after the end of the World War II. Prior to this, it had been called just "song," and the birth of a new term was strongly connected with the rise of democracy, which shed light on the lives of workmen and farmers in the countryside who had been ignored since the urban lifestyle came into favor in modern Japan. The Japan Broadcasting Corporation started broadcasting radio programs such as "Evening for Mining Towns" and "Evening for Farming Villages" just after the war in 1945, and they also broadcasted folk music from various different regions nationwide. These programs were intended to comfort communities of miners and farmers in various regions of Japan, who were working hard rebuilding war-wrecked Japan. Those working people loved the idea that their regional *min'yō* were broadcast throughout Japan, and the movement played a vital role in spreading traditional regional folk songs nationwide. Some songs also became nationally loved popular songs (Takeuchi 1981).

Min'yō, for Japanese people, evokes images of different regions of the country that are associated with one's hometown and the community back home. They link closely to local places, their specific locations, and landscapes as well as to the histories that lie behind them. In personal ways, *min'yō* summon up childhood memories and everyday life experiences, significant happenings in one's life such as marriage or the birth of children, and memories of loved ones, deceased family members, and friends (Hughes 2008).

As with other folk music traditions in the world, *min'yō* were composed anonymously within local folk communities and have been transmitted aurally and undergone unconscious and unintentional alterations (Asano 1966). The song's lyrics and melodies have been added or altered deliberately to fit the context in which they are sung. Expert singers often give their personal interpretations as well as some skillful variations in order to mark their ownership, and their particular ways of singing their specialty songs are praised. Singers who become highly regarded as artists often have their singing styles imitated by others. Thus, certain characteristics may become associated with particular songs and preserved in the transmission process. However, Onodera makes the point that, when the songs are handed down, the singer's thoughts and feelings are greatly reflected in the songs. She goes on to say that the singer's intention toward the songs determines the way they are sung (Onodera 2003, 106).

The most naturally arising *min'yō* are thought to be work songs and include songs for rice planting, woodcutting, horse leading, cow gathering, fishing, boat rowing, grass cutting, wheat beating, tea-leaf picking, weaving, sake making, and many other types of manual labor. Thanksgiving songs for harvests and for inviting the spirits of ancestors to spend time with family, known as *bon* dancing songs, are also included in this category. Other categories of songs are festival songs and congratulatory songs for occasions such as weddings. In so-called tatami room gathering, songs often associated with banqueting and drinking within family or close community settings are sung together (Japan Folk Song Association 2011).

These *min'yō* have been transmitted from place to place by traders traveling on ships or walking with horses carrying packs over long distances. Travelling musicians, either alone or in groups, have also played a role in the transmission of *min'yō,* and originally transported songs have been modified, accommodating and fusing various elements along the way (Takeuchi 1981). Broadly speaking, there are three styles of *min'yō* singing: solo singing, group singing in unison, and call-and-response singing, where the main solo singer sings a melodic line and another person or group of people sing calling parts.

Nationalizing the Repertoire

The Japan Folk Song Association was established in 1950, not just by scholars and dilettantes, but also by people who engage themselves with transmitting and preserving *min'yō*. It states that its aim is to "preserve, foster, spread *min'yō* and folk dances, and contribute to promoting the culture and arts of our country" (2014, 6). There are nine divisions of activities that organize various projects in order to achieve that aim. The first of all activities listed comes under the heading of "studying and diffusion," and its function is to organize various seminars for learning *min'yō* that encompass all aspects involved in its performance, which include lessons for accompanying instruments and folk dancing. The association states that it sends out "the supreme authorities of *min'yō* artists, folk dancers, and folklorists" (2014, 6) to teach at those seminars.

The second activity listed is "aural transmission, research, transcription, and recording," which implies organizing projects relating to ethnomusicological enquiry. The third activity is to "discover forgotten *min'yō* and folk dances," and these newly discovered ones are examined for authenticity and quality by the committee of authorities that is made up of the senior members of the association. If they pass the examination, they will be reintroduced to the public at the annual national competition. The fourth activity is "public relations and publishing" to produce newsletters for association members and various textbooks for teaching and learning *min'yō*.

The fifth aspect is "performing activity," and it is for this category that the association is best known nationally for its work. They hold various *min'yō* competitions "in order to raise the standard of the members' singing skills" (2014, 6). They organize eight events annually, among them five different competitions and three festivals to which winners of those competitions are invited to perform. The five competitions are organized in such a way that winners advance stepwise to successively win the higher prizes. For example, there is the alliance competition (at each prefecture, with several subdivisions within a prefecture). The winner goes on to the national competition as next step. Competitions are organized into categories based on age group so that competitors always compete against their contemporaries. There are several types of prizes at this national level, but the best singer across all age groups is also chosen at this event. All winners from the national competition are invited to compete against each other at the Japan *Min'yō* Festival that decides Japan's top *min'yō* singer of the year. There is a competition equivalent to that of the adults for children, and in the Tusgaru region (in the north of Japan), there is an annual shamisen (three-stringed plucked lute) competition to decide the top instrumentalist of the year that is also organized by the association.

The sixth activity of the Japan Folk Song Association is the "commendation and honoring" of people, who have contributed to the transmission and preservation of *min'yō*. Among the various awards they give, the *min'yō* singers with the highest medals are acknowledged as equivalent to national treasures. The seventh listed activity is "welfare work," which sends singers and accompanists to pensioners' homes or prisons to give informal concerts. They also perform at various festivals. The eighth activity is "international relations." For this, the association organizes Japan International Folk Arts Exchange Festival and invites folk musicians and artists from abroad. They also send musicians to other countries to cultivate mutual friendships and for cultural exchange. Finally, the ninth activity of the association is to certify teachers of *min'yō*. This includes not only singers but also dancers and all types of accompanying instrumentalists, with each category having its own certification. There are six stages of teacher qualification, starting from assistant teacher, then progressing to teacher, lecturer, assistant professor, professor, and finally to the highest stage, master professor.

As we see, the Japan Folk Song Association authorizes almost every aspect of *min'yō*. At each competition, technique, interpretation, and expression are strictly defined for each song according to the traditional or popular style of singing approved by the association. There are books that explain how the singers are judged at the competitions and how they can practice and win (see, e.g., Takeuchi 1981). Therefore, competitors often have formal lessons from certified teachers of the association. Highly qualified *min'yō* singers and teachers tend to establish their own societies, called *kai,* that maintain a close relationship with the association. They sometimes call themselves *iemoto* (literally, "head of the family," referring to a school of arts) and transmit their particular techniques and styles, called *ryu,* to their disciples.

In this way many *min'yō* have been standardized as soon as they reach national attention, and the most popular songs that are sung in the competition become national standard repertoire in their places of origin. They are subsequently modified from their original meanings of *volkslied,* songs of the people. Less familiar songs are forgotten unless the association happens to discover them and considers them worthy of transmission and preservation.

Going through the standardization and various controls by the authority, *min'yō* as traditional informal community singing has been replaced by performance on the stage. Furthermore, there are deliberately created conditions put forward by the association that has singers compete against each other. In this way ownership of *min'yō* has been shifted from people who sing their own *min'yō* in their local hometowns to the qualified skilled teachers who are the experts of *min'yō* as a whole but come from outside the place where a song originated. In this view, good *min'yō* teachers are the ones who are able to teach standardized repertoire to as many as possible and up to the standard demanded by the various competitions.

Introducing *Min'yō* in School Music Education

In March 2008, the currently practiced *Course of Studies for Music in Lower Secondary Schools* was published, which specifies that teaching materials are to include *min'yō* for singing activities. It states that first- through third-year students (thirteen- to fifteen-year-olds) should be taught to:

> Respond to the meaning of the verse and mood of the song, and sing with expression suitable for the song and to choose appropriate voice production to suit the genre of the song and sing with articulation bringing out the best of its verbal characteristics. . . . Among traditional singing styles of our country such as *min'yō* . . . teaching materials should include songs appropriate for the reality of region, school, and the students, that also represent characteristics of traditional singing voice. (Ministry of Education and Science 2008, 82–84)

The *Course of Studies* acknowledges that today's Japanese children should be aware of different world cultures as well as experience and understand their own music culture as the starting point (2008, 3). It has been implemented since April 2012, and music teachers nationwide have been incorporating traditional singing activities in their classrooms. The *Manual for the Course of Studies for Music* states that in order to understand characteristics of the traditional singing voice, the students should sing *min'yō,* noting its specific vocal tones and their production. They include various techniques for embellishing melodic lines and a special feature of stretching vowels (Ministry of Education and Science 2008, 35).

Authorized music textbooks for the lower secondary schools published by two companies incorporate pages of teaching *min'yō* to first-year students.

Both texts give a map of Japan and represent lists of famous songs, with lines pointing to their places of origin on the map. One explains very briefly about categories of *min'yō,* characteristics of the rhythm, and vocal techniques (Obara et al. 2012, 46–47). This textbook also presents photographs of a famous male *min'yō* singer and interviews him in the foreword. The interview article stresses that the purpose of *min'yō* singing is to express oneself and communicate one's feelings to others using one's natural voice. "Natural voice" means that children should not force the sound or feel tension in the jaw, vocal folds, and facial muscles (e.g., Callaghan 2000; Gackle 2000a, 2000b; Heyler 2003; Shewell 2009). However, there is no instruction for producing a "natural voice" as such in the textbook, and it only suggests listening to the recordings and then imitating the vocal character and sing along with them. The other textbook presents more extensive categories of *min'yō,* and their four different pentatonic scales are introduced (Miyoshi 2012, 40). It provides a score of a *min'yō* in five line staff notation and eight photographs successively showing how to use two wooden sticks to accompany the song (51).

The Japan Folk Song Association also published its own textbook in 2011 in order to support the teaching and learning of *min'yō* in the schools. The association states that it is for the qualified *min'yō* teachers that are sent by the association into the schools. It also gives a guide that the school music teachers can use to learn about *min'yō* by themselves, as well as instructions on how to teach them in the classroom (2011, 1). The textbook consists of chapters on background knowledge of *min'yō* and related historical information, vocal exercises and voice training, words, pronunciation and dialects, lyrics and words of *min'yō,* singing techniques, instructions for teachers, and the lists of *min'yō* repertoires recommended for the school use, written in staff notation.

Issues concerning the Teaching and Learning of *Min'yō* in the Classroom

As we have seen, the Japan Folk Song Association authorizes not only the repertoire but also many other aspects relating to the preservation and transmission of *min'yō.* Its ownership seems to have shifted from local people to the experts of *min'yō,* who are versatile specialists in standardized repertoire. In this way, *min'yō*'s original meaning as people's songs that were born anonymously in specific regions and sung by people in their communities is significantly modified, becoming just another genre of music, and little attention is paid to the original cultural context of each song. Various competitions and the certifying system of teachers organized by the association clearly show the shift from *min'yō* as an informal community music activity to a nationalized musical practice, even before it reaches the music classroom. In addition, within the schools' formal learning settings, if teachers are not careful, *min'yō* will become a performance-oriented activity where excellence in skills rather than informal community singing is the prime concern.

Another difficulty facing the teaching of *min'yō* in school is that music teachers lack familiarity with it. The secondary music teacher training courses are situated in the colleges of music or university departments of education that specialize in Western classical music. Therefore, music teacher education is based on the European classical model, where being competent in piano playing and singing with classical technique is the norm. They do not encourage music students to practice singing in a natural, strong voice with the special effects required by *min'yō* singing. After graduating from the music college with teaching certificates, newly qualified music teachers prepare to deal with teaching *min'yō* on their own. Most likely, they attend the seminars organized by the Japan Folk Song Association that offer hands-on experience and basic knowledge of *min'yō* using their textbooks.

Although the primary aim of teaching *min'yō* is to let the students experience characteristics of their voice production, there is no information or any suggestions on how to approach this educational aim in the authorized textbooks. Listening to recorded materials and imitating the singer's voice while listening is the only activity they recommend. If the music teacher has little experience in *min'yō* singing and is not confident about teaching it, this sort of activity is reduced merely to a listening activity. Although the association's textbook gives detailed descriptions of how the *min'yō* voice should be produced, their instructions are too specialized and difficult for the music teacher to use.

Creating New Meanings in the Classroom

The stories told through *min'yō* describe traditional ways of living in the countryside in years past, such as portraying lives of hard work in the fields and mountains. Songs relating to various festive occasions in farming villages and old-fashioned love songs, however, are not familiar subjects for young teenagers to sing and have little relevance to their own lives. The aim of teaching *min'yō* stated by the *Course of Studies* is to learn the characteristics of a traditional singing voice. However, singing is not just for producing characteristic vocal sounds but also to feel sympathy with something and to understand the meaning of the lyrics. Special care should be taken to motivate young students to learn this particular tradition of singing in order to make it relevant to their lives.

Teaching *min'yō* in today's music classroom is not an easy task and requires a lot of preparation on the teacher's part. It is crucial that music teachers choose at least one *min'yō* with which they can identify. More important, they should practice the chosen song and study it for themselves. This marks the starting point. Although this music may be unfamiliar to them, unless teachers make efforts to explore and value it, there is little chance that students will become interested in learning *min'yō*. It should be noted that the heart of *min'yō* singing lies not only in the technical matters involved in its voice production, but also in its emotional content, charged by generations of people who have loved it and those who continue to sing it. Thus, when the music is separated from its historical and cultural contexts, it may become meaningless.

Team teaching between the music teacher and a *min'yō* specialist who visits the classroom is ideal. However, the specialist does not need to be "the supreme authority of *min'yō*" suggested by the Japan Folk Song Association. The ideal specialist is someone who can sing well, but also someone who is the culture bearer of her/his own *min'yō* tradition. It should also be someone who has a lot of resources and ideas about how to communicate both musical and human values in a way with which the students can identify.

Strategies for teaching *min'yō* in the classroom could begin by having students listen to various recordings in order to become familiar with it. They should be encouraged to be imaginative about what is going on in the music as a whole. They could discuss the characteristics of singing styles as well as the meanings of the lyrics and the contexts in which they originated. They may notice that old recordings present different ways of singing the same song compared with recent ones. There is a range of voice production, from relatively simple to highly sophisticated. After such an introduction, all the students could choose a favorite song from the ones they heard.

It is important to create a communal environment for learning *min'yō*, as that was how they were originally created and transmitted. It is suggested that the students who choose the same *min'yō* as their favorite form a group for learning collaboratively. In this way they take responsibility for each other's learning. They can research the origin of the song as well as its history and follow its transmission and transfiguration process together. They should be encouraged to be imaginative and creative in their approaches so that, if they wish to, they can create a drama or a dance to explore people's lives and associate them with the song. Imagination and creativity are crucial in bridging the gap between classroom and the original contexts of *min'yō*.

After the group of students have listened to the recording of their chosen *min'yō* they may practice singing it together. While doing this they can discuss the characteristics of voice production and how they can create particular effects. This is where collaborative learning really works: they can learn from each other's findings and help each other to progress together. The music teacher should be available to help and advise students as the need arises, but as the teacher may not be able to deal with all issues, s/he can suggest saving them for when the *min'yō* specialist visits the classroom. In this way, the music teacher and the students learn *min'yō* collaboratively, and the students anticipate the visit of the specialist with clear ideas of which questions to ask to help them resolve their particular problems and issues.

It is recommended that after the students learn to sing their chosen *min'yō* they develop enough confidence to show what they have achieved together to the *min'yō* specialist when s/he is invited into the classroom. At this first meeting the specialist can talk about what *min'yō* means to her/him as well as the contexts in which it is learned. Significant life experiences associated with the song, as well as the stories of childhood experiences in their hometown can be shared with the students. The students may use their imaginations to identify their own life stories with them. Then the specialist demonstrates how *min'yō* sounds in a live performance. The goal of this performance should be to encourage the students to be interested in furthering their *min'yō* project rather than impressing them with brilliant and skillful singing.

The *min'yō* specialist goes to each group working on different songs, teaches necessary skills through demonstration, and supplies important information about the song they have been learning. The music teacher accompanies the specialist to each group and acts as a liaison between her/him and the students by helping them formulate questions and interpreting the answers. Because the music teacher knows the students and the *min'yō* specialist knows the music, how to sing, and possible ways to help others to sing like themselves, such a collaborative teaching effort is expected to be ideal.

An informal concert can be arranged to conclude the project wherein not only the students sing but also the music teacher. The *min'yō* specialist might then sing her/his own special song to close the session. Another possible strategy would be to have the class videotape their performance and upload it on YouTube to share with other classes or schools. They could also create a collaborative blog to share the art with other students and perhaps come up with ideas that marry traditional with modern singing, thus creating a new art form.

It is important that, through their experience of learning *min'yō,* students have explored the possibility of expressing themselves by using their voices in a special way. There really is no end to learning music, so the project is best left open-ended at that point. It is important, however, to make sure that the students have learned something from the experience that will motivate further learning, not only of *min'yō,* but of music as a whole.

As already discussed, *min'yō* have been standardized and subsequently modified from their original communal meanings. Traditional informal community singing is being replaced by performances and competitions among *min'yō* singers that stress skillful performance on stage. This chapter has presented possible ways in which these traditional Japanese folk songs could be taught in the music classroom while striving to maintain their originally intended essence.

Music teachers' familiarity with *min'yō* singing is still seriously lacking in the teacher education system in Japan, but this can be remedied by inviting *min'yō* specialists who are sensitive enough to care about the original essence of *min'yō* and are sympathetic to students' ownership of the music they learn to participate in the system. This assumes that a collaborative effort on the parts of the music teacher and the specialist is a crucial element for a successful classroom teaching of *min'yō.* The most important thing to be expected of music teachers is that they be receptive to new territories of music and open to expanding their own possibilities as musicians.

References

Asano, Kenji. 1966. *Japanese Folk Song (Nihon no Min'yō).* Tokyo: Iwanami Shoten.

Callaghan, Jean. 2000. *Singing and Voice Science.* San Diego, CA: Singular Publishing.

Gackle, Lynne. 2000a. "Female Adolescent Transforming Voices: Voice Classification, Voice Skill Development, and Music Literature Selection." In *Bodymind and Voice: Foundations of Voice Education,* edited by L. Thurman and G. Welch, vol. 3, bk. 5, pp. 814–820. Rev. ed. USA: The VoiceCare Network, the National Center for Voice and Speech, Fairview Voice Center, Centre for Advanced Studies in Music Education and the contributing authors.

———. 2000b. "Understanding Voice Transformation in Female Adolescents." In *Bodymind and Voice: Foundations of Voice Education,* edited by L. Thurman and G. Welch, vol. 3, bk. 4, pp. 739–744. Rev. ed. USA: The VoiceCare Network, the National Center for Voice and Speech, Fairview Voice Center, Centre for Advanced Studies in Music Education and the contributing authors.

Heyler, Mary. 2003. "Vocal Health—Looking after Your Voice." In *Bluebirds and Crows: Developing a Singing Culture in and out of School,* edited by A. Paterson and E. Bentley, pp. 22–25. Matlock, UK: The National Association of Music Educators.

Hughes, David W. 2008. *Traditional Folk Song in Modern Japan.* Kent: Global Oriental.

Japan Broadcasting Corporation (Nihon Hōsō Kyōkai). 1944. *Survey of Japanese min'yō. Vol.1 Kanto Region (Nihon Minyo Taikan, Dai 1kan, Kantōhen).* Tokyo: NHK Publishing.

Japan Folk Song Association (Nihon Minyo Kyokai). 2011. *Manual for Teaching Min'yō (Min'yō Shidou Manyuaru).* Tokyo: Nihon Minyo Kyokai.

———. 2014. *Program for National Competition of Min'yō and Folk Dancing (Min'yō Minbu Zenkoku Taikai Puroguramu).* Tokyo: Nihon.

Malm, William P. 2000. *Traditional Japanese Music and Musical Instruments.* Tokyo: Kodansha.

Ministry of Education and Science (Monbu Kagaku Shou). 2008. *The Manual for the Course of Studies For Lower Secondary Schools Music (Chugakkou Gakushushidou Youryou Kaisets Ongakuhen).* Tokyo: Kyouikugeijutsusha.

Miyoshi, Akira, ed. 2012. *Lower Secondary Music, Vol.1: Musical Offerings (Chugakuongaku 1 Ongaku no Okurimono).* Tokyo: Kyouiku shuppansha.

Obara, Kouichi, Nobuyoshi Iinuma, and Kenjiro Urata, eds. 2012. *Music for Lower Secondary Students, Vol.1 (Chugakusei no Ongaku 1).* Tokyo: Kyouikugeijutsusha.

Onodera, Setsuko. 2003. "Transmission of Japanese Songs." In *Science of Performing Arts,* edited by Tokyo Research Institute of Cultural Assets (Tokyo Bunkazai Kenkyujo), pp. 85–116. Tokyo: Tokyo Research Institute of Cultural Assets.

Scholes, Percy A. 1970. *The Oxford Companion to Music.* Oxford: Oxford University Press.

Shewell, Christina. 2009. *Voice Work: Art and Science in Changing Voices.* Paris: Lavoisier.

Takeuchi, Tsutomu. 1981. *Min'yō: Its Birth and Development (Miny'ō: Sono Hassei to Hensen).* Tokyo: Kadokawa Shoten.

Yanagida, Kunio. 1929. *Past and Present of Min'yō (Min'yō no Ima to Mukashi).* Tokyo: Chiheisha.

CHAPTER 5

Child's Play?

Teaching and Learning in Fijian Sigidrigi

Jennifer Cattermole

This chapter focuses on the teaching and learning methods used in a Fijian music genre known as *sigidrigi,* primarily focusing on a method labelled *vulitara* (learning by doing) by cultural insiders (emics). As in all ethnographic research, this chapter aims to represent primarily emic perspectives and understandings. For the purposes of cross-cultural comparison, it also compares and contrasts these emic perspectives with those of cultural outsiders (etics). In this case, the author—an etic researcher—utilizes the work of scholars of music pedagogy as the basis for this cross-cultural comparison. This comparison has been undertaken to highlight similarities and differences between the *vulitara* method and music teaching and learning methods used in Western cultures.

Vulitara, an experiential teaching and learning method, remains the prevalent method employed by teachers and learners of *sigidrigi* and is an important aspect of this performance tradition. Here, *vulitara* will be discussed in relation to self-tuition, peer learning, and tuition by proficient adults. In addition to discussing the actual teaching and learning practices used, this chapter also discusses the varying degrees of formality involved in *sigidrigi* tuition (ranging from casual observation to formal apprenticeship), as well as the variety of contexts in which *sigidrigi* teaching and learning take place (e.g., during public performances, in private, in schools, during child's play). The chapter also looks at some of the factors that restrict learners' engagement with the genre and thus threaten its sustainability (e.g., the use of teasing to enforce musical/social hierarchies, restricted amounts of leisure time, and restricted access to musical instruments). Though *sigidrigi* is performed throughout Fiji, this research is primarily concerned with its performance on the islands of Taveuni and Qamea.

This chapter utilizes data that was collected during ethnographic fieldwork on Taveuni, Fiji's third-largest island, and neighboring island Qamea from March to September 2005, as well as a subsequent fieldwork trip from mid-December 2005 to February 2006. The ethnographic data presented consists of observations of live *sigidrigi* performances as well as interviews with musicians. Interviews were mostly conducted in English,[1] except where indigenous terminology was used and explained by Fijian participants, or where participants were semifluent in English. As the researcher herself was not fluent in either Bauan (standard Fijian) or the Cakaudrove dialect spoken on Taveuni and Qamea, Taveuni resident Rafaele Waqa[2] (who was fluent in both Fijian dialects, as well as English) provided translation services during interviews where participants were not fluent in English. A semistructured interviewing technique was used, whereby some of the questions asked by the interviewer were determined in advance but others were asked based on the topics and issues raised by the interviewee. Interviews were conducted one-on-one in person, and each interview lasted approximately one hour.[3] They were audio-recorded and subsequently transcribed.

What Is *Sigidrigi*?

Before exploring teaching and learning methods it is necessary to have some understanding of the genre. Although this genre is known by a variety of names (e.g., *sere ni cumu,*[4] *sere ni verada,*[5] and *jinjig*[6]), *sigidrigi*[7] was the most commonly used term during the researcher's fieldwork and is therefore used throughout this chapter. *Sigidrigi* is an *i taukei* (indigenous Fijian) music genre featuring three- or four-part diatonic vocal harmony. The core group of singers[8] typically accompany themselves on guitar and/or ukulele, and must therefore master learning not only the repertoire but also vocal and instrumental performance techniques. Songs are most commonly performed by groups of men to entertain people during informal *yaqona*[9] drinking sessions. It is the oldest form of vernacular popular music still performed in Fiji, with its origins dating back to the 1920s (Goldsworthy 1998, 161). Although *sigidrigi*'s popularity has waned in recent years due to the introduction of alternative forms of entertainment (radio, music recordings, television, etc.),[10] the genre remains an important form of community music making throughout Fiji.

How Is *Sigidrigi* Taught and Learned?

There are three core practices employed in the teaching and learning of *sigidrigi:* self-tuition, peer learning, and tuition (either paid or unpaid) by proficient adult musicians. Of these three methods self-tuition is by far the most commonly used.

Self-tuition

Formal music tuition in Taveuni's and Qamea's primary and secondary schools predominantly consists of learning sacred songs (*sere ni lotu*). Little to no attention is given to *sigidrigi;* some schoolteachers lack the requisite skill and knowledge to teach this genre effectively, and others deem it inappropriate for the classroom. For these reasons, the majority of *sigidrigi* performers on these islands are self-taught.

Sustained contact with the genre over a protracted period leads to familiarity. Petero Kanawabu (personal communication, May 22, 2005), for example, described his learning process as one of osmosis—of gradually and unconsciously absorbing information through continual exposure to the music. Listeners, whether they are paying a great deal of attention to the music or not, may not be consciously aware that learning is occurring; enjoyment or entertainment rather than education is the focus of the activity. In other words, learning *sigidrigi* is not always a conscious, deliberate, or sought-out act, but takes place via enculturation in the musical environment. Musical skills and knowledge are acquired through immersion in everyday music making and music listening activities. Enculturation remains the most prevalent means of learning *sigidrigi* repertoire.

However, many musicians also learn the song lyrics, vocal parts, chord fingerings, and strumming techniques and rhythms through consciously observing and listening to accomplished musicians performing. In other words, their learning is focused, goal-oriented, and intentional. Green (2001, 23–24) labels this "purposive listening," which "has the particular aim, or purpose, of learning something in order to put it to use in some way after the listening experience is over." Solitarily and in private, learners subsequently copy what they have seen and heard, experimenting until they are able to replicate the sound. This certainly contrasts with teaching and learning conventions in many other cultures. As Robert Fripp (quoted in Green 2001, ix) notes, "customarily, the aspirant player seeks an 'elder' in their tradition for instruction."

Pio Taleiyawa (personal communication, May 1, 2005) called such learning *vulitara* or "to learn by doing it," and stressed that this was "a very Fijian way to learn." *Vulitara* is not only, therefore, a teaching/learning method employed in other spheres of Fijian activity, but is seen as a distinctive aspect of Fijian culture, a practice that distinguishes Fijian *sigidrigi* musicians from musicians elsewhere in the world. It is therefore a component of Fijian musicians' cultural identity, a way of distinguishing "us" from "them."

Vulitara requires intense concentration and attentiveness, as well as excellent visual and aural recall. Indeed, when recalling learning to play guitar, musician Leone Ranuve (personal communication, April 6, 2005) complained that he sometimes used to get headaches as a result of concentrating too hard on where the musicians were placing their fingers. In addition to concentrating on playing methods (fingering positions and strumming patterns in particular), purposive listeners and watchers also concentrate intently on various other aspects of performance, such as performers' facial expressions and body language. While *sigidrigi* performers may place greater emphasis on the aural than on the visual, spectacle is still an important aspect of *sigidrigi* performance and adds greatly to audience enjoyment.

Primarily, this kind of learning (via aural and visual memorization) takes place during live performances—most commonly at informal *yaqona* drinking parties. Although it has become increasingly permissible for children to attend such social gatherings, some mothers and other older female relatives still forbid them to attend, deeming *yaqona*-drinking an inappropriate activity for those younger than their mid-late teens. Two key objections are raised to children's presence at such events, both relating to men's role and social status.

First, various adult activities that take place at such parties (such as tobacco smoking, *yaqona* drinking, ribald joking, and flirting) are regarded as bad influences on young boys, an example of poor role modelling. Women try to raise their sons, nephews, or grandsons so they grow up to be healthy and good husbands and providers for their families. The *yaqona*-drinking gatherings at which *sigidrigi* is often performed contravene these aims, as smoking is unhealthy and excessive *yaqona*-drinking and staying up late can take a toll on family life and overall health. Such behavior makes husbands tired and lethargic and hence less productive gardeners and farmers, which is an important consideration given that Taveuni and Qamea's economy is subsistence-based. *Sigidrigi* performance also reduces the amount of quality family time husbands spend with their wives and children. Moreover, the ribald joking and flirting that is often directed towards musicians[11] can create tension and jealousy if those musicians are married. Again, married women see this as promoting inappropriate behavior, and as an example of poor role modelling for young boys.

Second, it is generally considered ill-mannered for children to sit around with their elders. Elders, in Fijian culture, are accorded great respect: the greater one's age, the greater one's social status. For children to include themselves among adult company is therefore regarded as presumptuous. For example, Victor Bibi (personal communication, August 1, 2005) remembers being chastised by his aunties and called *viavia qase* (wanting to be old; presuming a higher social status than that due to him on the basis of his age).

Despite such objections, most *sigidrigi* performers on Taveuni and Qamea described learning the genre as children by watching and listening to their older male relatives and other elders performing at *yaqona* drinking parties.[12] Victor Bibi (personal communication, August 1, 2005), for example, displayed such a persistent interest in the music that he eventually overcame his aunties' objections; after watching for some time he was encouraged to join in. A child's active musical interest can, therefore, be rewarded; indeed, this is often a source of pleasurable pride for performers who are adult male relatives of the child (i.e., a sign that they are taking after them, following in their footsteps by emulating their behavior). In informal, family settings, even very young children, if they take an interest in *sigidrigi,* may be indulged by being allowed to strum the instrument's strings under adult supervision.

That most Taveuni and Qamea musicians I spoke with indicated they learned *sigidrigi* by attending *yaqona*-drinking gatherings as children seems indicative of broader cultural shifts. Married men, priests, and chiefs, during the researcher's fieldwork, were generally expected to act in a responsible and dignified manner, and a measure of societal pressure was brought to bear on such individuals to adhere to behavioral expectations. Over time, however, expectations regarding such decorum have been gradually relaxed. During fieldwork, the researcher encountered instances where chiefs, priests, and married men participated in *yaqona*-drinking gatherings as *sigidrigi* performers. Even though such individuals could be viewed as acting beneath their dignity by participating in such gatherings (and would thus be disapproved of by conservative elements in their communities), their status did not appear to suffer—at least, not in such a way that was observable or openly acknowledged to an etic researcher. *Yaqona* drinking itself has become markedly less formal over time. Previously the preserve of the highest-ranking men in the *koro* (village), *yaqona* may now be drunk by women, and even by children.

The way in which the *yaqona* is served is also changing. While serving the most highly ranked individuals in a group first was the norm during fieldwork, the researcher attended parties where people simply served themselves and ignored customary *yaqona*-serving protocols. All these factors indicate a gradual democratization of Fijian society, and it is this breaking down of social barriers that has made it possible for the current generation of *sigidrigi* performers to learn the genre as children.

While most musicians learn *sigidrigi* at informal *yaqona*-drinking gatherings, learning also occurs in other contexts. Some Taveuni musicians described listening to songs over the radio or on music recordings and experimenting with guitar chord fingerings until they were able to replicate the sounds. Popular music learning on Taveuni has therefore, to date, been the inverse of common global practice, which Green (2001, 60) describes as follows: "Live music is encountered much less. By far the overriding learning practice for the beginner popular musician . . . is to copy recordings by ear." She notes the ubiquity of this practice across the world (Green 2001, 61), and indeed there are signs that popular music learning on Taveuni is following this global trend. The growing accessibility and affordability of recording technologies and media, and the decline of live performance in favor of recorded alternatives, means that recordings are becoming increasingly influential learning tools for Taveuni popular musicians. Hence, aural learning is assuming greater importance than more experiential practices based on both listening *and* looking.

On Taveuni, *sigidrigi* is also learned through the construction of imitation musical instruments. Green (2001, 60) notes that "children not only *copy the behaviour* of adults and other children, but they also *make copies of objects* which they find in the environment" (italics in original). Prior to picking up real musical instruments, some Taveuni children, in an application of the *vulitara* method, learn about *sigidrigi* by making toy instruments and using them to mimic adult behaviour.[13] Sirilo Seru (personal communication, July 5, 2005), for example, used a home-made ukulele when he was a young boy. It consisted of a small wooden board from a wooden crate. At the "body" end, an empty tinned meat can was nailed onto the back to form a closed resonating chamber; on the front, a wooden bridge with four notches for the strings was attached. Four holes were drilled through the board at the "neck" end and the strings stretched tight and knotted at the back. Sirilo used to sit beside his father during *sigidrigi* performances and play his toy ukulele. Although his father chased him away, this was how he learned to play the instrument.

Many of Tavenui and Qamea's current *sigidrigi* performers also learned various musical skills (e.g., singing, playing in time in a group, leadership skills) by playing a game in which they pretended to be members of a band featuring electrified instruments.[14] In other words, while not imitating *sigidrigi* performance directly, this activity was still part of these musicians' formative musical development. Boys ranging from six to fourteen years of age, individually or in groups of three to six members, would go into the bush and construct instruments from available materials. Guitars (bass, rhythm, and lead) were made from the thick ends of fallen coconut palm fronds (*drau ni niu*) or pieces of wood, cut to an appropriate length and shaped using a knife. String or vine would be used for guitar straps. Vine could also be used to represent electric cable, and biscuit tins as amplifiers. Keyboards were imitated using a row of sticks laid on the ground. Microphones were represented by sticks or small felled trees, sometimes with nuts or fruits stuck on top to represent the head of the microphone. Drum kits were made using empty metal containers (e.g., biscuit tins, tin cans), and/or cardboard boxes, with two to three pot lids with holes in the middle stuck on top of sticks, or tin plates nailed to tree trunks forming the cymbals. Sticks were used as beaters. A tambourine would be made from a stick or a piece of plywood with metal bottle caps nailed on it.

The boys would imitate playing on these instruments, and all (including the percussionists) would vocalize the instruments' sounds. One member of the group would sing, sometimes sitting on a tree branch above the other band members. As spatial elevation conveys and confers elevated social status, the solo vocalist was thereby—consciously or not—replicating the "star" system hierarchy found Western popular music. Sets of instruments were usually kept in a private and secluded place (e.g., beneath a small tree covered in vines), far from adults. This game occupied the boys primarily during school holidays and after school; it was so appealing that sometimes they would shirk their after-school chores, or even skip school, in order to play. If discovered by parents or other adult relatives, such behavior was punished. The disappearance of these bands from Taveuni means that such games (and the type of musical learning they involved) are a thing of the past.

In addition to watching, listening to, and imitating other players (using real or imitation instruments), some Taveuni musicians have taught themselves to use Western tunings and chord fingerings by using chord books. This is particularly the case for those who perform in resorts on the island, where the repertoire predominantly consists of covers of English-language pop songs, as Western chord fingerings are considered most appropriate for this repertoire. In many cases, chord books were not the primary source of information but supplemented existing knowledge. Some musicians also learn about playing techniques and music theory from reading instructional books. Generally speaking, however, this kind of book learning is very uncommon.

Mentoring/Apprenticeship

Individuals wishing to learn how to sing and/or play guitar/ukulele may ask to apprentice themselves to a performer they admire (a *dau ni lagasere*—expert singer, or a *dau ni qiriqiri*—expert instrumentalist). Similar kinds of apprenticeship training take place in other musical performance traditions around the world (see, e.g., Berliner 1994; Nketia 1975; Merriam 1964), but are uncommon in Western Europe. As Green (2001, 16) notes: "Most young popular musicians in the West are not surrounded by an adult community of practicing popular musicians, and therefore 'legitimate peripheral participation' of the sort studied by Lave and Wenger (1991) is largely unavailable to them . . . in so far as a community of practice is available to young popular musicians, it tends to be a community of *peers* rather than of 'master musicians' or adults with greater skills." On Taveuni and Qamea, a learner may learn both singing and playing from one performer or may develop these skills separately with two individuals (i.e., one singer and one instrumentalist). These experts may be respected musicians from an individual's own or a neighboring *koro* (village); they are commonly family members.

A "situated learning" (see Lave and Wenger 1991) approach is used during a musician's apprenticeship to a musician who has mastered the genre. During live *sigidrigi* performances, the learner will sit beside her/his mentor, often leaning close so they can hear the part clearly. Before the beginning of the song (e.g., during a break for a round of *yaqona*), the singing teacher may first demonstrate the limits of that part's vocal range to make sure the learner can handle the part and/or the vocal line itself; if teaching instrumental performance, the teacher may use that time to demonstrate the tuning, chord fingerings, and strumming patterns and techniques—they may also verbally communicate information about the song's tempo and key. The students are expected to memorize what they see and hear and be able to replicate it either immediately or at a later time.

Learners may then take their teacher's place in the ensemble, with their teacher only joining in if they are insecure or struggling with their part; or they might play and/or sing along with their teacher—quietly, and a little

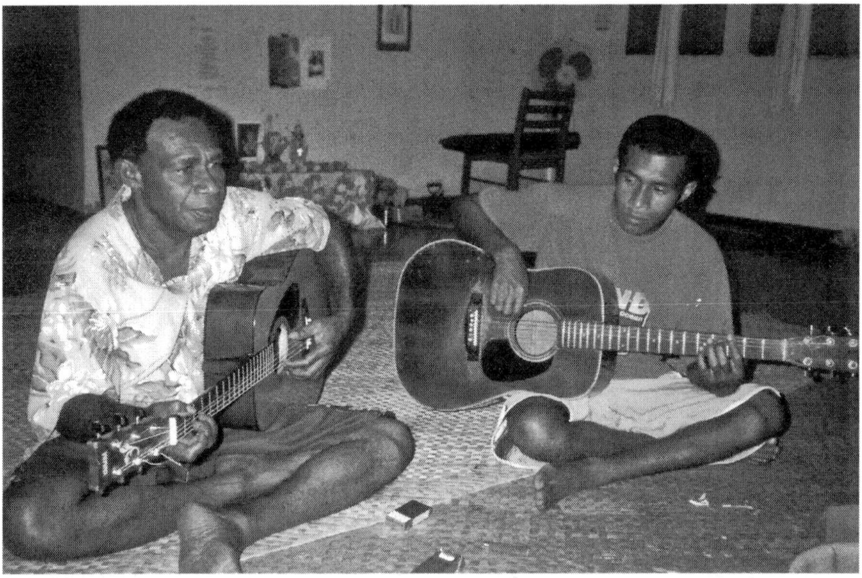

Figure 5.1. Photo of Pete Tavaya (right) being taught to play guitar by his father, Petero (left). Particularly interesting is the fact that Petero is left-handed, whereas Pete is right-handed. Thus, unlike his brother Mika who is also left-handed, Pete has not been able to imitate his father's playing exactly but has had to think in terms of creating a mirror image. Photo taken by Jennifer Cattermole at Tutu, Taveuni.

behind the beat, conscious that their every mistake will be audible. A singing teacher will sometimes indicate the melodic contour using hand gestures as a visual aid for the learner. I also frequently witnessed instances where a teacher acted as a prompt if the learner was unfamiliar with the song lyrics—speaking the words quickly immediately before the line was sung. To assist learners to change chords in the correct place, a teacher may call out the names of the chords (or hold up the correct number of fingers to represent the chords *dua*-tonic, *rua*-subdominant, or *tolu*-dominant),[15] or signal the time to change chords using eye contact or nodding. Alternatively, they may shake their head or point to indicate that the musician is performing an incorrect chord, or perform the correct chord until the learning musician has changed his fingering. Key changes, or temporary rests (e.g., just prior to the beginning of a new verse) may also be visually or verbally cued.

Learning performers often rely on established musicians to correct any significant errors in their performance. The teacher will provide feedback during or after the performance, tapping the learner on his shoulder or thigh to gain his attention, and—in a whisper—identifying the mistake and advising how to correct it. Alternatively, they may stop the learner's performance and demonstrate the correct part while the student pays close attention. Sometimes, they may even physically place the learner's fingers on the correct frets and strings on the fret-board when teaching chord fingerings. This type of teaching and learning is essentially the *vulitara* "watch, listen, and imitate" method, albeit with expert and intentional guidance. Learners are provided with immediate feedback on their singing and playing in a live performance context, and therefore do not have to memorize what they see and hear and try to reproduce that at a later time. It can be viewed as an extension of traditional *sigidrigi* teaching/learning practice and is, in my opinion, a much more effective learning practice in that it involves direct rather than indirect tuition.

Peer-group Learning

As Green (2001, 83) notes, "as with listening and copying, peer-directed learning and group learning form central components of popular music informal learning practices." Learners commonly perform with others of a similar age and skill level. This kind of peer learning usually begins when boys reach their late teens—the age when they are usually permitted to drink *yaqona* at the *yaqona*-drinking gatherings where *sigidrigi* is often performed and hence gain exposure to the music.

The key exceptions to this are boys who grow up in musical households. Abaramu Tivikea, for example, is a well-known composer and performer on Taveuni, and his wife Vitalina also composes and comes from a remarkably musical family. Their three youngest sons, Aca (fifteen years old), Benito (fourteen), and Lorosio (twelve) usually perform together as a trio. The support, help, and encouragement provided by Abaramu and Vitalina have been pivotal in their sons' musical education. As with popular music performance traditions elsewhere, "due to the increased emphasis on enculturation in popular music learning practices, it is *more* likely that popular musicians will come from musically interested families" (Green 2001, 24; italics in original).

On Taveuni and Qamea, the most accomplished and experienced musicians (usually older men) perform earliest at *yaqona*-drinking gatherings; the least proficient musicians perform either at the very end of the evening's entertainment or immediately prior to the arrival of the most highly esteemed musicians at the beginning of the event. Group learning occurs primarily at such gatherings.[16] These group practices are particularly significant for beginners, who seldom practice in the company of their peers outside of such occasions, as work/chore demands can make coordinating leisure time somewhat difficult. The opportunities for learning musicians to practice are limited by the amount of free time learners have available. In a subsistence economy, productivity is essential and leisure time scarce.

Individuals typically learn to sing and play *sigidrigi* songs by spending hours on their own, in private, attempting to recall and imitate what they have seen and heard during live performances. Therefore, the rare opportunities to perform with and learn from one's peers provide a valuable means to develop confidence in playing in front of an audience as well as ensemble performance skills (e.g., learning to sing and play in time with others, when to change chords, and how to sing in harmony).

Accomplished musicians emphasize the need for learning musicians to put in lots of practice. However, practice opportunities for learning musicians are limited not only by available leisure time but also by factors such as their status within the musical (and, more broadly speaking, social) hierarchy. One particular challenge learning musicians need to come to grips with is the teasing that enforces the existing hierarchy. Elders may give younger groups of musicians insulting or demeaning names to make fun of them and discourage them from performing. As Tui Rabe (personal communication, July 29, 2005) jokingly remarked: "for the young musicians, it can be dangerous when these old men are around." There is a wide range of insulting expressions that can be used. Singers may be accused of talking or shouting rather than singing, or of being *mateni* (the state when one has drunk too much *yaqona*). The expression *ari niu* (scraping coconut) may be used to liken voices to the harsh sound of the flesh being scraped from the inside of a coconut. Those doing the insulting may also pretend to call their chickens in a more covert reference to the sound of scraping coconut (chickens enjoy pecking at the inside of a coconut whose flesh has been mostly scraped away). Singers' voices may also be compared to the sounds of animals such as horses, goats, dogs, cows, or cats. For example, a group might receive the unflattering moniker of *tagapusi* (bag of cats), after which listeners may begin mimicking the sound of these unfortunate animals. Alternatively, groups may also be crudely compared to the sounds of flatulence or a flushing toilet.

Younger musicians expect to be criticized by their elders, and insults such as these are seldom taken to heart. Indeed, such playful teasing and joking is regarded as contributing to the overall fun of the social gathering. If taken seriously, however, this kind of teasing can discourage younger musicians from performing in the presence of their elders. For example, Wani (personal communication, May 17, 2005)—a young musician from Lovonivonu, Taveuni—and his peers can join in when his father and older cousins are performing, but are criticized and insulted by the older musicians the following day. As he states: "the next night, you find somewhere else to sing." Wani does want to learn the repertoire and develop his skills as a singer and guitarist but finds the discouragement by and lack of support from his elders to be a deterrent. Tenacity, determination, and emotional resilience are required if musicians are to become proficient enough to perform for the enjoyment of others.

In addition to time constraints and considerations of social status, learners' ability to practice is also determined by the availability of instruments (which are prohibitively expensive for many). Learning musicians sometimes borrow instruments belonging to relatives, even if they have been expressly forbidden to do so. If a member of their household does not own an instrument, learning musicians might ask to borrow someone's instrument the day after the *sigidrigi* performance so they can practice while the memory of what they have seen and heard is still fresh in their minds. If they want clarification on particular aspects of the playing or singing, they may ask the musicians next time they perform.

Occasionally, learners participate in more advanced groups, where they have the chance to learn playing and singing from their elders rather than their peers. A lesser-skilled musician may, for example, take the place of an older, more accomplished musician during their temporary absence when a performance is taking place (caused, for example, by a visit to the toilet). Infrequently, an experienced musician may lend his instrument to a learner and encourage him to take his place during a performance.[17]

Occasionally, an exceptionally talented *cauravou* (youth) may be invited to perform with the musicians of highest social rank; this is considered an honor. Precocious, talented children may be encouraged to showcase their talent in adult performance contexts. For example, Iowani, Kasiano Ramuala's eleven-year old son was once included in a core group of performers for a couple of songs. Such performances are, however, unusual.

To briefly summarize, *vulitara,* or "learning by doing" is by far the most common learning and teaching practice used for *sigidrigi.* Aspiring musicians typically watch and listen to those proficient in the genre and then experiment on their own using borrowed (or, less commonly, bought) instruments until they can reproduce what they have heard and seen. For young boys, this imitation of adult musical behavior tends to occur in play via the use of toy instruments, either individually or in small groups. If a younger family member wishes to learn, an older male relative will often step in and become a tutor and mentor. Alternatively, a learner may pay a nonfamily member to provide tuition, although this situation is rare. Even where expert teaching is provided, *vulitara* remains the essential method employed. Given restrictions on leisure time and instrument availability, opportunities to learn from one's peers and to develop ensemble performance skills are rare and are primarily limited to the very end of *yaqona*-drinking gatherings. The teasing that takes place on such occasions, albeit good-natured, is an additional challenge learning *sigidrigi* musicians must face. Learning *sigidrigi* is therefore challenging; students need to have well-developed aural and visual memory skills, as well as persistence, dedication, and resilience, to master the genre.

While the peer-directed and group learning and learning through children's play documented on Taveuni and Qamea appear to be fairly ubiquitous Western music learning practices, the emphasis on learning in live music contexts—that is, memorizing what has been seen and heard and attempting to replicate it during or after the performance event—is not. Although *vulitara* is not in fact a unique Fijian music teaching/learning process, it is perceived as being so by Fijians, whose only bases for comparison are the Western music teaching/learning practices they see in formal educational settings as well as in encounters with Western musicians—often in touristic environments. On this basis, *vulitara* can be regarded as an important aspect of vernacular popular music making on Taveuni and Qamea and as a signifier of cultural uniqueness.

Notes

1 English is one of Fiji's three official languages, the other two being Fijian and Hindi. Fiji was a British colony from 1874 to 1970.

2 Rafaele Waqa was a member of the family who hosted the researcher for most of her stay at Wairiki, Taveuni. Kusitino Marawa, the head of that family, is his uncle (*momo*). Rafaele acted as translator during interviews where needed and also translated song texts for me. He remains an invaluable teacher and friend.

3 Some interviews were shorter or longer than one hour (the shortest was around twenty minutes, and the longest around two-and-a-half hours). The duration was always at the discretion of the interviewee, and some interviewees were interviewed more than once (but no more than three times).

4 "*Cumu* songs." *Cumu* has a variety of meanings in the Standard Fijian language (*vosa vakabau*, or Bauan). It means "leaning up against," or "bumping or hitting against," and is most often said to refer to drinking or dancing activities associated with this music genre.

5 "Veranda songs" refers to one of the common performance contexts for this genre: under the eaves of people's verandas.
6 An onomatopoeic term referring to the sound of guitar and/or ukulele strumming.
7 Often believed to be a conflation of the English words "sing" and "drink," although *drigi* also has a range of indigenous meanings referring to people being in close physical proximity (e.g., when people lean against or rub up against one another).
8 Up until around the mid-1990s, the *sere bass* (bass song) style of *sigidrigi* was popular. This featured a trio of vocal soloists, along with a large group of bass singers. Since that time, a newer style called *trio,* featuring only the three solo singers, has overtaken the older style in terms of popularity. During the researcher's fieldwork, *sere bass* songs were still being performed, although not as frequently as *trio* songs.
9 *Yaqona* is an infusion of powdered *Piper Methisticum* roots and stems; its Polynesian term is *kava.*
10 This gradual decline in music making is also occurring in other areas around the globe (see Hayward 2006, 65; Nwezi 1999, 77; Oehrle 1991, 164).
11 On Taveuni and Qamea, being a *sigidrigi* musician is viewed as increasing one's sexual appeal. Young men sometimes learn music in order to try and attract sexual partners, and wives may expect their husbands to give up *sigidrigi* performing after their marriage (although in practice few adhere to this ideal of Fijian husbandly behavior).
12 This teaching/learning method is not restricted to *i taukei.* Pasemaca (personal communication, June 14, 2005), a woman from Betelema, Taveuni, learned guitar by watching Dileep, the Indo-Fijian shopkeeper who works at the Maqaiviti store. Before dinner they would share a *beseni* (basin) of *yaqona,* watch a movie, and then Dileep would perform songs while Pasemaca observed.
13 For further discussions of children's learning music by mimicking adults, see, for example, Campbell, 1991, 1998; Harwood, 1998a, 1998b; Marsh, 1995, 1999; Wemyss, 1999; Glover, 2000.
14 Such bands, playing rock, pop, and country hits, were popular during the 1970s and 1980s.
15 When I was learning how to play ukulele in Naivivi, Qamea, Taniela would sometimes call out the names of the chords (e.g., *dua, rua, tolu*). During a performance I witnessed at Qali, Abaramu was helping his sons Aca, Benny, and Lorosio by calling out the chords to "E na loma ga ni nomudrau vuvale lomani." Vitalina, their mother, would sometimes hold up one, two, or three fingers to indicate the chords *dua, rua,* or *tolu* respectively.

16 They can also occur during music classes at primary and secondary school in the absence of suitably skilled/knowledgeable adult teachers.

17 The researcher taught herself how to play some chords on the ukulele by watching and listening to experienced players at a performance at Naivivi, Qamea. These musicians were very supportive and encouraging of her efforts, and insisted that she play the instrument during a song's performance for a group of tourists visiting the *koro.* This was a gesture of respect and hospitality.

References

Berliner, Paul. 1994. *Thinking in Jazz: The Infinite Art of Improvisation.* Chicago: Chicago University Press.

Campbell, Patricia S. 1991. "The Child-Song Genre: A Comparison of Songs by and for Children." *International Journal of Music Education* 17 (1): 14–23. doi:10.1177/025576149101700103.

———. 1998. *Songs in Their Heads: Music and Its Meaning in Children's Lives.* New York: Oxford University Press.

Glover, Joanna. 2000. *Children Composing, 4–14.* Brighton, UK: Falmer Press.

Goldsworthy, David. 1998. "Fijian Music." In *The Garland Encyclopedia of World Music: Australia and the Pacific Islands,* edited by Adrienne L. Kaeppler and J. W. Love, 774–776. New York and London: Garland Publishing.

Green, Lucy. 2001. *How Popular Musicians Learn: A Way Ahead for Music Education.* Aldershot, UK: Ashgate Publishing.

Harwood, Eve. 1998a. "Learning in Context: A Playground Tale." *Research Studies in Music Education* 11: 52–61. doi:10.1177/1321103x9801100106.

———. 1998b. "'Go on Girl!' Improvisation in African-American Girls' Singing Games." In *In the Course of Performance: Studies in the World of Musical Improvisation,* edited by Bruno Nettl and Melinda Russell, 113–126. Chicago: University of Chicago Press.

Hayward, Philip. 2006. "Localisation and Local Song Repertoire on Norfolk Island." *Paper presented at the 2nd International Small Island Cultures Conference,* edited by H. Johnson, 61–67. Sydney: The Small Island Cultures Research Initiative (SICRI).

Lave, Jean, and Wenger, Etienne. 1991. *Situated Learning: Legitimate Peripheral Participation.* Cambridge: Cambridge University Press.

Marsh, Kathryn. 1995. "Children's Singing Games: Composition in the Playground?" *Research Studies in Music Education* 4: 2–11. doi:10.1177/1321103x9500400102.

———. 1999. "Mediated Orality: The Role of Popular Music in the Changing Traditions of Children's Musical Play." *Research Studies in Music Education* 13: 2–12. doi:10.1177/1321103x9901300102.

Merriam, Alan P. 1964. *The Anthropology of Music.* Chicago: Northwestern University Press.

Nketia, Joseph H. K. 1975. *The Music of Africa.* London: Gollancz.

Nwezi, Meki. 1999. "Strategies for Music Education in Africa: Towards a Meaningful Progression from Traditional to Modern." *International Journal of Music Education* 33: 72–87. doi:10.1177/025576149903300109.

Oehrle, Elizabeth. 1991. "An Introduction to African Views of Music Making." *Journal of Aesthetic Education* 25 (3): 163–73. doi:10.2307/3333001.

Wemyss, Kathryn. 1999. "From T.I. to Tasmania: Australian Indigenous Popular Music in the Curriculum." *Research Studies in Music Education* 13: 28–39. doi:10.1177/1321103x9901300104.

CHAPTER 6

Gathering to Study

The Case of the Myōan Shakuhachi's Benkyō-kai

Christian Mau

Well known for its connections to Zen Buddhism, the Japanese *shakuhachi* has spread internationally, often along with its Zen or "spiritual" aspects. Yet even in Japan, this end-blown notched bamboo flute is often heard performed on stage in a concert context rather than with the backdrop of a temple. This chapter looks at a particular community of *shakuhachi* players who gather regularly at a temple in Kyoto to pursue activities all of which are centered around the instrument, and examines the various factors that contribute to forming, defining, and maintaining it as a self-contained community. A brief overview of a problematic history will serve to situate the instrument and its Zen legacy firmly in the present by paying particular attention to understanding how the historical aspects contribute to defining the community known as the Myōan Kyōkai. The chapter continues by examining current practice in order to understand how members' activities function, not only to further define the community, but also to sustain it. Because all activities revolve around the *shakuhachi* and a set repertoire, the focus will be on understanding how group learning in the form of the *benkyō-kai* contributes to defining and reinforcing the community of the Myōan Kyōkai.

Overview of a Problematic History

Due to many inconsistencies, gaps, and unverifiable facts, a history of the Zen legacy of the *shakuhachi*—and even the instrument itself—can never be fully accurate or complete. A self-defined history of the tradition is outlined in a document called the *Kyotaku denki* (History of the False Bell) and its contents have been analyzed, strongly questioned, and even criticized for their lack of historical consistency and complete veracity. Presenting and discussing all of these points will not aid in understanding the current study, but at the same time a basic history serves to situate the study in the present.

The Fuke sect of Rinzai Zen Buddhism takes its name from the Tang Dynasty Chinese priest Fuke (d. 860), who rang a bell while proclaiming: "If attacked in the light, I will strike back in the light. If attacked in the dark, I will strike in the dark. If attacked[1] from all quarters, I will strike as a whirlwind does. If attacked from the empty sky, I will thrash with a flail"[2] (trans. Tsuge 1977, 49). This poetic verse (*gatha*) serves as the basis for the Zen *shakuhachi* tradition as a whole and is still recited at Myōan Temple today. Even though Fuke did not play any type of flute, an admirer who wanted to become his disciple fashioned a bamboo flute and named it a "false bell" (*kyotaku*) to emulate Fuke's bell. Thus a flute-playing tradition was born and transmitted from generation to generation. While in China studying Zen (Chinese: Ch'an), the Japanese priest Kakushin (1207–1298) encountered the sixteenth generation flute player and began to learn it. He is then purported to have brought the tradition, along with the instrument, on his return to Japan in 1254.

Historically, the *shakuhachi* or any flute cannot be linked to Kakushin, however, nor is there any trace of any similar flute-playing tradition in China. Even the precursor to today's instrument that had originally come from the mainland as part of the *gagaku* imperial court ensemble in the latter half of the seventh century was short-lived, having disappeared from the orchestra by the middle of the ninth century. The *shakuhachi* subsequently evolved appreciably, with little doubt (and actually without much trace) inside Japan. This is based on the fact that many of its physical traits cannot be found in any flute back on the continent excluding its more recent exportation from Japan. The first hard evidence of an organized Zen flute-playing tradition in Japan, however, does not appear until 1677.

During a time when religious organizations and their creation were strictly controlled by the Tokugawa Shogunate that ruled the country during Japan's Edo period (1600–1868), many scholars believe the history to be a fabrication in order to legitimize it (cf. Nakatsuka 1936; Sanford 1977; Kamisangō 1974, 1988; Deeg 2007). For the purposes here, however, detailing the exact origins are far less important than recognizing that an organization calling itself Fuke and aligning itself with Rinzai Zen Buddhism certainly existed from 1677 until its proscription in 1871, just three years after imperial rule was restored. This also coincided with a period that saw Buddhism as a whole under strong attack in the country, with thousands of temples razed and priests forced into the laity (Ketelaar 1990; Collcutt 1986; Hane 1986).

Before the proscription, correspondence between the Tokugawa government and the Fuke sect[3] declared that the *shakuhachi* was the sole domain of its adherents and that membership was exclusively reserved for the warrior (*bushi*) class. With an official monopoly on the instrument, adherents of the sect called themselves *komusō,* meaning "monks/priests[4] of emptiness and nothingness." They were easily recognizable by a distinctive raiment that included a hive-shaped basket covering their faces, which they wore outside the temple to perform mendicancy.

Contemporizing the Past

While the overall history is somewhat sketchy at best, it is clear that a *komusō* flute-playing tradition that aligned itself with Rinzai Zen certainly did exist during the late seventeenth through late nineteenth centuries before being outlawed in 1871. A lot of the documentation about the *komusō* and their wonderings while performing mendicancy is iconic or included in isolated anecdotal episodes. There is, however, very little documentation on actual ideology other than the *History of the False Bell* (*Kyotaku denki*) that outlined the contentious history briefly described in the preceding section. Nothing really appears until the early nineteenth century in the form of three essays written by Hisamatsu Fūyō (1791–1871).[5] Furthermore, if anything actually did exist, virtually nothing survives about what actually took place within the confines of a temple.[6] Yet even with this problematic history, when a new constitution was promulgated in 1889 that included religious freedom, the tradition was able to revive itself in Kyoto the following year, when the Myōan Kyōkai[7] was established within the compound of the Rinzai Zen Temple, Tōfuku-ji.

Myōan Temple is a freestanding headquarters and has no satellite temples directly affiliated with it. Of the Fuke sect's three main temples, it is the only one that was reestablished, although at a different location from its original. Today there are over four hundred members nationwide, about half of them certified teachers.[8] The repertoire is organized into seven stages before a member is considered to have had all pieces transmitted to him/her. With the completion of each of the first six steps, certification is issued by the temple and awarded directly to the student by the teacher. It is not unusual, therefore, for a student not to have visited the temple, especially if not residing within close proximity to Kyoto. Once all of the prescribed repertoire has been received, the final level is known as *kaiden,* literally translated as "everything transmitted." Once this final stage has been achieved, a special ceremony is held at the temple in which the student is conferred *kaiden* status along with being inducted into the *dōshu-kai,* or association of certified teachers.

Many, if not most, arts in Japan are divided into similar graded stages, and in addition they are organized into a pseudo-kinship arrangement known as the *iemoto* system. This hierarchical structure has at its top the *iemoto,* which translates as "household head." This leader bears the name of a particular style or school. Once a student is considered to have achieved mastery, he/she takes the name (*natori*) of the school and is often given an additional name. Relationships thus take on familial characteristics, and a lineage can be traced back to the person who is the household head. Matsumoto (1960) uses the term "simulated family" and points out that this sort of group identity manifests itself in other facets of Japanese life. Hsu describes it as "kin-tract," by which he means: "a fixed and unalterable hierarchical arrangement voluntarily entered into among a group of human beings who follow a common code of behavior under a common ideology for a set of common objectives" (Hsu 1975, 62).

The Myōan Kyōkai shows similar characteristics to the *iemoto* system, but with some important and notable differences. A corresponding relationship to the teacher exists and students take what is referred to as a "bamboo name" (*chikumei*), which includes one character (*kanji* or Chinese ideograph) of the teacher's bamboo name. This sets up a lineage that is traceable to the teacher, the teacher's teacher, and so forth. Inter-student relationships are actually verbalized with familial designations. For example, a senior student (defined in terms of length of time he/she has studied rather than age) would be the older brother/sister of a junior student. These kinship features are often used in other areas that are based on the *iemoto* system, which, as mentioned, also carry the style or school within the name that can be tracked back to a specific person. This is missing in the Myōan Kyōkai, as there is nothing to identify a particular school or style of playing contained within the name, only a way of tracing teaching lineage. Unlike in the typical *iemoto* scheme, however, there is no single traceable lineage but rather several. In effect, the head of the household would be the house itself, in this case Myōan Temple, as aptly observed by Nishiyama (1997, 206).

Still, this does not mean that any kind of hierarchical structure is absent from Myōan Temple and the Myōan Kyōkai.[9] A resident priest takes care of the temple, its grounds, and many of the administrative functions related to the operations of the Kyōkai. He is ordained and tonsured and also presides over the *suizen-kai.* An abbot is seen as the main culture bearer and overall leader, but though he takes on students, he cannot be considered a father figure in the traditional *iemoto* sense. A head teacher oversees the *dōshu-kai,* the association of certified teachers. Like the *komusō* of the Edo period, who were not ordained or tonsured, the Myōan Kyōkai is essentially a lay organization, except for the resident priest, as just noted. Finally, there is no professionalism associated with the membership. While fees are paid for lessons, members usually have other professional occupations or are retired. For example, the current abbot is a medical doctor. It should be added that there are fees associated with membership. These, other than covering operation costs, represent a commitment to membership of the community.

Activities

Activities of the Myōan Kyōkai do not generally include performing on stage in concert situations,[10] but rather take place within the setting of a temple. The most frequent is the *suizen-kai,* or "blowing Zen gathering," which is completely closed to the nonmembership. Notices regarding the date and time of these gatherings are sent via the postal system to all certified teachers (*dōshu*), thus filtering the information through teachers and attracting for the most part certified teachers, who may invite some of their more advanced students to join. The *suizen-kai* is a fixed ritual, led by the priest, that involves sutra chanting, reciting Fuke's poetic verse (*gatha*), and playing the *shakuhachi* together as a group, facing the altar. Participants are on the floor, kneeling on cushions *seiza* style (sitting on the soles of the feet). During the chanting and recitation, the blowing end of the participants' *shakuhachi* rest in front of them on cinnabar-colored folded fans. The ritual concludes with each participant approaching the altar in turn to offer incense (*shōkō*). Some participants wear a black robe over their clothes, but all wear a *kesa* (Sanskrit: *kasaya*—a Buddhist apron-like stole) and *juzu* (rosary beads bracelet). This not only adds to the formality of the occasion but also serves to unite the group through attire and accessories, moving beyond just the *shakuhachi* as a sole binding agent.

Other more occasional assemblies, called *kensō-kai* (dedication-playing gatherings), involve each participant playing a piece, in turn, before the altar. These take place at the home temple, Myōan-ji in Kyoto, or at various other temples in Japan. They are often held over a weekend, with some participants spending the preceding afternoon dressed as *komusō* and collecting alms, which are donated to a civic cause. All participants dine together and share rooms at a nearby inn or hotel that has been reserved for the occasion. There are two types of *kensō-kai,* one in which only Myōan Kyōkai members take part and the other open to participation by *shakuhachi* players of other styles. Both, however, are available to observation by the general public.

Teaching, Learning, and the *Benkyō-kai*

The preceding section described the various ways in which members of the Myōan Kyōkai engage with the *shakuhachi* and a fixed unaccompanied solo repertoire.[11] The pieces are initially learned privately with a certified teacher and are graded into seven levels as already mentioned. Learning in one-on-one situations can vary with each teacher, and it would be misleading to attempt a generalization about private teaching methods. There are, however, group learning situations, known as *benkyō-kai.* This is not a temple-specific term and can be translated as study (*benkyō*), with *kai* signifying "gathering" or "assembly." Some of these are organized by individual teachers outside the temple and are akin to a master class, with focus on the organizer, who leads and oversees the instruction of the group.

The *benkyō-kai* that take place in the temple differ significantly in this regard. Even though they are presided over by the abbot, they are considerably more cooperative and collaborative in nature than a master teacher instructing a group of learners. These sessions are always held following a short break after the *suizen-kai,* and the atmosphere is considerably less formal. No robes are worn and most participants remove their *kesa* and *juzu.* Except for the priest, who does not play the *shakuhachi,* the event is attended by all participants who attended the *suizen-kai.* In this sense, rather than considering it a separate and independent event, it can really be considered as part of the *suizen-kai.*

The *benkyō-kai* takes place in the same area of the temple, with participants again seated on the floor in a squared horseshoe formation whose open end faces the altar. The session begins with the abbot ringing a small bell (*inkin*), signaling a brief period of silent meditation punctuated by another ringing of the *inkin.* This same procedure is repeated at the end of the session, just after reciting Fuke's *gatha,* thus framing the proceedings. The abbot introduces the day's piece, which he had chosen and announced to all *dōshu* along with the date and time for the *suizen-kai.* He explains some of the piece's historical background and then demonstrates by playing it. During his introductory remarks, after his demonstration, and throughout the session, he continuously solicits questions and comments from the participants, thus creating a very open and cooperative atmosphere. Sometimes he enlists the help of another participant, who may help lead the teaching of the piece or part of it. The session continues with all participants working on the piece together, sometimes divided into smaller groups.

The fixed repertoire of thirty-three pieces limits the range of material covered during the *benkyō-kai.* Yet with a tradition that does have written notation, there is still considerable variation in the ways that the repertoire is notated. Transmission combines the written with the oral/aural by notating syllables that represent fingerings on the *shakuhachi.* Unlike a Western score, for example, the written score is used here as more of a skeletal guide or mnemonic device. Pieces cannot be properly interpreted or learned without the aid of an instructor, and teachers will sometimes write out their own scores or use the ones provided by their own teachers. This would account for differences and varying degrees of prescriptive detail, even though they all share the same overall system of notation. While the temple does publish a set of scores, interestingly these are not strictly adhered to or accepted as completely standard or as the de facto official set. At the beginning of each *benkyō-kai,* a copy of the day's material is distributed, thus providing some unity to the proceedings, but participants will invariably compare their own notation to the one given out, and much discussion revolves around interpreting the distributed copy, at times even calling into question the way it was notated.

Although the text itself is often discussed, the purpose never seems to move towards reaching any sort of full consensus on either what constitutes a definitive textual representation or even proper execution of it. With a repertoire that is largely nonmetrical and rhythmically free, a single standard rendition of any of it is doubtful, and with variations in notation it is virtually guaranteed not to occur. This is not meant to imply that stylistic tendencies are not pointed out and adhered to, but here too, without a single teaching lineage as well as a geographically dispersed teacher base, differences are not only bound to occur but are also accepted. Given also that all participants of the *benkyō-kai* are experienced players, no material covered in these sessions can really be considered new. This indicates that, rather than learning new music, those present participate in order to further their knowledge of something already known. This also equalizes the participants, creating an atmosphere of single purpose and a spirit of cooperation.

There is little doubt that this sense of collaboration is influenced by the abbot's personality and approach to the proceedings. While his authority and leadership is already tacitly accepted, he seems to relinquish most of it during these sessions by continuously soliciting questions and comments, and even enlisting help from others in the group. He also seems to take on a learner's role by carefully and actively listening, and most technical aspects and pointers he leaves to the group. He projects an image of "facilitator, coach, or midwife rather than a 'sage on the stage'" and shares both the teaching and learning experiences with all present (Matthews et al. 1995, 37).

At their most fundamental level, communities are created and defined by commonalities. This chapter has identified seven interdependent components that both define and sustain one particular community, the Myōan Kyōkai:

1. Music
2. History
3. Space
4. Ritual
5. Attire
6. Family
7. Learning

Music-related components are at the core of the Myōan Kyōkai and its activities. Without the *shakuhachi* this community would not exist, for all activities do not simply include the instrument but revolve completely around it. Yet at the same time, the *shakuhachi* does not stand on its own; it supports the activities while, in turn, it is supported by them. Its fixed repertoire, although showing differences and therefore some flexibility in interpretation, also contributes to binding the group by the simple fact that it is still a set and fixed corpus. At the same time, however, because the repertoire itself is fixed and taken from the past without any new additions, it relies on the historical past that created them.

Historical components contribute, as just remarked, to the repertoire of the Myōan Kyōkai. Yet history—even a problematic one—has also served to define the community in other ways. By invoking Fuke's *gatha,* the Myōan Kyōkai maintains a link with a past movement that was inspired and started in his name. Dressing up as *komusō* and performing mendicancy links past to present. Although a voluntary—and therefore relatively minor—activity, it maintains a portion of an old tradition, but rather than trying to replicate it, acknowledges and perpetuates it in a contemporary form. Reviving one of three main temples of the Fuke sect also clearly demonstrates roots in the past and the transplanting of them to the present.

The dedicated space in which all the events take place is an important defining and sustaining component. By confining activities to a temple as backdrop rather than displaying them on a stage (exceptions already noted), the Myōan Kyōkai sets some boundaries on its practice by confining and sometimes closing them to the outside. Yet borders ultimately serve to clearly identify any community and, if permeable enough, to include "visitors" (as can be demonstrated by the gatherings that include "foreign" *shakuhachi* players and allow the public at large to observe), thus connecting the tradition to contemporary circumstances.

"Ritual" can be a heavily loaded label, but for present purposes, I take it in Rappaport's sense of "denot[ing] *the performance of more or less invariant sequences of formal acts and utterances not entirely encoded by the performers*" (Rappaport 1999, 24; emphasis in original). The *suizen-kai*'s formal, fixed structure creates bonds partly due to its familiarity. In fact, the very act of gathering regularly in a dedicated and familiar space can in a sense be seen in itself as ritual. Framing the varying content of the *benkyō-kai* with the familiar act of bell ringing, meditation, and recitation also acts to bind the proceedings and its actors. Catherine Bell has observed that "ritualization tends to make ritual activities effective in grounding and displaying a sense of community *without* overriding the autonomy of individuals or subgroups" (Bell 1992, 221–222; emphasis in original).

The way members dress not only unites and identifies the community but also adds formality and thus another element of cohesion to the various activities. This extends beyond attire to include the accessories they use, such as the *juzu* and folded fans. The removal of some of these, as in the *benkyō-kai,* when robes, *kesa,* and *juzu* are taken off simultaneously, removes the formality of the *suizen-kai* that preceded it and effectively elevates the status of the *suizen-kai* by reserving some implements for exclusive use there.

Although not necessarily in the foreground, by essentially employing the model of family, a different type of belonging is affirmed. Its very presence in the background helps to underpin an overall sense of tacit group membership in a way comparable to membership in a family related along blood and genetic lines. Unlike the *iemoto* model that describes a singular family, by bringing several families together, the Myōan Kyōkai forms a true community rather than just one family.

Finally, learning in its widest and most ideal sense—one that includes studying and furthering the learning of something already familiar—supports and sustains the Myōan Kyōkai as a community. Furthermore, collaboration equalizes and democratizes the group. The tradition surrounding the *shakuhachi* of the Myōan Kyōkai is essentially a musical one, and upholding it requires training and working towards reaching an understanding—or new understandings—of the music that is central to it. As we have also seen, a diversity of interpretations also endows a static and set repertoire with life and relevance. Accepting this diversity also corroborates Catherine Bell's observation that individual and subgroup autonomy is not sacrificed.

Notes

1 Here, Tsuge's translation "attached" is treated as a typographical error.

2 No doubt another typographical error. Tsuge's text reads "flail."

3 The first of these documents dated 1614 is called 'Keichō Era Statutes' (*Keichō no okitegaki;* the Keichō era covered the period 1596–1615). The authenticity of this document is questionable; government records show no existence of it, and sect elders reported that the original was destroyed in a fire. Subsequent similar documents outlining regulations and codes of conduct were in government possession. All are translated into English and analyzed by Takahashi (1990, 54–74).

4 The *sō* suffix does not make a distinction between priest or monk.

5 Gutzwiller provides all three essays in Japanese, along with German translations. He also gives English summaries (Gutzwiller 1983, 164–198, 249–250).

6 Kamisangō (1974, 17; 1988, 110) describes daily activities in a Fuke temple but gives no source, raising doubts as to the veracity; others, in turn, cite Kamisangō (Lee 1986, 54; Lee 1998, 129–130; Takahashi 1990, 112–113; Shingūji Hōsankai 1996, 91).

7 *Kyōkai* is often mistranslated as "association," but here is written with the same characters used to denote "church," taking on more a meaning of collective education/learning.

8 Based on temple documents, as of the end of 2012 the overall membership was 438, of whom 220 were certified to teach. For information on geographic distribution of the membership, see Mau (2014, 246–248).

9 For the sake of readability, I have chosen to use titles rather than names throughout the text. My intention is not to leave them anonymous however. The position of priest is presently held by Hirazumi Gyozan; the abbot is Kojima Hōan; and the current head teacher is Yao Byakuren (following Japanese custom, names are listed with family name first).

10 To my knowledge there are two special exceptions to this principle. In 1996, the current abbot and several members participated in a concert entitled *The*

Mystery of Religious Shakuhachi (*Shūkyō Shakuhachi no Shinpi*). The program included players of other styles who also share repertoire attributed to the *komusō*. More recently, members appeared in a concert showcasing the various styles of *shakuhachi* playing as part of the 2012 World Shakuhachi Festival. Because the sixth such international festival was held in Kyoto, the organizers wanted to ensure the presence of the Myōan style, which had been completely absent from all prior festivals.

11 One piece, *Shika no tone,* is intended as a call-and-response duet, but is sometimes played solo.

References

Bell, Catherine M. 1992. *Ritual Theory, Ritual Practice.* New York: Oxford University Press.

Collcutt, Martin. 1986. "Buddhism: The Threat of Eradication." In *Japan in Transition: From Tokugawa to Meiji,* edited by Marius B. Jansen and Gilbert Rozman, 143–167. Princeton, NJ: Princeton University Press.

Deeg, Max. 2007. "Komusō and 'Shakuhachi-Zen': From Historical Legitimation to the Spiritualisation of a Buddhist Denomination in the Edo Period." *Japanese Religions* 32 (1 and 2): 7–38.

Gutzwiller, Andreas B. 1983. *Die Shakuhachi der Kinko-Schule.* Studien zur Traditionellen Musik Japans. Kassel: Bärenreiter.

Hane, Mikiso. 1986. *Modern Japan: A Historical Survey.* Boulder, CO: Westview Press.

Hsu, Francis L. K. 1975. *Iemoto: The Heart of Japan.* Cambridge, MA: Shenkman Publishing Company.

Kamisangō, Yūkō. 1974. *Shakuhachi Gaku Ryakureki: Suizen No Rikai No Tame Ni* (A Brief History of Shakuhachi Music: In Order to Reach an Understanding of Suizen). Tokyo: Nippon Columbia KX-7001–33.

———. 1988. "The Shakuhachi—History and Development." In *The Shakuhachi: A Manual for Learning.* Translated and adapted by Christopher Yohmei Blasdel, 69–132. Tokyo: Ongaku no Tomo Sha.

Ketelaar, James Edward. 1990. *Of Heretics and Martyrs in Meiji Japan: Buddhism and Its Persecution.* Princeton, NJ: Princeton University Press.

Lee, Riley Kelly. 1986. "Blowing Zen: Aspects of Performance Practices of the Chikuho Ryu Honkyoku." MA thesis, University of Hawai'i.

———. 1998. "Yearning for the Bell: A Study of Transmission in the Shakuhachi Honkyoku Tradition." PhD diss., University of Sydney.

Matsumoto, Yoshiharu Scott. 1960. "Contemporary Japan: The Individual and the Group." *Transactions of the American Philosophical Society,* n.s. 50 (1): 1–75. doi:10.2307/1005846.

Matthews, Roberta S., James L. Cooper, Neil Davidson, and Peter Hawkes. 1995. "Building Bridges between Cooperative and Collaborative Learning." *Change* 27 (4): 34–40. doi:10.1080/00091383.1995.9936435.

Mau, Christian Theodore. 2014. "Situating the Myōan Kyōkai: A Study of Suizen and the Fuke Shakuhachi." PhD diss., SOAS, University of London. http://eprints.soas.ac.uk/18260/.

Nakatsuka, Chikuzen. 1936. *Kinko Ryū Shakuhachi Shikan* (A Historical View of the Kinko-Ryū Shakuhachi). Tokyo: Nihon Ongaku.

Nishiyama, Matsunosuke. 1997. *Edo Culture: Daily Life and Diversions in Urban Japan, 1600–1868.* Translated by Gerald Groemer. Honolulu: University of Hawai'i Press.

Rappaport, Roy A. 1999. *Ritual and Religion in the Making of Humanity.* Cambridge Studies in Social and Cultural Anthropology 110. Cambridge: Cambridge University Press.

Sanford, James H. 1977. "Shakuhachi Zen: The Fukeshu and Komuso." *Monumenta Nipponica* 32 (4): 411–440. doi:10.2307/2384045.

Shingūji Hōsankai. 1996. *Sagami no Kuni Komusōdera Isehara Jingūji shi: Suizen Shakuhachi* (A Komusō Temple in Sagami Country Isehara jingū Temple: Suizen Shakuhachi). Tokyo: Shingūji Hōsankai.

Takahashi, Tone. 1990. "Tozan-Ryû: An Innovation of the Shakuhachi Tradition from Fuke-Shû to Secularism." PhD diss., Florida State University.

Tsuge, Gen'ichi. 1977. "The History of the Kyotaku." *Asian Music: Journal of the Society for Asian Music* 8 (2): 47–63. doi:10.2307.

CHAPTER 7

Hei te pō, hei te ao—Singing in the Dark

The Revival of an Indigenous Teaching Methodology

Karyn Paringatai

Prior to European arrival to New Zealand, Māori (the Indigenous people of New Zealand) had developed a highly sophisticated knowledge system that relied on the intergenerational transference of information based on the fact that pre-European Māori society was an entirely oral culture. Chanted and recited forms of music, such as *waiata* (song) and *haka* (posture dance accompanied with rhythmically chanted/shouted words), were used as mnemonic devices to ensure that screeds of information were passed, error-free, from one generation to the next.

Waiata and *haka,* in their many forms, were a part of everyday life and were used in all aspects of traditional Māori society—from birth rituals to ceremonies associated with bidding farewell to the dead, from the planting of crops to the harvesting and gathering of food supplies, the welcoming of visitors, and the recruitment of friendly neighbors in times of war. They were used to attract members of the opposite sex, to warn others of impending danger, and in educating children about tribal histories. Thus they served a functional purpose and were not always used for entertainment. However, a number of *waiata* and *haka* became redundant soon after European arrival to New Zealand when the reasons for their original purpose no longer existed or they were systematically rationalized out of use by early missionaries.

Māori Pedagogies

Waiata and *haka* were also used as tools in the intergenerational transfer of knowledge within Māori communities. From a Māori perspective, Rangi-nui (Sky Father) and Papa-tū-ā-nuku (Earth Mother) clung to each other, while in between them their multitude of children lived in a world of darkness. One of their children, Tāne-mahuta (the god of the forest), eventually separated his parents and in doing so created a world of light. This world was originally void of superior forms of knowledge. It instead resided in the realms of the gods who dwelt in the heavens or within the realm of Io (the supreme god) who inhabited the uppermost of the twelve heavens. This knowledge was obtained by Tāne, who then brought it back to earth to be used by mankind (Buck 1966).

Tāne retrieved three baskets of knowledge: *te kete aronui* (knowledge pertaining to good, all things humane and peaceful); *te kete tuatea* (knowledge pertaining to all evil arts, warfare, and black magic); and *te kete tuauri* (knowledge of ritual and all ceremonies designed to remove the restrictions that are placed on the relationships that connect all things on earth and in the heavens) (Best 1986). In all cases this knowledge helped create a balance between good and evil, between the godly and human realms, and among those who dwelt within each. Because this knowledge was obtained from the gods, it was shrouded in *tapu* (sacred, prohibited, restricted). Once brought back to earth, in order to utilize that knowledge, certain rituals and procedures had to be followed to make that information safe to use to avoid offending the gods lest they exact revenge in their anger. That knowledge was used in all aspects of Māori society and was passed down from generation to generation.

In pre-European Māori society much of the education of children took place informally. Children acquired skills and knowledge by watching, observing, and mimicking the activities of adults in the village (Buck 1966). Some types of knowledge, though, were regarded as too important to be taught in these informal environments; such was the sacredness of this information that it became the subject of formal study in the *whare wānanga* (pre-European institutions of learning of esoteric knowledge and occult lore) (McLean 1996).

The *whare wānanga* differed from tribe to tribe and was not always an actual physical location or space but also a curriculum. The teaching was divided into two divisions. The first was *te kauwae runga* (the upper jaw), which included everything pertaining to the gods, the heavens, the origin of all things, and the creation of man. The second was *te kauwae raro* (the lower jaw), which included the history of the people, their genealogies, migrations, and knowledge pertaining to terrestrial matters (Smith 1913). By learning both curricula, students were able to see how the celestial guided the terrestrial and vice versa.

Because of the nature and content of the knowledge and where it derived from, students who were initiated into the *whare wānanga* went through a ritualistic process that made them *tapu* while they were being infused with this knowledge. Young children, who were usually members of high-ranking families or who were seen to be exceptionally gifted in their abilities to remember things, were selected to be students of the *whare wānanga,* where they would become receptacles of tribal knowledge. In a preliterate society, the aural receptive and recollection skills of the Māori population were finely tuned. Screeds of information could be retained and repeated after hearing it only once. The development of these skills was particularly crucial for the students selected to participate in the *whare wānanga.*

> A word as to the powers of memory possessed by the Maori, upon which hinged the success of the School of Learning. Highly developed were the memorising powers of these folk. . . . The Maori depended entirely on memory, on oral tradition, on verbal teaching, in preserving all prized lore and in passing it on to his descendants. The School of Learning was the result of the strong desire to conserve such matter in its original purity. (Best 1986, 5)

While students were being instructed, the gods were invoked to make the children's minds clear and receptive to the knowledge that they were about to receive. Any lapse in concentration could prove disastrous in the long term if the material was not learned correctly and was subsequently recited with errors in it.

A strategy employed in the *whare wānanga* to develop ways in which information was encoded and retrieved at a later time involved the recitation of knowledge in some mnemonic form. Information was imparted to the student using some sort of rhythmic verse with regular and repeated rises and falls in pitch, and often with drawn-out endings. The use of mnemonic strategies has proven to be effective in helping people remember things and enhancing the recall of information transmitted in any given lesson (Mastropieri and Scruggs 1998).

Whare wānanga operated during the winter months of April to August. Therefore, the amount of sunlight hours would have been limited. Teaching in the *whare wānanga* sometimes took place in the middle of the night, when the students' minds were said to be free of distractions (Hemara 2000). It was thought that limiting external stimuli and keeping students isolated were more conducive to developing their mnemonic abilities and enhancing their retention skills. This type of teaching method was used particularly in the teaching of the dark arts. The intention of the dark arts was to attack the spiritual and mental state of another person, ultimately, but not always, ending in death. Any mistake in the recitation of the incantations required to inflict this type of damage would mean certain doom for the priestly expert in charge of this practice. It would then make sense that the best time period in which to teach this knowledge would be in the dead of night when there was limited light available to illuminate objects that could distract the students. While this particular teaching method was only used for certain subjects, the methodology proved beneficial for the aural-receptive and retention skills of the learner.

Changes in Māori Society

European arrival in New Zealand changed Māori society dramatically. One of the early institutional changes was the introduction of a new religious conviction coupled with a missionary desire to educate the Māori. By the 1830s the missionary school system was firmly entrenched, and at this time a number of Māori could read and write their own language, as the view was that literacy skills would enhance their traditional lifestyle. However, the texts available for them to read at this point in time consisted of religious material. In these particular texts the focus was on European values, which further served to undermine traditional Māori culture and knowledge. Subsequent literacy in English also played an important part in the conversion of Māori to Christianity, which missionaries hoped would lead to total abandonment of their traditional lifestyle (Openshaw, Lee, and Lee 1993). State involvement in the schooling of Māori from the mid-1840s onward only served to perpetuate the abandonment of Māori customs and signaled the beginning of the colonial policy of assimilation (Simon 1998). *Whare wānanga* and the knowledge contained within these institutions were soon abandoned in favor of European knowledge and skills, as were Māori methods of learning and teaching.

Some types of *haka* and *waiata* also suffered a similar fate at the hands of the missionaries and the subsequent onslaught of colonization, although to a much lesser extent than being abandoned completely. A number of *haka* and *waiata* were described as too lascivious for the newly converted Christians to continue dancing and singing, and so were forbidden to be performed. As the Reverend Henry Williams (a pioneer missionary in New Zealand) wrote in 1845: "I feel it is necessary to prohibit all the old (Maori) customs, their dances, singing, and tattooing, their general domestic disorders. In Auckland the people are fond of assembling in large parties for the purpose of exhibiting their horrible dances. Of course this has a most serious moral effect on their conduct as Christian people" (Williams, in Carleton 1877, 87).

The cessation of certain practices also caused particular types of *waiata* and *haka* used for these occasions to stop being performed. For example, the *peruperu* is a type of *haka* done on the battlefield during war when face-to-face with the enemy. A feature of this *haka* is a continual vertical jump. This stirred up the dust, insinuating that the war party was more numerous than it was and also demonstrating the physical prowess of the men performing the *haka*. When muskets became a feature of Māori warfare, the *peruperu* ceased to be so performed, as the enemy would no longer be intimidated by such a display. Instead it has been relegated to ceremonial use during the *pōwhiri* (welcoming ceremony of visitors on to a *marae*), as an entertainment item in competition, or to express objection to certain issues, which in a way could still be seen as a metaphorical battlefield.

Tohunga (priestly experts) were charged with the task of being the lead teachers in *whare wānanga*. The 1907 Tohunga Suppression Act prohibited Māori spiritual leaders from practicing all forms of *karakia* (prayers), *mākutu* (sorcery), and *mōteatea* (generic term for all types of traditional forms of music).

> Every person who gathers Maoris around him by practising on their superstition or credulity, or who misleads or attempts to mislead any Maori by professing or pretending to possess supernatural powers in the treatment or cure of any disease, or in the foretelling of future events, or otherwise, is liable on summary conviction before a Magistrate to a fine not exceeding twenty-five pounds or to imprisonment for a period not exceeding six months in the case of a first offence, or to imprisonment for a period not exceeding twelve months in the case of a second or any subsequent offence against this Act (Tohunga Suppression Act 1907).

The *haka* and *waiata* associated with the esoteric knowledge these experts possessed also stopped being performed.

The post–World War II migration of Māori from rural areas to urban centers has been described as the most rapid movement worldwide of any sub-ethnic population group (Gibson 1973). The dispersal of Māori populations around the country, far from tribal homelands, called into question the relevance of one's ethnic identity. Māori performing arts (commonly called *kapa haka*) have been used to help discover, construct, and negotiate Māori cultural identity among performers in urban areas. It has become an essential mechanism from which participants can derive a sense of who they are as Māori, particularly those living outside of their tribal area:

> Coming together to practice *Kapa Haka* has become another way of practicing tribalism, even if participants no longer maintained active connections to their *iwi* [tribe]. Indeed, over time, *Kapa Haka* has not only served as a substitute for *iwi* and the practices that formerly served to reinforce *whakapapa* [genealogical information] and *turangawaewae* [a place to stand], it has actually played a role in rebuilding and reinforcing the value of these vital components of Māori culture and identity. (Mazer 2011a, 47)

For those eager to maintain their cultural identity in the urban centers a number of tribal and pan-tribal Māori performing arts groups were formed (also known as cultural clubs or *kapa haka* groups). These groups also acted as a mechanism through which their members could integrate into an urban lifestyle more easily. Community-based *kapa haka* groups include the whole *whānau* (extended family). Practices operated using Māori processes, and a sense of *whānau* with reciprocal obligations was instilled in the members. Children were active participants, performing and learning alongside their older siblings, parents, and other senior members. They learned cultural practices, language, and history, all of which are embedded in the *haka* and *waiata* taught, and became proficient performers from a young age (Eriksson 2003). Children then moved through the ranks, and when they reached a certain age would fill performing spots in the senior group, already possessing the necessary performance skills (Grant 2014).

The establishment of these groups and their popularity was enhanced by public performances that were the pinnacle of months of practice, hard work, and dedication. Local festivals, cultural events, school fund-raisers, concerts, and competitions ensured that people kept going to practices and learning new items that were displayed for the community, critiqued by watching elders and perfected at subsequent practices. Regular practices and constant performances not only improved the performance skills of the performers but also ensured the longevity of the groups.

These senior groups were pivotal throughout New Zealand, where participation in Māori performing arts has increased and active performers now number in the tens of thousands. However, their prominence and usefulness as an integrative mechanism dissipated in the lower half of the South Island in the 1990s. Therefore, the communities in this part of the country are lacking opportunity to participate in this art form. Most people in Dunedin do not have any connection with Māori performing arts. Nor do they have the opportunity to take part in this particular art form within the wider Dunedin community other than in schools. Because of the cultural dimension associated with Māori performing arts—the physical coordination necessary, the emotional sentiments, and *whakapapa* found in the words of the compositions, the complexity of the language, and the time and effort required of each individual to be proficient in all areas of performance—many people in Dunedin do not participate in the opportunities that are available. Currently, for adults in Dunedin the ability to learn about and participate in Māori performing arts is limited to formally taught courses (beginner, intermediate, and advanced) offered by Te Tumu—School of Māori, Pacific, and Indigenous Studies, at the University of Otago.

Revival of Māori Pedagogies

Typically, when learning *haka* or *waiata* the words are either projected onto a wall or are handed out on a piece of paper. Either way an emphasis is placed on the written form of the composition. It is easier for those with no Māori language skills to have a visual aid to assist them in learning the item. An English translation of the *haka* or *waiata* is also usually given, either verbally or written down, so people know what they are singing about. This is a common way for groups of people to learn *haka* and *waiata* in both formal and informal learning environments throughout the country.

A number of people who are engaged with Māori performing arts at a very basic level are concerned with learning the actions and choreography because they are the easiest part of *haka* and *waiata* to learn. They are also the most visual aspects of *kapa haka,* and it is noticeable if mistakes are made during performance. However, a number of Māori performing arts experts reiterate that the words and the messages conveyed within the *haka* or *waiata* are the most important aspect of Māori performing arts (Karetu 2013).

The beginner course offered by Te Tumu has a classroom size of approximately forty-five to fifty-five students. Over half are international students and over 80 percent of them have no background in Māori language, culture, and/or performing arts. This has always made for slow, labored learning of the words of the *haka* and *waiata*. Students have always struggled to remember the words, tune, actions, and choreography, and then they would be asked to connect emotionally with the item and perform it with appropriate facial expressions and body movement, and do it in a language that the majority of them did not understand. As a consequence, the correct pronunciation of Māori words became secondary. Once an item is learned incorrectly, it is very difficult to get a group of this demographic to change. One way to combat this is to teach by ear only.

> Before writing was introduced there was only one way and that was through memorizing through the ear. It was and still is the best way. Not only do you learn the actual words themselves, but also the sound of them, the tone or intonation, the accent or emphasis, the way the words are strung together, some clipped short, others drawn out. And in the constant reiteration through the ear you get to give each word its proper value and by hearing experts intone or recite you get the "tune" or "rangi" of the lines and verses. (Ngata 1944, 8)

The content of what can be learned in this way is not only restricted to *haka* and *waiata*. A myriad of information can be transmitted in the dark. In *wānanga* (immersion residential style of learning where people stay overnight), elders will often recite genealogical information and tribal histories late into the night or their teaching will begin in the early hours of the morning.

In order for the language to be placed philosophically at the center of the classroom and not on the periphery, it was decided to remove all visual stimuli while teaching the words and tune of the *haka* and *waiata*. In order for students to be able to connect emotionally with the songs they needed to have a greater understanding of what they were singing about and more confidence and command of the language. This then would enhance the physical performance of each item.

> I learnt one outstanding feature in the education of a Maori, that he must know a thing in one lesson; in two lessons, if his teacher is indulgent. To learn a song in one lesson, words, air and all its graces seemed

> an impossible feat. But it was demonstrated in many cases within one's knowledge. There were illiterate elders among my relatives in the sense that they read with great difficulty and could barely sign their names to paper. But they could memorize genealogies, land boundaries and strange songs with ease. They took no written notes, showed in fact from the commencement of any narration or recitation that they were committing to and holding the matter by an effort of memory. In that way they acquired the expression, the intonation, the rhythm, all the graces which reveal the meaning of the composition in its many shades. Words received their full signification from the stance of the bodies, the play of the eyes and the movements of the heads of the singers. (Ngata 2004, xxxv)

Technology has also made an impact on those who participate in Māori performing arts. Videos are made and sound files are captured and made readily available to those who need them to practice in their own time. The same occurs in this course, but the words in their written form are never given to the students, although this does not preclude them from accessing the words themselves if they choose to do so. It is expected that students will practice on their own time to consolidate what is learnt in class.

Removing external stimuli to free students to focus just on the words and the way they are said, using correct models of pronunciation from tutors, empowers learners in a number of ways. Students were initially dubious that they would be able to learn in this way. This was a method that they had not encountered before. Within the first two hours they learned two songs in the dark. Their doubts were thus laid aside and they became more receptive to enjoying the experience rather than fearing it. One of the first songs taught prior to learning in the dark took eight hours of class time over a period of four weeks before people felt comfortable singing the song without the words. The same song could now be learned in just two hours. The speed with which students now acquire the songs has meant that the number of items learned has doubled from four items in thirteen weeks to eight items in the same amount of time, thus expanding their repertoire of songs and their abilities to perform in a wider range of events in the community with other groups.

More time is also spent explaining what the items mean to help students connect with them emotionally. This, in turn, enables them to display the necessary facial emotions and body movements and expressions to enhance the performance. The faster the items are learned the more time there is to perfect actions, particularly of the *poi* (ball on the end of a string swung in time to some sort of musical accompaniment) and *haka*. Prior to learning in the dark the males did not have the time to learn the *poi* and the females to learn the *haka*. Although in community-based groups that have higher-level performers, most with Māori language abilities and considerable performance experience, it is standard that all performers learn all items, this was not the case in this course. Limited time constraints meant that it simply could not be done. Using this method, all students learn both the *haka* and *poi,* which has enhanced the overall performance of these items.

First-time performers also make mistakes—in pronunciation, timing, saying the correct words, and singing in tune. The majority of the class do not have experience participating in an art form that requires singing in another language, particularly a minority language spoken mostly only in New Zealand. The embarrassment of making mistakes in the dark is minimized by the fact that others cannot see who made the mistake. The confidence of the students is boosted, and they are not afraid to continue singing and practicing in the dark. When they emerge from the darkness to learn the actions and choreography, they are more confident in their knowledge of the lyrics, which, for most people, is the hardest part of Māori performing arts.

Secure in their knowledge of the words and actions, and with extra time to become more familiar with the other aspects of performing *haka* and *waiata,* there is extra time to spend with those who are in leadership positions. These positions are usually taken on by people who already have experience with *waiata* and *haka*. In terms of *haka,* assuming the role of *kaitātaki tāne* (male leader) means learning more words, making sure the group maintains an appropriate tempo and slowing them down if they speed up in a way that does not make them go out of time, and executing a commanding presence on stage by walking up and down the ranks of the male performers, urging them on. These are skills that cannot be acquired easily over the course of four weeks, the time it usually took for the men just to become confident with the group words and actions. This role was usually the responsibility of an experienced performer who either already knew the *haka* or could pick it up easily. This role can now be taken on by others with significantly lesser performing skills because of the extra time available for them to practice: "To this day, whenever I think I'm not confident enough to do something, I remember that I once lead a *haka*. It's an unstoppable feeling. That the audience and my fellow performers were primarily Māori and seemed to like what we did made it all the more special" (International student of Māori performing arts, 2012).

For those of Māori descent this is a method that enables their epistemologies, their language, and their cultural practices to be placed at the center of how the class operates. These things are not left on the periphery but are pivotal to how we learn. For those who already have Māori language fluency and experience in Māori performing arts it is one of the few opportunities in Dunedin where their experience and talents are valued and highly sought after by the non-Māori majority of the group. This creates an environment of success for all concerned.

From the moment we are born we listen to things around us. We learn by mimicking the sounds we hear. But as we age we stop listening and ignore the lilting grace of song, the powerful force of *haka,* and the subtle nuances of speech. We doubt our abilities to learn by ear and to retain information only by listening to it. Learning in the dark forces people to trust themselves and retrain their memories. In the darkness of our minds there are flashes of brilliance teasing us to explore our potential. Institutionalizing the method of teaching in the dark within a tertiary institution, the oldest university in New Zealand, is empowering for others who want to explore older, Indigenous methods of teaching and learning that were suppressed in the wave of Western ideas and developments. Teaching Māori performing arts in the dark is bringing new life to a venerable form of learning, with benefits that can be felt across all spectrums.

References

Best, Elsdon. 1986. *The Maori School of Learning: Its Objects, Methods, and Ceremonial.* Wellington: Government Printer.

Buck, Peter. 1966. *The Coming of the Maori.* Wellington: Whitcombe and Tombs.

Carleton, Hugh. 1877. *The Life of Henry Williams, Archdeacon of Waimate.* Vol. 2. Auckland: Wilson & Horton Printers.

Eriksson, Anitha. 2003. *Maori Music and Culture in New Zealand: Report from Studies at Waikato University in Hamilton, New Zealand, August 2001.* Department of Pedagogic and Humanist Subjects, Finnmark University College, Alta, Norway.

Gibson, Campbell. 1973. "Urbanization in New Zealand: A Comparative Analysis." *Demography* 10 (1): 71–84. doi:10.2307/2060751.

Grant, Donna. 2014. "Shaping Mātauranga Māori Opportunities through Kapa Haka." In *Enhancing Mātauranga Māori and Global Indigenous Knowledge,* edited by Taiarahia Black, 60–67. Wellington: New Zealand Qualifications Authority.

Hemara, Wharehuia. 2000. *Māori Pedagogies: A View from the Literature.* Wellington: New Zealand Council for Educational Research.

Karetu, Timoti. 2013. "Te haka." In *Kia Rōnaki: The Māori Performing Arts,* edited by Rachael Ka'ai-Mahuta, Tania Ka'ai, and John Moorfield, 85–90. Auckland: Pearson Education.

Mastropieri, Margo A., and Thomas E. Scruggs. 1998. "Enhancing School Success with Mnemonic Strategies." *Intervention in School and Clinic* 33 (4): 201–208. doi:10.1177/105345129803300402.

Mazer, Sharon. 2011a. "Performing Māori: *Kapa Haka* on the Stage and on the Ground." *Popular Entertainment Studies* 2 (1): 41–53. doi:10.1353/tj.2015.0072.

———. 2011b. "You Talkin' to Me? Eavesdropping on the Conversation at Te Matatini Māori Performing Arts Festival." *Performance Research: A Journal of the Performing Arts* 16 (2): 44–49. doi:10.1080/13528165.2011.578729.

McLean, Mervyn. 1996. *Maori Music.* Auckland: Auckland University Press.

Ngata, Apirana. 1944. *Rauru-nui-a-Toi Lectures and Ngati-Kahungunu Origins.* Wellington: Victoria University of Wellington.

———. 2004. *Ngā Mōteatea.* Auckland: Auckland University Press.

Openshaw, Roger, Greg Lee, and Howard Lee. 1993. *Challenging the Myths: Rethinking New Zealand's Education History.* Palmerston North: Dunmore Press, 1993.

Simon, Judith. 1998. *Ngā Kura Māori: The Native Schools System 1867–1969.* Auckland: Auckland University Press.

Smith, S. Percy. 1913. *The Lore of the Whare-wānanga; Teachings of the Maori College on Religion, Cosmogony, and History: Part I—Te Kauwae-runga, or "Things Celestial."* New Plymouth: Thomas Avery.

———. 1915. *The Lore of the Whare-wānanga; Teachings of the Maori College on Their History and Migrations, etc: Part II—Te Kauwae-raro, or "Things Terrestrial."* New Plymouth: Thomas Avery.

PART II

Broader Social Justice Considerations and Interdisciplinary Intersections

CHAPTER 8

Developing a Performance Involving People with Intellectual Challenges during the 2012 Beijing Traditional Music Festival

Phil Mullen

An unfair society is doomed to suffer from instability and discord.

—Former Chinese Premier Wen Jiabao

This chapter provides details of a concert given as part of the Fourth Beijing Traditional Music Festival in October 2012 by a music group from the An Hua Li (Happy Sunshine Home) center in Beijing, led by visiting community musicians Don DeVito and Phil Mullen, in partnership with Professor Xie Jiaxing and his students from the China Conservatory. This was the first time there was a performance by people with intellectual challenges in the Beijing Traditional Music Festival and represents a significant event in the development of community music in China.

This chapter is also an auto-ethnographic account of the project, essentially a report on what happened according to how the author saw it. It was also filtered through Don DeVito's views of the events and issues expressed in a number of informal discussions, before, during, and after the event. As such it is a detailed and accurate account of the project and the issues the project raises from the perspective of these two community musicians; but the chapter does not attempt to take into account the experiences or understandings of the Chinese participants, their key workers, the students from the China Conservatory, or the concert audience. In that sense the chapter is best seen as raising issues from a particular (if quite involved) set of viewpoints rather than as a comprehensive 360-degree investigation into the event.

Events Preceding the Project: Seminars and Summits

While there are no doubt many community music education projects throughout China, the visibility of these various projects to the global music education community was sparked by the 2010 International Society for Music Education (ISME) World Conference in Beijing. In particular, the Commission for Community Music Activity's (ISME CMA) seminar on community music hosted by the Open University of China in Hangzhou provided a point of first contact between the community music communities in China and internationally, opening up dialogue between Chinese community music practitioners and researchers and their counterparts from around the world (Coffman 2010). It was followed up in December 2011 by the first Chinese summit on community music held in the China Conservatory, Beijing. This brought together academics, researchers, music leaders, performing groups, and others with an interest in this emerging field for two days of discussions, workshops, and performances.

At this summit Professor Xie Jiaxing outlined some of the priorities for community music education in China. These included:

- Mom Music—music between mothers and young children
- Music with seniors, particularly senior choruses
- Music with migratory workers, particularly those from rural China now in large cities
- Music with people with intellectual challenges.

Guest keynote speakers at the summit were Don DeVito from the United States and Phil Mullen from Ireland. During the few days of the summit they were invited to run a workshop with members of the An Hua Li (Happy Sunshine Home) day center for adults with intellectual challenges. Don DeVito outlines how both Chinese adults and his American students could sample some of each other's cultures:

> During this trip we visited the Anhuali Centre, a day centre for adults with disabilities. I brought GoTalks, a communication aid device, adapted with visual aids to play recorded examples of instruments. The students would select an instrument, listen to the example and then we would teach

> each other the English and Chinese names. One of the participants was a young adult with Down's syndrome who selected "guitar" and after hearing the music and listening to the English verbalization, after two tries smiled, stated "guitar" and looked to her Chinese teachers for approval. I was then told the Chinese word for guitar and the social music activity was educational and collaborative for everyone. We used another GoTalk slide programmed with a variety of jazz and Motown music. The Chinese participants selected a numbered cell and listened to the music, creating dances for everyone to follow.
>
> Upon returning to Sidney Lanier, I had a GoTalk programmed with Chinese musical instruments and visual aids along with popular Chinese music so my students could have a similar encounter with the arts of a different culture. (DeVito 2013, 132)

When Professor Xie invited both Don DeVito and Phil Mullen back to a second community music summit in November 2012 it was an obvious move to also involve the An Hua Li center. This summit was to coincide with the fourth Beijing Traditional Music Festival, also hosted by the China Conservatory, and Professor Xie extended the invitation to perform in that event.

Shared Values through ISME

It was clear throughout both summits that the work of the two international community music leaders and the values of community music espoused by Professor Xie and his Chinese students showed similarities across the cultures. The role of the ISME CMA in acting as a forum for different understandings of community music was important in enabling everyone to have reference points that were not narrow or fixed in their vision. The CMA also had a useful role in disseminating both similarities and differences in the work across the world. The commission's vision statement states: "We believe that everyone has the right and ability to make, create, and enjoy their own music. We believe that active music-making should be encouraged and supported at all ages and at all levels of society" (ISME CMA 2006). This commission has been active for many years, fostering reflection, debate, and activity within the community music community globally. It is "[a] commission flexible in its definition of community music, watchful of political issues arising out of community music activities, and eager to connect with and learn from community music programmes worldwide, regardless of geographic location or socio-economic circumstances" (MacCarthy 2008, 45).

Preparation

From September 2012 through to arriving in China in December of that year, Phil Mullen and Don DeVito liaised with China Conservatory students to develop a partnership and make plans with the An Hua Li center to perform during the summit in December. This process raised a number of questions:

- How can foreign musicians with no knowledge of Chinese traditional music honor the intentions of the traditional festival?
- How can an event be organized across thousands of miles with major language barriers and cultural differences?
- How can people who have never put on a community music performance grasp the details of inclusive working?

While it could be argued that all of these questions were only partially answered, and that at times the logistical problems of working at such distances made both community musicians doubt whether the project could be successful, the goodwill shown to the project by all parties did allow people to raise their game and to trust in a positive outcome for all.

The musicians decided to combine some traditional Chinese material, some traditional material from other cultures and group-compose some new material, basing the compositions on traditional rhythms and Chinese poetry. All improvisations would use the five notes of the ancient Chinese scale: *gong, shang, jue, zhi,* and *yu*. The drum patterns used and developed by the group were from the music of the Uyghurs, a predominantly Muslim community with eight million people in China with ties to central Asia, whose drumming reflects an Arab influence in their culture (Harris and Muhpul 2002).

For the improvisation on a poem, a famous *gushi* poem written by Cao Chong during the Three Kingdoms Period was used. In Pinying this poem reads:

> Zhu dou ran dou ji,
> Dou zai fu zhong qi.
> Beng shi tong gen sheng,
> Xiang jian he tai ji!
>
> [Beans boil over beanstalk fire
> The beans cry in the pot.

We are born from the same root
Why are you so anxious to burn me?]

In the poem, the fire is made of dried beanstalks, so the beans are asking the beanstalks the question (Eoyong 1993, 73). The group wrote the melody for this poem in rehearsal at the An Hua Li center. Five of the group had a chime bar each, with one note of the scale for each chime bar. A sixth member decided (composed) which order the notes would go in by pointing as they wished at each of the chime bar players. This order was learned by the China Conservatory students, who then matched it to the words in the poem. This was then taught to the people in the group who wanted to sing. In this way, members of the group shared in the composition of the piece.

In addition the musicians decided to use the beautiful traditional Chinese song "Mo Li Hua," known in the West as "Jasmine Flower," which has English lyrics as follows:

What a beautiful jasmine flower
What a beautiful jasmine flower
Sweet-smelling beautiful full branch
Also good-smelling, also white everyone praises
Let me come take you, pluck you down
Give to others
Jasmine flower, oh jasmine flower

and, in Pinyin:

Hǎo yì duǒ měilìde mòlì huā
Hǎo yì duǒ měilìde mòlì huā
Fēnfāng měilì mǎn zhīyā
Yòu xiāng yòu bái rénrén kuā
Ràng wǒ lái jiāng nǐ zhāi xià
Sòng gěi biérénjiā
Mòlì huā ya mòlì huā
(Feifei 2013)

Interestingly, at the time of choosing this material, neither Phil nor Don knew if anyone in the group would be able to sing in tune or hold a rhythm beyond a basic pulse beat. The hope was that people would be able to sing at least a simplified version, and, if not, the group would make improvisations that would in some way be drawn from the original material.

Rehearsal

On arrival in Beijing the plan (in the minds of Don and Phil) was to work with ten traditional music students, a translator, and twenty-five An Hua Li center users to produce a ten-minute performance after two to three full days' rehearsal. In fact, the reality was that they worked with two China Conservatory students and twenty-five An Hua Li users for four-and-a-half hours to produce a forty-minute performance, with the translator not available for the first session.

The short amount of rehearsal time was probably the biggest challenge of the whole project. It was important to everyone involved to play in the festival, and to play well and have pride in the performance. The rehearsals had to be very meticulously planned to optimize how time was used, with roles clarified down to the minute. A key challenge here was how to ensure good-quality musical performance while not in any way sacrificing the enjoyment of the group and the sense of the group as a real team, with opportunity for their own input rather than just being told what to do by the leaders. In particular, the demands of time could have challenged the inclusive principles of community music practice, which "require that the working space be a safe space, in which the music facilitator attempts to create an atmosphere that is mindful of the participants' range of abilities but challenging enough to stimulate all concerned" (Higgins 2012, 150). Indeed, this author felt that his own principles might be challenged: "Because our working principles involve care for the group and individuals within it as more important than the resulting musical pieces it is more likely that participants will achieve a series of benefits on differing levels of human development, including increased self-esteem and a sense of belonging" (Mullen 2002, 3).

Being experienced community musicians, DeVito and Mullen understood that their role involved embracing the fact and boundary of the pre-organized performance as a showcase of the abilities of the group and musicians. They would have to do this even with the potentially stressful demands of a very tight schedule, while simultaneously encouraging the group to build their own confidence, have a substantial creative input into the material being performed, develop musical group skills in a very short time, and hopefully, and most importantly, enjoy the whole experience.

Without a translator in the first session, the first material was developed using improvised sign language, with signs for "watch me," "your turn," and so on. What became immediately obvious was that the group itself was primed and ready for performance. The An Hua Li center has a very caring and supportive atmosphere, helping adults with mild to moderate learning difficulties to raise their self-esteem and to be comfortable with independent living. There is a real sense of community, with everybody supporting everybody else.

Quite quickly the group, even lacking any shared verbal language with the music leaders, were able to follow visual cues and copy the patterns modelled. They developed simple rhythms, including keeping pulse, copying heartbeat, and some others. As there was a range of instruments with different timbres, it was easy to arrange the percussion instruments into sections and to bring the sections into the pieces at different times, thus creating layered arrangements. In one piece a number of members of the group took improvised solos. These solos, although all in time, were very basic, sometimes little more than a pulse, but this did not greatly matter. What mattered was that it was their own contribution to the piece; the group was working to give a sense that everyone could have their moment in the spotlight, even if it was quite short. ("We need to understand that all musical experiences are valuable—that there may be advanced and beginner experiences and all manner in between, but there are no lower or higher experiences" (Allsup 2013, 2).) For the leaders, working in a group all of whom clearly had high expectations of the project was helpful in bringing out their best efforts and it was easy to create a situation that mirrored Higgins' intention: "As a music facilitator, one might aim for group togetherness, respectful collaboration, and open negotiation" (Higgins 2012, 153).

One piece featured Uyghur rhythms with improvisations on chime bars and also on iPad instruments.

When it came to "Mo Li Hua," there were five women in the group who knew the song and who clearly wanted to be featured singers. They came out in front of the group and sang the song well. Although there was a language barrier it was clear from the focus levels and expressions of this small group that this performance was very important to them. After the actual concert it was translated to the leaders that this had been "the best night of their lives."

The Concert

The concert was held in the China Conservatory and was well attended. The audience was appreciative and the group performed well in a very focused way.

Throughout the session they kept their eyes on Phil and Don, watching for clues and nuances of volume, tempo, or expression. What was certainly clear was that, while two days ago they had been users of a day center who were often seen as not very capable and on the margins of society, now they were a performing group with every right to be onstage. The performance, although simple, was very effective and was appreciated by the audience, who gave them a rapturous reception. The performers all clearly felt it was important to them and ended in a celebratory mood. This included the music students from the Conservatory, who had never worked with this type of group before and felt it was a profound experience for them, reminding them that these people had as much a right to make music as they did. After the event they told the music leaders that this event had really made them think about music education and performance in a different way from how they had before. David Elliot states: "I believe we need to empower music students and music education majors as artistic and socially just musical citizens. What this means is that we need to enable our students to develop musical replies to the social/moral/political dilemmas of today and tomorrow by creating musical (or hybrid musical/bodily/visual) expressions of social problems" (2007, 87).

Some Implications

For this author, the specifics of this project raise questions in three areas:

1. What are the fundamental skills/qualities required in community music practice? In other words, in a project with such demands and short time constraints, which ways of working cannot be sacrificed in order to maintain the integrity of something like this as a community music project?
2. Who has a right to public performance and who, if anyone, has not? This raises separate questions about the purpose and nature of performance in human society and also about issues of musical quality within performance.
3. What are the possibilities/challenges for community music education in China?

Community Music Skills and Qualities

In a community music workshop it is necessary for the leader to be fully present with the group and to invite them to share what it is to be human. As Silverman states, "all forms of music teaching and learning should consider people's humanity first and foremost" (2009, 189). While this basic call to consciousness is of course common sense for all situations, the urgency for this approach is heightened when working with people who are vulnerable and have rarely been included in music-making activities in the past: "Not everyone can access music-making activities, and it is disadvantaged people who face the biggest barriers. Musical inclusivity recognises that, and actively dismantles those barriers to create a more culturally democratic society" (Deane et al. 2014, 10). Working in sensitive situations with sensitive people requires certain qualities to be always at the forefront of the leader's approach: "Key qualities needed in this work are being open-minded and tolerant, kind, calm, empathetic and patient" (Cartwright 2013, 2). Higgins confirms: "The facilitator enters the relationship without presenting a front or a façade and encourages the participant to do likewise. This opens the possibility for both to journey together, a chance to venture 'safely' into the unknown" (2012, 161).

When working with disadvantaged groups the leader is aware that the program may have many aims—some musical, some personal and social. They recognize that, while there is a need for a professional music project always to work towards high-quality performance outcomes (if a performance is required as part of the program of work), this should not be at the expense of the holistic development of the group. The implication is shared ownership, with the leader not always knowing in advance what the finished music will sound like, as it will most likely be created by the group, albeit with the leader's support and guidance:

> The majority of my work is in settings where offering a meaningful musical experience is the tool or intervention by which there can be a range of social outcomes including confidence, the ability to communicate, make decisions, be part of a group and in fact build a community. My goal is to balance social and artistic outcomes, while very consciously ensuring that the process is socially driven. I don't tend to arrive knowing what the artistic outcome will be—the participants will decide—but I have yet to see a project produce a piece of work that the participants are not proud of. (Abrams 2013, 62)

The leader has a role to keep the workshop and group "on track," or at least not too far "off track" for too long: "In any music workshop activity there is a need to maintain a balance between order, enough for the session to function without descending into chaos, and freedom, which releases the powerful playful inner child and its accompanying energy" (Pestano 2013, 122). Perhaps the key role for the leader here is to use his or her judgement as to when and how to intervene and when to let the group run with what they are creating. The leader's range of communication can be expanded far beyond the transmission of musical skills to a range of responses that include questioning, supporting, creating humor, acknowledging contributions, lifting the mood, taking risks, giving affirmation, believing in the group and sharing that belief, and celebrating both failure and success.

Higgins acknowledges that

> Facilitators are able to find a comfortable balance between (1) being prepared to lead and able to lead and (2) being prepared and able to hold back, thus enabling the group or individuals to discover the journey of musical invention for themselves. Facilitators are never static in one approach or another but move in and out of roles as the group dictates. Facilitation necessitates trust in the ability of others as well as submission to the inventiveness of others (2012, 14).

So, in a community music performance, the leader must balance the needs of the group and the audience for a performance that is satisfying musically without ever losing the sense of the community created through the workshop process. In a sense, the leader is ethically bound to maintain her/his own humanity and love for the group as something that supersedes all other considerations. In practice the twin demands of sound and self require a very broad and mature set of skills, which may not be that developed through conventional musical training programs.

The Right to Perform

Both DeVito and Mullen had previously been involved in a concert given by teenagers with intellectual challenges in Carnegie Hall in New York (DeVito 2013, 130–131) as well as similar performances in a range of less prestigious venues in America and the UK. They operate from the belief that everyone should get the opportunity to perform onstage and that we should celebrate the achievements of all of us, especially those of the more vulnerable and traditionally excluded in society.

This approach to integrating performance venues is not a commonplace across the world. For many, performing is synonymous with a showcasing of musical excellence, achieved over many years of practice by those with a special "talent." The exclusive pursuit of that model would deny access to well-known venues for most, if not all, children and adults with intellectual challenges. The author argues that this leads to a form of discriminatory thinking—namely, that these people's music is not good enough for these venues and thus by extension they are in some way deficient. It is therefore a social justice issue, something of a political act, to enable people with intellectual challenges to perform in prestigious venues, places where they have hitherto not been expected to play.

This becomes more pronounced in societies like China where, though attitudes towards disability are changing for the better both at the government level and among ordinary people, there are still major hurdles to overcome in terms of inclusion and equality. Recently Human Rights Watch reported: "Many families, fearing social stigma and 'loss of face,' continue to keep their (disabled) adult offspring under wraps at home, suffering the difficulties and isolation of their situation in silence." And where "people with disabilities in China remain a vulnerable group of citizens, encountering specific difficulties in a society with an economy under enormous market-oriented transition. There is still a great deal to be accomplished in order to realize the full equality, participation, and sharing of people with disabilities in China" (Weiss 2010).

The Beijing concert was perhaps an example of what David Elliott calls the ethical spectacle: "An ethical spectacle 'demonstrates' legal, distributive, procedural, and associational justice, and challenges oppressions. Ethical spectacles disrupt cultural hierarchies, build safe communities, promote diversity, and engage with reality while asking what new realities might be possible" (Elliott 2007, 89). Such concerts can act in at least two ways: first, by giving the audience exposure to what up to now would be an unusual experience, seeing and hearing the joy of musical performance expressed by people who previously were not thought to have the capacity for either music or concert making; and second, by making it a commonplace for disadvantaged people to feel joint ownership of public performance spaces, that they have an equal right to access and so to experience all the internal benefits of this enhanced sense of citizenship: "Rather than explicitly tackling the conditions of material poverty, physical illness, or disability often experienced by young people facing additional challenges, the music project serves as a way of raising consciousness and expressive ability, facilitating a deeper understanding amongst the young people of their own abilities and providing opportunities to communicate and connect with other people" (Lonie 2013, 10). Through integrating concert halls, festivals, media events and all aspects of public music making we can help establish the rights of people with intellectual challenges, and other marginalized groups, to play a full role in the cultural life of our societies, to be honored for their contributions as artists, and to receive the respect they deserve.

Possibilities and Challenges

The second community music summit in Beijing (including the performance discussed in this chapter) showed that there is an understanding among some Chinese music educators of the processes and intentions of community music. It also pointed to a need within marginalized communities to make and celebrate their own music and benefit from the goodwill among audiences for such performances. Can this work develop further, and what are the challenges to that development?

First, it is clear that the models of community music activity developed around the world and documented through the ISME CMA have resonances in China. People respond to the same type of intervention; there is Chinese material that is suitable to be adapted and used by participants. However, as yet there is no organization, network, or forum beyond the two summits that can act as a catalyst for the development of community music in China. There is no professional body or, at this time, sense of a profession, although Chinese music therapists who spoke to this author at the summit made it clear that there was much in common between the two fields in China at this time. So these questions arise:

- Who will champion community music in China—in terms of individuals, institutions, and policy makers?
- How (if at all), will community music and music therapy develop their joint relationship?
- How will music educators and institutions embrace working with new populations/groups such as people with intellectual challenges, those with dementia, autism, and so forth?
- How can the system embrace and support the grassroots nature of the community-music approach?
- How best to develop a skilled professional workforce and provide them with resources?
- How can the work be made strategic so as to cover all of China over time?

This chapter, while being the place to ask such questions, is not the place to answer them. That can only be done in China, over time, by musicians, educators, and policy makers who are committed to the goal of creating equal access to culture for all as a cornerstone of developing a more inclusive society, one that honors the contributions made by everyone, no matter what their starting point. In the words of David Elliott, "Practices of school and community music education as/for social justice require personal and political persistence over a long period, the skills of building musical community solidarity, specific social and musical-social aims, the "commissioning" of help from local, regional, and national musicians, and the courage to push for legal, distributive, procedural, economic, associational and anti-discriminatory justice" (2007, 84). Importantly, the answers to the questions raised here will require work over what may turn out to be generations, fuelled by a hunger for lived equality and social justice for everyone.

Note

Epigraph. Quoted in *Chinese People's Daily,* May 5, 2010.

References

Abrams, Jess. 2013 "Social and Artistic—A Reflection on Balancing Outcomes." In *Reaching Out: Music Education with "Hard to Reach" Children and Young People,* edited by P. Mullen and C. Harrison, 62–66. London: Music Mark.

Allsup, Randall. 2013. "Engaging the "Hard to Reach": Issues and Challenges." In *Reaching Out: Music Education with "Hard to Reach"Children and Young People,* edited by P. Mullen and C. Harrison, 1–2. London: Music Mark.

Cartwright, Jim. 2013. "Working with Children in Challenging Circumstances." London: Sound Connections. http://www.sound-connections.org.uk/wp-content/uploads/CCC-Research-FINAL-BRIEFING-PAPER.pdf.

Coffman, Don D., ed. 2010. *CMA XII: Harmonizing the Diversity That Is Community Music: Proceedings from the International Society for Music Education 2010 Seminar of the Commission for Community Music Activity.* Nedlands, Western Australia: International Society for Music Education.

Deane, Kathryn, Anita Holford, Rob Hunter, and Phil Mullen. 2014. *The Power of Equality; Interim Evaluation of Musical Inclusion.* UK: Sound Sense and Youth Music.

DeVito, Don. 2013. "Developing a Grassroots International Community Music Network Serving People with Disabilities." In *Reaching Out: Music Education with "Hard to Reach" Children and Young People,* edited by P. Mullen and C. Harrison, 127–134. London: Music Mark.

Elliott, David. 2007. "Socializing Music Education." *Action, Criticism, and Theory for Music Education* 6 (4): 60–95.

Eoyang, Eugene Chen. 1993. *The Transparent Eye: Reflections on Translation, Chinese Literature and Comparative Poetics.* Honolulu: University of Hawai'i Press.

Feifei, Feng. 2013. "Jasmine Flower." *Learn Chinese Songs.* September 18, 2013. http://easywaytolearnchinese.blogspot.co.uk/2013/09/moli-hua-jasmine-flowers-by-feng-feifei.html.

Harris, Rachel, and Yashin Muhpul. 2002. "Music of the Uyghurs." *London Uyghur Ensemble.* http://www.uyghurensemble.co.uk/en-html/nf-research-article1.html.

Higgins, Lee. 2012. *Community Music: In Theory and in Practice.* New York: Oxford University Press.

ISME CMA. 2006. "Vision." Community Music Activity Commission (CMA). http://www.isme.org/cma (accessed April 20, 2016).

Lonie, Dougie. 2013. "Why Music? A Research Rationale for Making Music with Children and Young People Experiencing Additional Challenges." In *Reaching Out: Music Education with "Hard to Reach" Children and Young People,* edited by P. Mullen and C. Harrison, 3–12. London: Music Mark.

McCarthy, Marie. 2008. "The Community Music Activity Commission of ISME, 1982–2007: A Forum for Global Dialogue and Institutional Formation." *International Journal of Community Music* 1 (1): 39–48. doi:10.1386/ijcm.1.1.39_1.

Mullen, Phil. 2002. "'We Don't Teach, We Explore': Aspects of Community Music Delivery." International Society for Music Education Community Music Activity Commission Conference, Rotterdam, Holland, July 2002. http://www.worldmusiccentre.com/uploads/cma/mullenteachexplore.PDF.

Pestano, Catherine. 2013. "Music Group Work with LGBT youth." In *Reaching Out: Music Education with "Hard to Reach" Children and Young People,* edited by P. Mullen and C. Harrison, 117–126. London: Music Mark.

Silverman, Marissa. 2009. "Sites of Social Justice: Community Music in New York City." *Research Studies in Music Education* 31 (2): 178–192. doi:10.1177/1321103x09344384.

Weiss, Thomas C. 2010. "Overview of Disability in China." *Disabled World.* http://www.disabled-world.com/news/asia/china/disability-china.php.

CHAPTER 9

Community Music Therapy

From the Clinical to Community

Kirstin Robertson-Gillam

Community Music Therapy (CoMT) is a community-based music therapy approach that addresses the multiple needs of marginalized, disadvantaged, and socially isolated people, and operates alongside the clinically based traditional consensus models of music therapy (Ansdell 2002, 2014; O'Grady and McFerran 2007). CoMT acknowledges the cultural and social needs of isolated people with reference to their health and well-being. In contrast, Community Music (CM) takes a more educational approach and is dedicated to cultural and social betterment and developing music proficiencies (Atkinson 2001). CM attracts groups of people, from young children to older adults, in community projects focused on developing group music proficiencies primarily through music education. In contrast, CoMT belongs on a continuum of music therapy interventions, with acute care and individualized treatments at one end and communal *musicking* at the other (Small 1998). Because medically oriented interventions within acute care are highly confidential, music performances do not normally take place. However, in CoMT settings, performances are an integral part of communal *musicking,* showcasing personal and group achievements.

Atkinson put forward a definition of Community Music as

> A participatory music-making activity in which community musicians work with a given community to enable them to make music which is inspired by their own interests and ideas. Some Community Music

> activities seek to address the issues of social difficulty experienced by the participating communities, whilst others pursue music-making for its own sake. (2001, 7)

Ansdell (2002, 12), in contrast, proposed an early working definition of CoMT:

> An approach to working musically with people in context: acknowledging the social and cultural factors of their health, illness, relationships and musics. It reflects the essentially communal reality of musicing (originally described and spelt by Nordoff and Robbins, 2007) and is a response to overly individualized treatment models and the isolation people often experience within society.

Christopher Small's definition (1998, 9) fits nicely into both of these concepts:

> To *music* is to take part, in any capacity, in a musical performance, whether by performing, by listening, by rehearsing or practicing, by providing material for performance (what is called composing), or by dancing.

Furthermore, the term "co-musicking" was coined and spelled by Christopher Small in 1998. In this chapter Small's spelling of "musicking" will be used throughout.

Historically, Rudd (2010) believed that music therapy as an allied health profession was more socially oriented because of its tool, music, which has the ability to engage groups of people in cooperative activities. Rudd argued that the traditional biomedical and psychological approaches for treating health conditions musically excluded social and cultural considerations, leaving gaps in the service delivery of the clinical models within traditionally accepted music therapy practices (Rudd 2010; O'Grady and McFerran 2007). Because music therapy was establishing itself as a health-care profession in the late twentieth century, alignments with contemporary medical and health practices were very important and remain relevant to this day.

Music therapy as a profession has evolved in developed countries as a university-trained, clinical, research-based profession since the Second World War. Traditionally, clinically based music therapy is a confidential interaction between client and therapist and has deep psychological roots with equal emphasis on music and therapy (Ansdell 2014, 65). These factors helped to develop the profession of music therapy in the latter part of the twentieth century.

In Australia, music therapy as a profession was born in the 1970s with the formation of the Australian Music Therapy Association (AMTA) in 1975 and the first training course at Melbourne University in 1978. Today, the two university courses in Melbourne and Sydney offer music therapy training at a master's degree level for registration with the AMTA. Music therapists can also undertake higher degree research master and doctoral programs. Music therapy clinicians work in many settings: special schools, clinics, hospitals, mental health facilities, disability centres, forensic facilities, and aged-care centers. They employ a variety of clinical approaches from active music making to receptive music models, depending on their suitability for meeting clients' needs. The master's in CoMT at Western Sydney University (Kingswood campus) collaborates with the Nordoff Robbins Music Therapy Centre located on the same campus. This center employs both clinical and CoMT approaches within the Nordoff Robbins method.

CoMT engages the social, cultural, physical, psychological, and political aspects of an individual and provides a way for disadvantaged, disenfranchised, and socially isolated people to feel they belong. It offers participation in community-based groups such as choirs, drumming circles, and instrumental and drama groups. This builds artistic expression as well as developing individual and group identities through music making and music performances. Aldridge (2005, 46) theorized the idea of a "performed identity" in which "we can offer contexts of expression and understanding where gesture, movement and vocalization make communicative sense and . . . that perception of self is dependent on coherence in time." The ultimate goal is to promote quality of life and well-being through music participation across the continuum from individual to communal health care.

CoMT engages the community that it serves, and thus the community becomes a consumer of CoMT services (Ansdell 2014). Furthermore, within institutions exists a living and breathing community that is unique to that organization and its function. Each of these communities connects in some way with the wider community, creating multifaceted ways for CM therapists to work *with* people (Pavlicevic and Ansdell 2004). Some examples of this are discussed later in this chapter.

The health-care continuum places illness at one end and well-being at the other, and Australian practice is to involve both clinically based music therapy models and CoMT approaches (O'Grady and McFerran 2007). For instance,

CoMT operates within a *salutogenic* (defined by Antonovsky 1991 as supporting health and well-being) nonmedical environment. In contrast, clinically based music therapy is more likely to work within a *pathogenic* medically oriented environment (Antonovsky 1991). Although it is focused on healing medical conditions, the pathogenic environment in which clinical music therapy operates does aim to achieve a sense of well-being and quality of life for patients through clinically based interventions, addressing medical and psychological symptomatologies (Ansdell 2014). Accordingly, clients can move back and forth along the health-care spectrum depending on their state of health. This concept was originally described by Antonovsky 1991).

Music in itself is a vital motivating force, forming connections between people and their environment through its various elements and activities. McMillan and Chavis (1986) suggested that individuals can come together and interact through a common activity over a period of time in a specific geographical location that is itself connected to its wider community. In this way, people can sense belongingness to and membership in a group that offers an enjoyable and motivating activity. They can also experience having their needs met by the group as well as emotionally connecting with each other. This type of connection may involve histories and similar experiences that, when shared, promote a sense of validation and well-being. One example occurred during the research for my doctoral research with a cohort of depressed middle-aged community-dwelling adults with comorbid medical conditions who were socially isolated. Their depression and social isolation were significantly decreased by their participating in a Community Music Therapy choir. Their story is told later in this chapter.

The Social, Ecological, and Evolutionary Benefits of Music

Music by its very nature is socially and culturally based. It exists in every culture and society throughout the world. Small (1998, 94) asserted, "*musicking* is about the creation and performance of relationships . . . a type of ritual situation, enacting ideal relationships which then become the foundation of community." It brings people together, creating community events such as marching military bands, hymn singing, funerals, weddings, and national celebrations (Mannes 2011). Mithen (2006) said that music builds personal and national identities, fostering a sense of purpose and well-being for individuals, groups, and societies. He believed that unless we engage in musicking, especially with and for our young people at an early age, we limit opportunities to develop an important aspect of what it is to be human, thereby threatening the ongoing well-being of societies. *Musicking* affirms our connectedness to and belongingness with others.

Ansdell (1997) viewed music as an ecology, which balances in such a way that it sustains and creates diversity. As Bruscia postulated, "the basic ecological premise is that changes in one area will lead to changes in the other" (1998, 231), so that helping a person develop becomes a communal activity to bring about changes at both environmental and personal levels. Because music therapy extends beyond the therapy room, there are also transformational changes that can take place in the client–therapist relationship, including both personal and community aspects (Bruscia 1998).

Stige and Aaro (2012) believe that CoMT can enhance the culture and context in which a client lives. This in turn increases personal and cultural identities, creating positive social changes between individuals and groups and building communicative networks. In this way, CoMT works at the level of many interlinking histories between culture, society, and the individual, empowering participants and humanizing communities (Rudd 2010). As such, these aspects increase understandings and acceptance of all people within societies in a field of mutual caring and health promotion.

From an evolutionary perspective, protomusicality refers to the ability of humans to relate to movement and sound when communicating with others (Malloch and Trevarthen 2009). This suggests that there is an innate, evolutionary capacity in humans to make music (Stige and Aaro 2012). Furthermore, early man could have developed music for communication, as a form of social control, and as a mechanism of sexual selection (Miller 2001) in order to ensure the survival of tribal and nomadic societies (Mithen 2006).

Dissanayake (2009) asserted that the evolutionary nature of music carried a survival factor along with its social attributes for bringing people together in communities. Thus, early music making could have provided evolutionary benefits for survival, building and sustaining relationships, and creating diversity for skill and knowledge building. This appears to be the beginnings of musical communication, or *musicking,* as we know it today.

Registered and board-certified music therapists (in Australia and the United States respectively) use music skills as their primary communication tools in order to meet their clients' needs and promote states of well-being. Community musicians also use their music skills to bring people together in groups with an emphasis on the "social betterment of individuals, communities and societies at large" through an educational model (Yerichuk 2014, 130). Its social rationale is that of a tool that works towards social betterment, such as making improvements in family and work life, improving leisure pursuits, articulating political agendas, promoting educational opportunities, and generally working towards providing musical opportunities for people from all walks of life (Yerichuk 2014, 130).

Concern focuses on clients' physical, mental, and social well-being. These three factors are also related to the health of a community, a group, or a nation (Stige and Aaro 2012, 67). In terms of CoMT, the overall health and well-being of an individual can be related to the well-being of others in the community through shared music making. Stige proposed that human coexistence depends upon how well we can care for each other in a spirit of mutuality, "building resources of the individual, the community and the relationship between individual and community" (Stige 2003, 207). By building a *co-musicking* environment, we partner with each other, expressing ourselves through the process of musical communication.

As a nonmedical approach within health care, CoMT focuses on personhood, enablement, and empowerment as primary factors of communication in order to realize the goals of ultimate good quality of life and well-being, with performance growing out of these goals (Procter 2001).

Community Music Therapy and Disabilities

CoMT exemplifies Small's *co-musicking* notions (Small 1998). Accordingly, community music therapists' work with clients in a shared interaction implies a levelling of power imbalances between individuals when making music together in spontaneous improvisations and structured music learning conditions. Procter argued that in "Community Music Therapy, aesthetic objectives *are* social objectives," and that "playing together increases possibilities for action" and social capital (2004, 228).

The following case vignette illustrates this point:

> A large institution was re-structuring and preparing for their young adult residents to move into community homes. These residents had regularly attended individual and group music therapy sessions from various areas of their community. They primarily engaged in clinical improvisation and structured music making. A local eisteddfod provided a disabled section for music performers in their competition.

> One twenty-six-year-old man with Down Syndrome had become extremely skilled in drumming improvisations during his individual music therapy sessions. I decided he was ready to apply his skills in an improvisation to a Spanish dance "Minueto" from *Danzas Españoles,* Op. 5, composed by Enrique Granados to which I provided live accompaniment on the piano. We practiced twice weekly and he was able [to] cue in with correct drum patterns, keeping the rhythm while throwing his beaters in the air dramatically between musical pauses in the composition. At the Eisteddfod, he received much applause and acclaim at his expertise in keeping the beat and throwing the beaters. He won the competition and came home with a trophy. His story and the recording of his performance were later incorporated into the ABC radio program *Music of the Pacific,* 1987. When he finally left to live in a community home, he was well equipped to cope with community life.

Institutional life embraces its own community and, in this instance, Community Music Therapy played a role with regular performances and an adolescent dance and coffee-shop club. One Christmas, a musical play based on the song "The Twelve Days of Christmas" was performed, bringing all sectors of the facility together from the school principal (who played the role of the lord), a teacher (who played the page), a physiotherapist (who played the lady) and psychology, nursing, and care staff (who formed a choir to sing between each act). The residents performed each day of Christmas that showcased their learned musical and dramatic abilities (even though they were extremely disabled). This production exemplified the idea of creating a "level playing field where everyone was equal and all shared in the communal spirit of *musicking*" (Small 1998).

Embracing the Nordoff Robbins Approach

The Nordoff Robbins method (2007) embodies the notion of a core musical self that is creative and spontaneous. This approach focuses on drawing out and developing the client's own inner music and leading to transformations in perceptions, movement, speech, and motivation. Nordoff and Robbins theorized that individualized musicality is the essence of the universality of human musical sensitivity (Nordoff and Robbins 2007). It is through the *co-musicking* interaction of spontaneous music making that the language of communication occurs. A *musicking* community with those who have disabilities, mental health issues, and are culturally and socially disenfranchised can then develop. Tommy's story highlights how disabilities can be transcended in a musical relationship.

> Tommy was a seventeen-year-old Tonganese boy, born with microcephaly (small brain) and quadriplegia. He was unable to speak and was blind but had extremely acute hearing. His life prognosis was poor. He attended the Nordoff Robbins Music Therapy Centre following his completed school program. Tommy learnt to play the drum on cue with limited muscle movement in one arm. He learnt to vocalise during improvisations as he built a trusting relationship with me as his music therapist. When his adopted mother expressed concerns about his inability to sleep, I created a music and relaxation recording for him which helped him to relax and divert his distress at night. Tommy's exuberant participation in musicking drew the attention of his previous school and local community which [was] reported in the local newspaper and his Nordoff Robbins community.

Community Music Therapy in Hospice Care: Whatever Next?

People who are dying have a lot of living to do, and music is one way of offering moments of connection and interaction in the reality of *present time.* I was the first music therapist in Sydney to embark on work in palliative care. Initially, I encountered resistance and dubiousness from the staff, with many asking, *Whatever next?* They felt that music therapy would upset their palliative care routine. No one could imagine how music would work with dying people.

My work relied on referrals from medical, nursing, and allied health staff, relatives, and self-referrals from the patients themselves. Equipped with a trolley containing a keyboard, autoharp, recorded music, CD player, music materials, art materials, poetry, and stories, I would do my rounds, visiting referred patients and building a presence on the wards. As I interacted with patients through discussions, songs, live instrumental playing, music-based relaxation, art work, and recorded music, I began to see a way forward. With my nursing background, I was able to integrate myself well into the existing medical model.

Hospice work includes community work, and this meant travelling to other aged-care facilities and private homes. An open channel between the community and the hospice was evident, with patients mostly being admitted for symptom management. They would always be pleased to see me when I visited them in their homes and later, after admission to the hospice for symptom management. Connections were made between community and hospice staff, bringing a viable role for music therapy in both settings. Religious services were provided in the hospice by the chaplain every three months to celebrate the lives of those who had passed on. As the music therapist, I provided appropriate live music, offering a valuable community role for family, friends, and staff.

The following case vignette illustrates a music therapy intervention along the health-care continuum.

> Adam was a twenty-three-year-old arts law student who suddenly collapsed one night in his university room. He was rushed to hospital where a non-malignant tumour was found lodged in the frontal lobes of his brain. He underwent radical surgery and came to the hospice for rehabilitation. Even though he now had a seriously impaired short term memory, he maintained a sense of self and personal insight. He knew that his life was permanently changed with a limited future. He had difficulty fitting into the hospice routine and knew that he was living with "very sick people." He had been involved in a Pentecostal Christian group at the university so at our initial meeting, when I introduced an upbeat gospel song called "Praise the Lord," he immediately clapped and sang with me. The next day, he remembered me and started to sing the same song again. Gradually, over a period of six weeks, Adam and I built a *musicking* relationship which included singing songs, instrumental improvisation (to release tension and grief) and a musical life review (to re-build his memory, accompanied by a journal of memorabilia and a CD of songs) with lots of verbal discussions. On discharge, he went home to his mother who was struggling with severe asthma. She was very supportive of his music therapy and brought him back to the hospice as an outpatient each week. Over the next five months, with the help of his mother, Adam learnt to re-build his memories using the life review journal and music recordings. He learnt to find his new bedroom to the song "Rock Around the Clock," by replacing the lyrics with words of instruction. His mother suffered a cardiac arrest and died five months later and Adam went to live with his aunt, who brought him to Community Music Therapy sessions with me at a local medical centre. He called these sessions "music lessons." We worked through many issues of low self-esteem, lack of confidence and grief; coming to terms with his disabilities and working towards a future. One highlight was a visit to the local Anglican church for a rock-style worship service where he shouted and clapped, calling out "Yey, Jesus!" We

> followed this by a dinner at McDonald's where he devoured a hamburger with relish! He eventually went to live with another aunt in Queensland, working as the gardener for an aged care facility.

Adam initially received individualized music therapy while in hospice care for six weeks. These sessions involved his mother. Later, after his mother's death, community-based sessions involved his wider family. He traversed the health-care continuum from a pathogenic to salutogenic environment. This increased his sense of self and motivation. Adam's memory returned to an acceptable level in present time (much to the surprise of his doctor) and he began to come to terms with the limitations of his abilities. Through his newly "performed identity" (Aldridge 2005), he built meaning, purpose, and motivation for living. Community Music Therapy followed Adam from the pathogenic environment of hospice care to a nonmedical, salutogenic environment. His music therapy program was adjusted to meet his needs at every stage, strengthening him to develop coping strategies for adjusting and rebuilding his life (Ansdell 2002).

The "Whatever next?" question became a "Why not!" statement within the hospice setting. Music therapy services in palliative care were delivered along the continuum of health care from individual interventions to community care, depending on patients' current states of health. Each interaction aimed to enhance a sense of well-being and build social relationships. Staff appreciated input for symptom management such as pain, constipation, and breathing difficulties. They also began to request after-hours assistance for distressed patients, particularly those who were close to dying. Additionally, music therapy became an integral part of the community outreach service and the rehabilitation ward. The role of music therapy services became well established within the hospice and the community.

From Aged Care to the Community

At fifty-four years' old Sharon had suffered a severe mental breakdown eight years previously, and had moved around various mental health communities until she was admitted into aged care. She began to attend a music therapy improvisation group, and after a few sessions I arranged an individual session in which she expressed her sense of complete hopelessness and futility. She had not been able to cry or express her emotions freely for many years. However, during her first drumming interaction, she expressed her anger and frustration, bursting into tears. She drew an art mandala in response to an improvisation that I played to her, in which she discovered that she had an empty center inside. Subsequent sessions revolved around vocal as well as instrumental improvisation in order to address her various needs, including low self-esteem and confidence.

During one dramatic vocal improvisation session, Sharon wailed, "I have no mouth, I have no voice. R. is in charge of me, I am perfectly useless" while beating perseveringly on a drum. This gave her a cathartic release and was the turning point in her rehabilitation. She eventually joined the facility-based Blue Jays choir and began to participate in music making at local and wider community events. She continued with her individual vocal improvisation and counselling sessions.

Eventually, Sharon left aged care to live in a community flat, and she continued with her music therapy sessions in my private practice for twelve months. She set about rebuilding her life within the wider community, creating a future for herself that she had never thought possible. Today, she works as a mental health consumer advocate and says she loves her life. She continues to keep in contact with me.

Choir Work with Older People

Choir singing is a group activity that requires cooperation in order to produce a good sound. My initial research into choirs with older people began thirteen years ago with the Blue Jays choir in an aged-care facility in the Blue Mountains, west of Sydney. I had formed this choir for residents who were demonstrating social isolation and depressive symptoms. I had been visiting each resident and engaging them in individual music making and counselling conversations. The Blue Jays choir grew into a living entity, like a family, where members bonded and became caring towards each other through singing activities. They were able to join in wider community activities through the choir, feeling that they still had a role in society for the first time since their admission to aged care.

The combination of singing, verbal discussion, and mindfulness meditation proved highly beneficial, as regular surveys demonstrated. This choir grew into a close community in which many life events were celebrated and performed at, including deaths of members, birthdays, and performances in the wider community. The members requested three practices per week and could be seen eagerly rushing to choir practice on their walkers. While I recognized the needs of each individual member, I began to see, through the group process, a new perspective emerging—that of the choir as its own entity with communal sharing and togetherness. This was especially evident when the wife of R., one of the choir members, suddenly died. R., having been a church organist and composer, asked them to sing one of his compositions that they had learned at her funeral. We all went, out into the snow on a wet and cold day, to the church. The choir sang beautifully as they honored one of their own, who sat with tears pouring down his face.

Similarly, Ramsey (2002) came to view his group of aphasia patients as restoring the communal experiences during music therapy. His study highlighted how a music-making group can become a cohesive community that shares the raw emotions and experiences of life together, supporting each other by giving emotional and social support.

Blue Jay choir members became interested in attending concerts offered in the wider community and increased their music-listening pleasures. One highlight was their participation in a local jazz festival where they *brought the roof down* with their rendition of *The Marching Saints*. They also visited and performed in other nursing homes. This made them feel useful by contributing to the wider community. They built an important role within the facility, providing music for fetes, religious and secular events, and, at one stage, the opening of a new section to their facility. One major highlight was their joint performance of an abridged version of Andrew Lloyd Webber's musical *Joseph's Amazing Technicolor Dreamcoat* with a seniors' choir from another aged-care facility. The Blue Jays became a vital group that derived support and comfort from each other, increasing their quality of life, motivation, sense of purpose, and personhood.

Hearing the Voice of People with Dementia

I later engaged in researching the effects of a choir on depression in elderly people with severe dementia, comparing it to a reminiscence and control group (Robertson-Gillam 2008). The following results in both choir and reminiscence groups are described below in p (probability) scores. This means that any score below $p < 0.05$ will reject the null hypothesis and show significant positive results. The lower the score below 0.05, then the more significant will be the value of the results. Accordingly, depression scores for both groups showed a high significant p value of $p < 0.001$. Furthermore, levels of responsiveness to the therapy programs, such as expression of feelings, had a highly significant p value of $p < 0.013$. Similarly, positive mood changes showed a significance value of $p < 0.010$ as well as engagement in sessions with a p value of $p < 0.015$. In summary, both choir and reminiscence groups showed highly significant results, indicating that social engagement is an important factor in the well-being of people with dementia.

The following two case vignettes illustrate how "the creative and spontaneous nature of music is ideally suited to match the state of mind of a person with dementia who lives mostly in the present moment but whose potent memories are from the past" (Robertson-Gillam 2011, 102). Both vignettes also demonstrate how a community spirit was generated by meeting individual needs within the choir group and contributing to the formation of a cohesive and connected small community.

Case Vignette No 1

When Vera joined the dementia choir she had been unable to adequately communicate for some time. Her speech was gradually deteriorating into one to three word sentences. Her contact with myself began during the first choir meeting when I asked each choir member to "sing their song" with me individually. When I came to Vera, she burst forth singing "Summertime" (Gershwin) in a beautifully trained voice! It seemed that no-one knew she had been a trained singer in her past. She watched my lips when she stumbled on some of the words and lent over to me, patting my cheek and kissing me during the section of "hush little baby, don't you cry." She communicated a world of thoughts and feelings in that one song which became the starting point of communication between us. Whenever she saw me outside the choir room, she would swoop upon me singing the song! Over time, her vocabulary gradually increased into coherent statements with correct syntax. She learnt all the words of "Summertime" and many other songs. She began to join in other activities outside the choir and take part in conversations with fellow residents as well as enjoying positive interactions with her family. Her world opened up and expanded into the community in which she lived.

Case Vignette No. 2

Rob had late-stage dementia and was unable to adequately speak or interact with others. He was only able to utter one to two words at a time. Initially, he was unable to sit still in choir sessions for more than twenty minutes. He never sang any of the songs but kept walking around with me, holding onto my arm. I felt that by transforming his movements into music he might be able to express himself better. So, I asked him to dance.

> He gracefully took my hand and twirled me about the room. He surprised me by verbally enquiring whether he was treading on my toes during the first dance! His rhythm and timing were precise and his movements were musical. I discovered that Rob had previously been a well-known jazz musician who also loved to dance. After this, I always asked him to dance and he would wait for the invitation instead of wandering around in an agitated fashion. He was subsequently able to stay for the full sixty minutes and began playing jazz scales on the piano following choir practices.

Even though Rob's dementia had taken away his ability to connect with others socially, he managed to integrate his past music skills within the choir group by dancing. The choir members recognized his abilities and accepted him. A choir comprised of people with dementia is necessarily small and restricted within the confines of a locked facility. However, it remains a community and can offer a sense of Aldridge's notion of a "performed" identity and connection with others. In this way, the community choir can become stable and cohesive, affording people with dementia a sense of self-identity and the opportunity to interact with each other in a safe and socially appropriate environment.

Singing to Reduce Depression

As part of my doctoral studies, I formed a choir for middle-aged depressed people living in the community of the Blue Mountains, west of Sydney, Australia. These people were socially isolated because they suffered from many psychosocial and medical problems. Social isolation was the main focus of concern. Over time, choir members formed a cohesive support group who cared about each other, expanding their social environment. They shared similar histories and discussed common experiences. In order to demonstrate the efficacy of choir work for addressing mental health, I conducted two pilot studies, triangulating quantitative data (testing for depression, quality of life, and well-being), qualitative data (interviewing and recording responses), and biophysical data (quantitative electroencephalograms—QEEG, $N = 9$) with a sample of thirty-two participants aged between fifty to seventy-three years (Petchkovsky, Robertson-Gillam, Kropotov, and Petchkovsky 2013).

Figure 9.1 shows the sequence of activities within the program. Depression decreased significantly, and a sense of wellness increased following the eight-week choir program.

Before the choir intervention, the QEEG readings showed a state of chronic hyperarousal and brain asymmetry, whereas after the choir

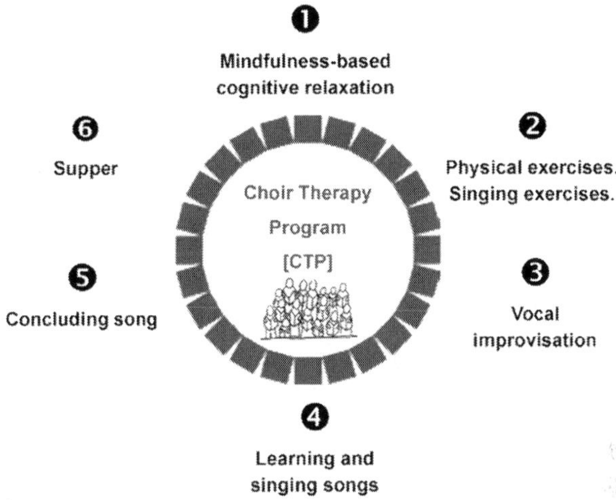

Figure 9.1. An illustration of the Choir Therapy Program, which addresses the symptoms of major depression and generalized anxiety in middle-aged people.

intervention the amount of alpha activity was more widespread frontally (Fp1), with a significantly lower novel response in the P3a Novelty Event Related Potentials (ERP) at $p < 0.05$. This is considered to be consistent with the reduction of depression (Budzinski et al. 2008).

The weekly choir surveys demonstrated significant improvements in two areas: increased comfort with singing ($p < 0.01$) and enjoyment of social interactions ($p < 0.01$). Comments from choir participants supported these results: "I didn't know I had a voice"; "Singing speeds up getting to know people"; "Singing has given me power; I feel happy again."

This white Caucasian group became more bonded and socially integrative within their community after they had participated in the choir program. They reported enhanced social and family relationships, and many of them joined other community groups such as bush walking, ukulele, and drumming groups as well as philosophical discussion groups, with increased confidence and enjoyment.

Music therapists have developed and expanded their practice models to include community music therapy services. They work alongside community musicians, providing a valuable resource and service for the marginalized, disabled, and disenfranchised in our society. Community Music Therapy allows for professional flexibility, adaptability, and cooperative partnerships with community musicians. Music therapists can still maintain their ethical standards within this cooperative paradigm and defend their values of respect, freedom, equality. and solidarity (Stige and Aaro 2012).

Community musicians are focused on building and developing music proficiencies within an educational approach, building social capital and social justice. Community music therapists focus on the importance of meeting individual needs within community-based therapeutic groups and one-on-one settings. This focus is a major contributor to CoMT in Australia (Threlfall 1999). Community music therapists and community musicians can learn a lot from each other. Within the health-care continuum, music therapists can flexibly provide services, ranging from acute to community care in a circular fashion, constantly adjusting to the individual needs of clients in a large variety of settings (O'Grady and McFerran 2007).

Community musicians and community music therapists play important roles in society by providing aesthetically oriented musical experiences for the enjoyment, achievement, social betterment, and the political advancement of society. Musicians and therapists can work alongside each other, offering education, achievement, and life enhancement through *musicking* relationships. Ideally, as community music making develops and grows, the ecological balance in society and culture will change for the better, creating a spontaneous and cooperative musical relationship that flows between people and places, and possibly marking the beginning of a less violent world.

References

Aldridge, D. 2005. *Music Therapy and Neurological Rehabilitation: Performing Health.* London and Philadelphia: Jessica Kingsley Publications.

Ansdell, Gary. 1997. "Musical Elaborations: What Has the New Musicology to Say to Music Therapy?" *British Journal of Music Therapy* 11 (2): 36–44. doi:10.1177/135945759701100202.

———. 2002. "Community Music Therapy and the Winds of Change: A Discussion Paper." *Voices* 2 (2). doi:10.15845/voices.v2i2.83

———. 2014. *How Music Helps in Music Therapy and Everyday Life.* Farnham, UK: Ashgate Publishing.

Antonovsky, Aaron. 1991. *Unraveling the Mystery of Health: How People Manage Stress and Stay Well.* San Francisco, CA: Jossey-Bass Publishers.

Atkinson, J. 2001. "Survey of Community Music in the UK." Unpublished report for the Speedwell Trust.

Beck, Aaron T., Robert A. Steer, and Gregory K. Brown. 1996. *Manual for the Beck Depression Inventory-II.* San Antonio, TX: Psychological Corporation.

Bruscia, Kenneth E. 1998. *Defining Music Therapy.* 2nd ed. Gilsum, NH: Barcelona Publishers.

Budzinski, Thomas H., Helen Kogan Budzinski, James R. Evans, and Andrew Ababarnel, eds. 2008. *Introduction to Quantitative EEG and Neurofeedback: Advanced Theory and Applications.* 2nd ed. Burlington, MA: Academic Press.

Daaleman, Timothy P., and Bruce B. Frey. 2004. "The Spirituality Index of Well-Being: A New Instrument for Health-Related Quality-of-Life Research." *Annals of Family Medicine* 2 (5): 499–503.

Dissanayake, Ellen. 2009. "Root, Leaf, Blossom, or Bole: Concerning the Origin and Adaptive Function of Music." In *Communicative Musicality. Exploring the Basis of Human Companionship,* edited by S. Malloch and C. Trevarthen, 17–29. Oxford: Oxford University Press.

Malloch, Stephen, and Colwyn Trevarthen, eds. 2009. *Communicative Musicality. Exploring the Basis of Human Companionship.* Oxford: Oxford University Press.

Mannes, Elena. 2011. *The Power of Music: Pioneering Discoveries in the New Science of Song.* New York: Walker Books.

McMillan, David W., and David M. Chavis. 1986. "Sense of Community: A Definition and Theory." *Journal of Community Psychology* 14 (1): 6–23. doi:10.1002/1520–6629(198601)14:1<6::AID-JCOP2290140103>3.0.CO;2-I.

Miller, Geoffrey. 2001. The Mating Mind: How Sexual Choice Shaped the Evolution of Human Nature. London: Random House, Vintage.

Mithen, Stephen. 2006. *The Singing Neanderthals: The Origins of Music, Language, Mind and Body.* Beverly Hills, CA: Phoenix.

Nordoff, P., and C. Robbins. 2007. *Creative Music Therapy.* Gilsum, NH: Barcelona Publishers.

O'Grady, Lucy, and Katrina McFerran. 2007. "Community Music Therapy and Its Relationship to Community Music: Where Does It End?" *Nordic Journal of Music Therapy* 16 (1): 14–26. doi:10.1080/08098130709478170.

Pavlicevic, Mercedes, and Gary Ansdell, eds. 2004. *Community Music Therapy.* London and Philadelphia: Jessica Kingsley Publishers.

Petchkovksy, L., K. Robertson-Gillam, J. Kropotov, and M. Petchkovsky. 2013. "Using QEEG Parameters (Asymmetry, Coherence, and P3a Novelty Response) to Track Improvement in Depression after Choir Therapy." *Advances in Mental Health* 11 (3): 257–267.

Procter, Simon. 2001. "Empowering and Enabling: Improvisational Music Therapy in Non-medical Mental Health Provision." *Voices: A World Forum for Music Therapy* 1 (2). doi:10.15845/voices.v1i2.58.

———. 2004. "Playing Politics: Community Music Therapy and the Therapeutic Redistribution of Music Capital for Mental Health." In *Community Music*

Therapy, edited by M. Pavlicevic and G. Ansdell, 214–232. London and Philadelphia: Jessica Kingsley Publications.

Ramsey, David. 2002. "The Restoration of Communal Experiences during Music Therapy." PhD diss., School of Education, Health, Nursing, and Arts Profession, New York University.

Robertson-Gillam, Kirstin. 2008. "Hearing the Voice of the Elderly: The Potential for Choir Work to Reduce Depression and Meet Spiritual Needs." In *Ageing, Disability and Spirituality: Addressing the Challenge of Disability in Later Life,* edited by E. MacKinlay, 163–182. London and Philadelphia: Jessica Kingsley Publications.

———. 2011. Music Therapy in Dementia Care. In H. Lee and T. Adams, *Creative Approaches in Dementia Care,* 102. Basingstoke: Palgrave Macmillan.

Rudd, Even. 2010. *Music Therapy: A Perspective from the Humanities.* New Braunfels, TX: Barcelona Publishers.

Small, Christopher. 1998. *Musicking: The Means of Performing and Listening.* Hanover, NH: Wesleyan University Press.

Stige, Brynjulf. 2003. "Elaborations toward a Notion of Community Music Therapy." Doctoral dissertation. Oslo, Norway: University of Norway.

Stige, Brynjulf, and Leif Edvard Aaro. 2012. *Invitation to Community Music Therapy.* New York and London: Routledge.

Threlfall, Catherine. 1999. "Community Music and Music Therapy—Partnerships and Possibilities." Australian Music Therapy Association Network, November 10–15.

Yerichuk, Deanna. 2014. "Socialized Music: Historical Formations of Community Music through Social Rationales." *Criticism and Theory for Music Education* 13 (1): 126–154.

CHAPTER 10

Exchange and Common Ground

"The Big Sing in the Desert"

Julie Rickwood

In an essay on music and social being, Ian Cross argued that social justice is not produced by musicality in itself, but is made manifest through music making's capacity for shared intentionality; that is, music making provides "space for the emergence of concepts that bear on how humans can, and ultimately perhaps should, interact" (Cross 2005–2006, 124). In his conclusion, Cross refers to Inga Clendinnen's *Dancing with Strangers: Europeans and Australians at First Contact* (2005), noting her comment that culture is a dynamic system of shared meanings that are rarely made explicit, and, in cross-cultural engagements, "understanding another culture's meanings is and will always be a hazardous enterprise" (Cross 2005–2006, 124). In some way, dance enabled an exchange and the creation of common ground so that members of the two cultures could "believe that they could begin to know" something of each other (Cross 2005–2006, 125).

The collective history of Aboriginal and Torres Strait Islander dispossession of land and clashes over resources that followed first contact played out its own distinctive pattern in every region of Australia. As a result, some 220 years later, in a very different social, cultural, economic, and political climate from that of first contact, understanding across the cultures of settler and the First Peoples[1] of Australia remains a hazardous enterprise. Exchange and the creation of common ground are now important means by which to enable reconciliation. Community singing has been used as one mechanism to do so.

This chapter will first explore community music and reconciliation in Australia, broadly discuss cross-cultural community choral activity, and then focus on "The Big Sing in the Desert," an ongoing workshop in Central Australia. This one site of cross-cultural community singing emphasizes exchange and common ground; the shared intentionality for interaction within Cross' schema.

Community Music and Reconciliation

Both the community music and reconciliation movements in Australia can be traced back to at least the beginning of 1990s. Broadly, both popular movements make contributions to community building and human vitality. Neither of them operates at the margins of popular conversations, although both are admittedly aligned with progressive rather than neoliberal views. These two movements have followed separate though parallel paths that converge in the space of cross-cultural choirs and choral events.

The Community Music Movement

The community music movement has witnessed a growth in community choirs over the last decade (Rickwood 2013b; Masso 2013). The popularity of community choirs in Australia can be largely attributed to the Australian a cappella scene, which was prolific from the mid-1980s up to the early twenty-first century (Rickwood 2013a, 2013b).[2] The scene challenged the capitalist-driven consumption of music and the entrenched institutional narrowing of legitimate musical practice. It saw community singing as a means to effect both musical and social change. It set itself apart from other choral traditions as a strategy, not a fact.

The a cappella scene also played an important role in first enabling and then contributing to the evolution of the community music movement, which is now widely supported by institutions, industry, and government. The community music movement actively promotes music making in line with current social and cultural agendas and is particularly aligned to the arts and health phenomena. The movement has greatly normalized community choirs and softened the political and alternative edge that existed during the a cappella scene.

The Reconciliation Movement

Over a similar period the relationship between the First Nations minority and the nonindigenous majority has been a recurrent national concern. The officially sanctioned process of reconciliation saw the establishment of the Council for Aboriginal Reconciliation in 1991 and subsequently, a nongovernmental foundation, Reconciliation Australia, to educate on cross-cultural relations. The focus has shifted from an investigation of a social history of disadvantage and reform to a mobilization of change in national attitudes (Merlan 2005, 486–487), or "from hostility and conflict to mutual acceptance, respect, and future cooperation" (Subasic and Reynolds 2009, 245). The "Apology to the Stolen Generations" by the then newly elected prime minister Kevin Rudd on February 13, 2008, was a historical and symbolic moment in this process and promised a new beginning for race relations.[3] The reconciliation project is hardly a smooth process, with shifting and fluid concepts and contexts, but it continues to carry currency within the Australian political, social, and cultural landscape. The current focus is advocating for recognition of First Nations in the Australian Constitution.[4]

While the reconciliation project provides purchase for political debate and contestation about First Nations' rights, it also operates as a focus for action and agency in the development of cross-cultural relations. It involves governments at all levels instituting policies and practices but also involves the wider Australian community, including through music making.

The Convergence of the Movements

The community music movement heralds inclusion and social cohesion, which can then capture the intent of reconciliation and massage the notion of Australian identity. Accessible songs from First Nation groups have become popular with many community choirs, often connected to the desire to express and perform the evolving and converging processes of reconciliation and national identity. The choral performances utilize songs founded by the nation's original inhabitants as a reference point of "Australianness." The rhythms, melodies, and harmonies of Aboriginal and Torres Strait Islander musics are potent to the desire or the imagining of a reconciled nation. Songs commonly performed include "Inanay" (traditional),[5] "My Island Home" by Neil Murray,[6] "Baba Waiar" by Miseron Levi,[7] and "Kulba Yaday" by Christina Anu, Jensen Warusam, David Bridie, John Phillips, and Michael Barker[8] (Rickwood 2014b).

These performances can be largely symbolic, however, as the choirs are often dislocated from the musics they sing. As a result, the singers and their audiences are often unaware of the full meaning and significance of the songs. While they cannot wholly be regarded as inauthentic acts of ideological celebration "devoid of pleasure, meaning or significance" (Stokes 2004, 6), these performances and the preparations beforehand rarely enable exchange and common ground.

Exchange and common ground are more readily found where music is shared and, importantly, where music making might unsettle assumptions regarding the musics of "others." These interactions also enable greater understanding of the role and meaning of music in peoples' lives. Exchange and common ground are more readily seen where community choral leaders are motivated by a desire to improve cross-cultural relations, to promote Aboriginal and Torres Strait Islander musical cultures, and to present social cohesion through community music making.

Various projects have been created that invite singers to come together as overt acts of reconciliation. At the same time, they serve to "solidify indigeneity as a distinct identity but inevitably do so in terms that are grounded within a wider national—and, increasingly, international—public sphere" (Merlan 2005, 489). These cross-cultural interactions confront the dual narrative of celebration and anxiety about First Nations identity and its relationship to mainstream Australia (Barney 2005, 141), operate within the tensions of this dual narrative, and prompt a "shared intentionality" that can shift cross-cultural relations beyond the symbolic. Music is a compelling vehicle in this choral "common ground" (Nakata 2002, 2007), where the "histories, politics, economics, multiple and interconnected discourses, social practices and knowledge" (Nakata 2007, 9) that operate in diverse daily lives can become relational.

The Creation of Common Ground

My doctoral research project (2013b) was based on three case studies of cross-cultural community choirs or choral events from diverse regions: Victoria, southwest Western Australia, and Central Australia. Comparative analysis allowed recognition of a spectrum of engagement with First Nations' music by community singers. It enabled me to more readily discern the difference between symbolic celebration and a "shared intentionality" to music making.

"Shared intentionality" dwells within the space of interaction—the space of "singing in between,"[9] where engagement is shifting from an "interface" between separately conceived domains or bounded cultures towards a distinctive set of values and practices that can appreciate that diverse and different social forms are inextricably relational. It is a space where concepts that bear on interaction can emerge. The notion of "singing in between" has similarities with Martin Nakata's (2002, 2007) term "common ground," the term I have adopted to use in this chapter. As with "common ground," "singing in between" is the space where opportunities to engender the "cultural interface" identified by Nakata can occur (2002, 2007; see also Dillon 2007; Dillon, Bartleet, and Leong 2012). This "cultural interface" probes reconciliation, prompted by the "shared intentionality" created through an emphasis on exchange and common ground.

The creation of common ground varied as much as the geography and histories of the case studies. In Melbourne it was a one-off event, the Melbourne Millennium Chorus of 2009 with its artistic director Lou Bennett. Madjitil Moorna from Perth was a single community choir that had started as a one-time festival project in 2006 and subsequently developed into a group passionately sharing its example of reconciliation through music, stories, and more. In Central Australia there is an evolving cross-cultural singing environment, which has included the creation of community singing workshops and festivals that bring Aboriginal and other singers together to exchange and perform. The collective interests of singing and a desire for cross-cultural encounter are readily located in the common ground established by these interactions. All three regional representations shared a desire to revitalize or maintain languages, to promote cultures, to sing accessible songs, and to integrate storytelling into their practices.

To varying degrees, each of these regional dimensions brought a nonindigenous integration into the lives and knowledge of First Nations' people. The activists driving these projects inspired other actors with their vision, drawing from their charismatic and determined leadership. Each reinforced the profile of successful community music leaders suggested by Bartleet and colleagues (2009). With a belief in the power of music, matched by a desire for improved cultural relations, these activists passionately nurtured musical and social harmony. They encouraged community voices to merge and blend over a history of racial discord, a vocal process that attempted to shift the tension between the healing of wounds of the past and the imagining of a different Australia. They constructed community choral engagements that were "relational, interactional, intersubjective, dialogical and [a] mutually transformative process" (Ottosson 2010, 276) through an emphasis on exchange.

But there were differences in certain priorities. In Western Australia the journey of the Stolen Generations framed the choir's mandate to promote reconciliation through musical expression. The personal stories from the Noongar members that accompanied their music making were powerful motivators. In Victoria, the 2009 Melbourne Millennium Chorus concert series was a celebratory vehicle for a recently declared co-managed national park, which was linked to Yorta Yorta[10] knowledge of land management that could contribute to caring for the environment. And in Central Australia the desire was to hold tight to the tradition of Desert Gospel choral music and performance while exploring other choral possibilities.

The next section will discuss in greater detail one of the projects from this Central Australian field site, "The Big Sing in the Desert," to show in more detail how an emphasis on exchange and common ground is nurtured and how a "shared intentionality" is created. It begins and ends with a descriptive narrative of the 2012 workshop.

"The Big Sing in the Desert"

> There's nothing you can do that can't be done.
> Nothing you can sing that can't be sung.
> Nothing you can say but you can learn how to play the game.
> It's easy.
> (John Lennon and Paul McCartney, "All You Need is Love")

The Setting

We were all closely gathered in the communal room of the original Loves Creek Homestead, built in 1898 at Ross River as a working cattle station by the pioneering Bloomfield family.[11] The roughly sawn timber walls and heavy beams made it dark and cavernous at times, but beyond the high windows the sun was bright. In the late afternoons the deep-red rock of the steep hill behind the homestead glowed.

We were sitting and standing around the large screen that was playing through a series of photographs from the past two days. The young women who had put the photo story together were operating as a nongovernment organization (NGO) called Joining the Dots.[12] They had come to support "The Big Sing in the Desert 2012" by creating multimedia capture and dissemination of the weekend singing workshop. Unsurprisingly, they chose as its title the famous Lennon and McCartney song "All You Need Is Love," which we had learned to sing in four-part harmony. It captured the sentiment of the weekend workshop—the smiling, joyful faces of the singers and the few children who had accompanied some of the adults from nearby Central Australian communities or far distant parts of Australia.

Ross River is a modest resort, about eighty-five kilometers east of Alice Springs in the Northern Territory. Its simple green cabins tumble down a gentle slope near the homestead; over the river is a campground and bunkhouse with a communal cooking area. It sits within the stunning landscape of the Eastern MacDonnell Ranges, iconic geography in Central Australia. Nearby is the spectacular Trephina Gorge where the singers spent one afternoon singing in the resonant space and exploring its creek and paths, the Aboriginal women searching (unsuccessfully) for *ingkulpa*.[13] Closer still is N'Darla Gorge, which few were able to travel to, although one afternoon we all ventured to the nearby bluff at a turn in the Ross River, to sing with each other, to sing to the bluff (and hear our voices bounce back), to sing to country. At night the dingoes sang our lullabies; our morning chorus the twitter of budgerigars. In between, the hours were filled with our songs, our voices.

The Beginnings of "The Big Sing in the Desert"

"The Big Sing in the Desert" (henceforth "The Big Sing") was conceived by popular community singing leader, Rachel Hore.[14] Hore's musical leadership skills emerged during the a cappella scene. She was a member of the influential band Arramaieda and, together with other a cappella performers at the time, led singing workshops. She had been one of the musical leaders of the Central Australian Aboriginal Media Association's (CAAMA) community choir project "Many Roads One Voice." A collaborative project with the Alice Desert Festival in 2008, it also involved musicians Kavisha Mazzella, Kutcha Edwards, and Emma Donovan. The project brought together many of the choirs in and around Alice Springs in order to celebrate the music of CAAMA, which had supported, nurtured, and promoted Central Australian Aboriginal music making since its establishment in the 1980s. The intercultural, intergenerational choir of over two hundred singers was said to be the first of its kind.

Members of a choir from the community of Titjikala, located about 107 kilometers south of Alice Springs, were taken with Hore's musical leadership. Titjikala is a community of some two hundred people. It sits on the edge of the Simpson Desert, in the former cattle station of Maryvale. Capitalizing on the experience of "Many Roads One Voice," the community organized a project with Hore in order to further enable their musical development. "There was a desire to follow up ["Many Roads One Voice"] and have singers, black and white, spend more time singing together, learning repertoire and learning from each other," explained Hore (2009). Margaret Campbell, from Titjikala, saw this opportunity as helping "us to sing strong way, learning more about harmonies. I was a leader . . . that was good. I might teach all the other girls" (cited in Hore 2009).

The success of "Many Roads One Voice" also led to the Alice Desert Festival's "Desert Voice" concerts, which were coordinated by Morris Stuart from 2009 until 2012. Although not officially a leader in the CAAMA project, Stuart was instrumental to the success of the combined choral event, particularly with his Alice Springs choir, Asante Sana. Asante Sana is a town-based choir that sings a repertoire described as "Afro-fusion" enthusiastically led by Stuart, a staunch supporter of aural transmission. The choir brought solid harmony skills to the 2008 concert. Stuart's leadership skills in "Many Roads One Voice" were acknowledged by the organizers and he was approached to coordinate the "Desert Voice" concert from 2009. Stuart is now one of the coordinators of "Desert Song," a Central Australian festival of singing that began in 2013.[15] He continues to work regularly with many of the regional Aboriginal community choirs as well as Asante Sana.

Rachel Hore approached Morris Stuart in early 2010 to jointly lead "The Big Sing." Held over a long weekend in July, it presented an opportunity to bring the regional Aboriginal singers into a wide gathering of national singers. Songs were exchanged and shared and new material introduced. It gathered up the vitality of "Many Roads One Voice" and the inaugural "Desert Voice" and subsequently continues to contribute significantly to the ongoing musical development and performance opportunities for Central Australian choirs.

Reflections on the Inaugural Big Sing

At the inaugural "Big Sing," the introductory scene of communal engagement with images from the weekend in 2012 would have been less likely. In 2010 there had been both fewer women from the regional Aboriginal communities and fewer singers familiar with Central Australia. Most of those attending the weekend workshop had been attracted by Rachel Hore's reputation. Many of the participants had experienced her workshops previously. Some admitted to having attended multiple workshops both in Australia and overseas. Most of the Aboriginal singers, who had been fully or partially sponsored by many people within Hore's network of singers, had been attracted to "The Big Sing" because they had worked with both Hore and/or Stuart in the past, particularly through "Many Roads One Voice." A handful of nonindigenous singers were attracted specifically by Stuart's involvement, having been members of Asante Sana. Barbara Jackson (2010) admired Stuart's work and knew of Hore's reputation:

> I was blown out by his [leadership], how he directs music and all of the songs. We just had lyrics, we had no music. . . . I just wanted to do the workshop. And particularly because it was Rachel and Morris. And particularly because they were doing it together. I just thought it might be pretty amazing. Even though I'd never done a workshop with Rachel I'd heard from members of the choir I sing with back home that she was pretty great, special, so I imagined it would be pretty fantastic. So I was really excited.

"The Big Sing" in 2010 met its modest goal of bringing people together to sing. Hore had been enormously happy with the event, claimed it a great success, and hoped it would be an ongoing event in coming years. She summed up the weekend: "Over eighty singers (and a dog!) attended from around Australia sharing songs from different cultures, including learning songs in *Pitjantjatjara, Arrente* [*sic*], *Khosa* and English" (Hore 2010). Hore repeated the words of one of the singers, saying they really liked singing with everyone and meeting lots of lovely people: "Both *An̲angu* and white people living, eating, singing in harmony, learning and sharing songs in different languages, meeting people from different places, learning different harmonies" (Hore 2010). Stuart (2010) reported that he had also been pleased with the weekend and was assured the Aboriginal women had benefited from it:

> I had no expectations except hopefully. It exceeded them really. I think the presence of the Aboriginal women, not just being there, but being really present, being able to express themselves ostensibly—where they're coming from, being able to be received, and having the confidence to share and teach stuff. I just heard from Areyonga. I was on the phone with one of them yesterday and one of the Indigenous people there said they had a wonderful weekend, they're just raving about it.

Stuart later added that "a few people wondered because there's an air of inscrutability about them but, no, they loved it." A Darug/Gundungaran woman from urban Australia who had visited this remote area for the first time expressed her appreciation of the experience: "and listening to the ladies singing in language. I think that's the biggest thrill in my life because our language was taken away. I could sit there and just listen to the talk or watch and listen to them sing. To me it's just magical" (Cooper 2010).

On the other hand, there had been expectations left unmet, disappointment with the musical content, a social discontent, and less connection made than would happen in 2012; nor was there the presence of a group of enthusiastic skilled young people wanting to record it. In 2010 numerous singers throughout the weekend mentioned that they were frustrated by a lack of the musical development they normally received at a Rachel Hore workshop. Many were surprised by the syncretic tradition of the Lutheran hymns the Aboriginal women sang, uncertain of its place within "traditional" Aboriginal cultures. They complained about the "God-bothering," took a very dim view of the "durgy" hymns, and were disappointed with the lack of "authentic" traditional songs.

Assumptions, expectations, and ignorance became evident. Previous exposure to contemporary Aboriginal lives varied. Curiously, the experience of many of the nonindigenous singers in 2010 revealed that little had changed in expectations or preconceived notions of Central Australian Aboriginal music performance and cultural expression since the 1960s, when nonindigenous audiences were similarly challenged. Then, too, travellers from "down south" could make little of the Hermannsburg Choir's performances at "campfire concerts" in Palm Valley, nor during the choir's tour to southern states in 1967 (Hurley 2012).

The Desert Gospel Choral Tradition

The Desert Gospel choral tradition began in June 1877 with the arrival of Lutheran pastors W. F. Schwarz and A. H. Kempe at Finke River and the establishment of the Hermannsburg mission. The local Aboriginal communities came to the mission largely for strategic and practical reasons, seeking trade and to secure refuge from increasing pastoralism (Schwarz and Dussart 2010, 1–13). Music was an essential element of life at the mission. It emerged in the teaching of hymns translated into Arrernte from the early mission days. Moses Tjalkabota recalled that "Mr Kempe taught us the right melody with the violin. Schulze also taught us" (cited in Westwood 2007). Pastor Carl Strehlow continued the musical practice. By 1922 many Lutheran hymns were being sung in Arrernte, and by the 1930s performed by a four-part choir.

As in other colonial missionary and evangelical movements, "music served as a crucial vehicle for conversion" (Radano and Bohlman 2000, 20; cited in Ottosson 2006, 70). The sacred music of missionaries that accompanied the colonial process possessed power. Being the primary text in the encounter between missionaries and the Arrernte people, music opened up "the acquisition of new meanings, which grew in power because of their aesthetic differences" (Bohlman 2002, 14). Jon Rose noted that the music was "full of colonial cultural contradiction" (Rose 2008, 11), both being part of the dislocation and disruption of the Aboriginal population and having the capacity to nurture them through times of persecution and extreme physical hardship. Andrew Wright Hurley (2012) argued that the lack of appreciation of this paradox by nonindigenous audiences impinged on music's reception in the 1960s and, I suggest, continues today.

Over time, the Arrernte became composers of the music, setting new words to introduced melodies or to Arrernte melodies—"Black Lutheran hymns" (Hurley 2012). In effect, exchange and common ground democratized local musical production, taking song composition outside of traditional music. The music of the church was "reinterpreted, reworked, and new songs composed through Aboriginal people's everyday experiences, languages, singing styles and social organization" (Ottosson 2006, 70). In effect, it became Arrernte music, which provided contemporary forms of power and status within Central Australian communities (Myers 2010, 119). Field research shows that various members of the Aboriginal choirs have composed and continue to write gospel songs and/or translate hymns into Arrernte, Pitjantjatjara, and Luritja. Borgas (2010, x) also remarks on this continuing practice: "today, a new generation of song-writers and singers have once again been composing their own songs to worship and sing praises to God. About thirty songs from the Areyonga and Docker River Gospel Singers are included in this new *Pitjantjatjara* hymnal."

The choirs have been a constant across the Central Desert area for generations (Westwood 2007), an aspect of the "ongoing intercultural dynamic of interaction, mutual influences and continuous 'othering' in Central Australia" (Ottosson 2010, 282). Current choir members carry memories of singing with their grandparents, some of whom were members of the Hermannsburg Choir. Kathleen France (2010) explained her choral tradition: "It happens a long time, choir. From Strehlow choir they was singing." Singing the repertoire of gospel songs at home and at bush camps was part of the everyday, and singing remains important. Noreen Hudson (2010) explained: "because we love God, we love singing. That is our life, singing." Gwen Inkamala commented that "It makes me feel good inside. . . . Singing makes you busy from other things, bad things that you see and talk about" (cited in Westwood 2007).

These choral traditions reworked European hymn traditions into the "desert gospel" (Ottosson 2010) genre, a musical tradition that highlights

Aboriginal Christian beliefs and draws on the color and tones of their languages. As Rose (2003) has recognized: "This is a unique musical language only made possible when the traditional and emotive vocal lines of Central Australian voices are applied to Lutheran hymnal music. The sound comes from the throat and nose with little portamento glides from pitch to pitch and an organic sense of rhythm."

The syncretic reality of contemporary Central Australian Aboriginal musical expressions confronts constructed notions of "tradition," "authenticity," "musical assimilation," and "cultural imperialism." This was clearly evident at "The Big Sing" in 2010, although some singers did express their appreciation of the opportunity to be challenged, to have understandings shifted, and to have knowledge deepened.

"The Big Sing 2012"

The gathering in 2012 benefited from the return of about half the singers from the first "Big Sing." The new singers familiar with Hore's work were more aware that expectations were unnecessary, and more singers resident in Central Australia attended. The experience of African Grace—a week of musical exchange, workshops, and performances with the Soweto Gospel Choir—for many of those from Alice Springs and surrounding communities in the interim year had introduced another level of exchange and common ground.[16] "Desert Voice" and its preparations in 2010 and 2011 had also added to this evolving common ground.

Unlike at the previous "Big Sing," the Aboriginal women shared more of their music beyond that of Desert Gospel or popular folk songs translated into local Aboriginal languages. During the weekend, some of the workshop songs were rapidly translated into Arrernte and Luritja, including "Vuma," a South African gospel, and "Lay Your Burden Down" by Jane Christie-Johnson.

On the first night, after an evening of informal solo and small group performances by many of the workshop participants, Daphne Puntjina Burton from Areyonga led traditional dances in the light of the campfire. She had been unable to attend the previous Big Sing and her presence in 2012 was a positive force, as her position in the community meant that she was able to lead and explain traditional music and dance. Puntjina Burton briefly described the dances: two women being chased by men; women with digging sticks; the story of the seven sisters (Pleiades); looking for bush tucker;[17] and dancing with the *manguri,* the fur or hair head ring worn for carrying loads. Her thin, aged body was strong and knowledgeable; she danced with energy. Other women joined her. Like many senior women, Puntjina Burton sings, dances, and paints; law and knowledge is embodied in her. She also carries religious knowledge and has translated hymns or composed gospel songs. Elders of the church are most often those also responsible for upholding traditional law (Pybus 2012, ii).

On the second night, as kangaroo tail and damper cooked on the fire, the singing around the campfire found shared repertoire, including songs from childhood: "The Hokie Pokie," "Three Little Ducks," "She'll be Coming 'Round the Mountain," "Pokarekare Ana," and "Ghost Rider." We learned "Hands, Shoulders, Knees, and Toes" in Pitjantjatjara. "Nyanpi Matilda" was the big hit of the night, with Puntjina Burton playing the role of the swagman and two other women the jumbuck (sheep) and the policeman. The Areyonga women had taught the Pitjantjatjara version earlier in the day, and everyone sang and laughed with delight as the women enacted its lyrics. It would be a reference point for gentle teasing the following morning when Puntjina Burton led the church service and during the final session, which was full of "singing, dancing, so much joy" (Lambert 2012). The song would reemerge as a much appreciated addition to the Desert Voice concert later in the year. After the final group photo on the last afternoon the Aboriginal women gathered together to sing their "farewell song."

In 2012 there was little discontent. Singers from more distant parts of Australia framed their appreciation of the weekend based on its cultural and physical placement: "I came here to be in a part of the land I've never been before . . . to meet the people and understand their culture in a positive way . . . even more importantly for my daughter to experience this with me" (Anon. 2012). Regionally based singers also enjoyed the weekend, appreciating the opportunity to mix with a diversity of other singers. Others in the gathering expressed their reflections more effusively:

> As I witnessed the friendships form and people's confidence build (and the smiles enlarge!) I got to thinking about what it is that creates community. Amidst the allure of sweet harmony and bodily expression, there were other things that were happening, quite naturally. I began to discover that what connected us to each other was the children, the campfire, sharing meals, the vibrant yet mindful facilitation and a strong desire to learn from one another. We were nourished not only with the sounds from our combined voices but with heapings of laughter, dancing and hugs!
>
> In the process we may just have discovered how similar we are, how much we needed to laugh, that we each have a story and it's sacred, that

> language can be both a mystery and a trigger for unique insights to culture. (Elsey 2012)

Exchange and common ground had been found, nurtured, established. The singing workshop enabled a transformation for all involved. In the recognition of a shared humanity came a shared intentionality. The weekend spent together made lives relational.

At the end of the weekend, Hore commented on the laughter that had so marked the weekend. She also spoke of how she and Stuart believed in the power of community and creating community through singing. They also shared a desire, she said, to support the preservation of Central Australian choral singing, a music practice that demanded "a bigger space and value in the wider choral context of Australia" (Hore 2012). Stuart (2012b) similarly felt the weekend was positive for all:

> I think it's been a fascinating process we've entered into, with Aboriginal women making a contribution in a very direct and confident way. There was nothing tokenistic about their contribution this weekend. Often when groups gather together there is an underlying patronizing that goes on, but I think people really stepped up into their place, stood, took it and we've all reaped the benefit of that. I always think that with choral singing, the narrative is bigger than the music, much bigger than the music and it enables people to build a sense of community—break down barriers, actually cross barriers they normally wouldn't cross. I think it's a great opportunity for people to start reconfiguring their views about other people, on both sides, and finding common humanity.

Some Final Moments

The big screen flickered through photographs of heads bent together working over the lyrics or melody of new material; the nursing of small children; the two leaders, Rachel and Morris, dynamically conducting; hands being held; damper and kangaroo tail on the fire; singing around the campfire; but, most frequently, the circle of song and voice and movement. Concentration and joy were manifest in the photographs. As we watched the captured moments change there were shouts of awe, delighted laughter, and tears of joy. Before the weekend concluded this immediate visual documentation cemented the workshop's impact, making the hope for cross-cultural exchange and common ground that had been its aim real.

The tenor of "The Big Sing" in 2012 continues to resonate: the gatherings in 2013 and 2014 further strengthened the "shared intentionality" of cross-cultural musical exchange and common ground.[18] During the evolution of the workshop the specific agendas of Hore and Stuart within this Central Australian context have merged. Before the first "Big Sing" there had been more of a distinction between their goals for the Aboriginal singers. Hore's motivations had been based on inviting the Aboriginal singers to access material beyond their Desert Gospel tradition. Stuart had responded to the desire of the regional choirs to extend their musicality in order to improve their performances. There was therefore a tension in bringing together the preservation of a musical practice and an increase in its performative level with that of responding to a desire for greater exposure to different choral traditions and repertoire. The inclusion of the nonindigenous participants was designed around the known interest in attending workshops in exotic places, a desire for cross-cultural musical encounters, and an assumption of alliance with the progressive ideals of the project leaders. Present throughout, then, was the challenge to create community within a gathering where desires and motivations did not perfectly align.

This chapter has explored the ideas of exchange and common group through a narrative about "The Big Sing in the Desert" and its attempt to enliven and enrich community choral music in Central Australia and beyond. It did so with the purpose of revealing how a shared aim to support community music making that promotes and supports Central Australian musics, along with the creation of new opportunities, new performances, and even new musics, is possible when emphasis is placed on exchange and common ground. In the process a more informed understanding of Australian history, culture, and identity can also emerge, creating socially just relationships that extend beyond merely symbolic notions of reconciliation.

Notes

1 The population of the Australian First Peoples includes Aborigines (from the continent of Australia) and Torres Strait Islanders (of Melanesian descent). I use the term "First Peoples" when referring to the population group as a whole. Accordingly, the term "Aboriginal" is used for that specific group within the population, likewise "Torres Strait Islanders." It should be noted that many First Peoples identify primarily with their language group, which I also adopt where appropriate.

2 See also Rickwood 1997, 1998, 2010, 2011, and 2012.

3 On February 13, 2008, Prime Minister Rudd said "Sorry" to the First Nations' peoples of the country. The Apology to the Stolen Generations for their forcible removal from their families, communities, and/or country was for many Australians a long time coming. The previous government, led by John Howard, had refused to formally apologize, despite increasing pressure since *Sorry Day* in 1998.

4 See, for instance, http://www.recognise.org.au.

5 "Inanay" entered the a cappella scene when trio Tiddas, from Melbourne, became popular in the early 1990s. Women's choirs in particular were attracted to the song. Lou Bennett, a member of Tiddas, learned the song from her cousins and her grandmother in the late 1980s. Bennett has been instrumental in teaching the song to community choirs, but there is little known about the song itself. The liner notes for "Inanay" simply say that it is a "traditional aboriginal song (words not available)." Bennett has suggested that the song travelled on "song lines," which was evident from a version by the Mills Sisters from the Torres Strait. Discussions with TSI music researchers suggest the song may have travelled through the Pacific from Hawai'i.

6 It should be noted that "My Island Home" was rewritten with Christine Anu in 1995. Anu recorded the song, and it was given mainstream exposure during the closing ceremony of the Sydney Olympic Games in 2000. As a result, community choirs often source the song to Anu, and therefore associate it with the Torres Strait Islands. It was, however, originally written by Neil Murray, and first performed by the Warumpi Band, which included First Nations' musicians. The lead singer was George Rrurrambu (also known as Burarrawanga or Djilaynga), who came from Elcho Island off the Northern Territory, and on whose situation Murray based the lyrics (Murray 2008, 41).

7 Miseron Levi was from the St. Paul community on Moa Island, in the Torres Strait. Written in *Kala Lagaw Ya,* "Baba Waiar" ("Father we ask you") is one of the many Torres Strait islander *kores* (contemporary sacred songs written since the 1960s) that circulate within their Christian churches (Dan and Neuenfeldt 2013).

8 "Kulba Yaday" was first recorded by Christine Anu in 1994. Simply, the song title means "old words," although it is far more complex than that (see Rickwood 2014b).

9 "Singing in between" is a theoretical concept I developed in my dissertation (Rickwood 2013b). It is beyond the scope of this chapter to expand beyond the brief description given here.

10 Traditional Yorta Yorta lands lie on both sides of the Murray River (which divides Victoria and New South Wales). The area lies roughly from Cohuna to Albury/Wodonga and includes the towns of Echuca, Shepparton, Benalla,

Corowa, and Wangaratta, and extends northwards to just south of Deniliquin. See Yorta Yorta Nation Aboriginal Corporation, http://www.yynac.com.au/maps.php (accessed November 14, 2014).

11 See http://www.rossriverresort.com.au/about.htm (accessed January 15, 2013).

12 See http://www.joiningthedots.org; and http://www.rachelhore.com/bigsing_blogintro.html (accessed July 1, 2012).

13 *Arrernte* for "bush tobacco."

14 See www.rachelhore.com (last accessed March 14, 2014).

15 See https://www.facebook.com/desertsongcentralaustralia (last accessed March 17, 2014).

16 See Rickwood, 2014c.

17 "Bush tucker," also called "bushfood," is any food native to Australia and used eaten as sustenance by the Australian First Peoples. It is also often used to describe any native food used in contemporary culinary dishes.

18 See http://www.rachelhore.com for further information, including images and videos of "The Big Sing in the Desert" workshops.

References

Bartleet, Brydie-Leigh, Peter Dunbar-Hall, Richard Letts, and Huib Schippers. 2009. *Sound Links: Community Music in Australia.* Brisbane: Queensland Conservatorium Research Centre, Griffith University.

Barney, Katelyn. 2005. "Celebration or Cover up? 'My Island Home,' Australian Nation Identity and the Spectacle of Sydney 2000." In *Aesthetics and Experience in Music Performance,* edited by E. Mackinlay, D. Collins, and S. Owens, 141–150. Buckinghamshire: Cambridge Scholars Press.

Bohlman, Philip V. 2002. *World Music: A Very Short Introduction.* Oxford: Oxford University Press.

Borgas, R. 2010. Preface to *Nyiri Inmatjara Lutheran Uwankaraku* (Pitjantjatjara Lutheran Hymnal), vii–xvii. Alice Springs: Finke River Mission of the Lutheran Church of Australia Inc.

Clendinnen, Inga. 2005. *Dancing with Strangers: Europeans and Australians at First Contact.* New York: Cambridge University Press.

Cross, Ian. 2005–2006. "Music and Social Being." *Musicology Australia* 28 (1): 114–126. doi:10.1080/08145857.2005.10415281.

Dan, Henry, and Karl Neuenfeldt. 2013. *Steady Steady: The Life and Music of Seaman Dan.* Canberra: Aboriginal Studies Press.

Dillon, Steve. 2007. Maybe We Can Find Some Common Ground: Indigenous Perspectives, a Music Teacher's Story." *Australian Journal of Indigenous Education* 36 (S1): 59–65. doi:10.1017/S1326011100004713.

Dillon, Steve, Brydie-Leigh Bartleet, and Samuel Leong. 2012. "Editorial." *International Journal of Community Music* 5 (1): 3–9. doi:10.1386/ijcm.5.1.3_2.

Downie, Elaine. 1996. "Why A Cappella? Why Women? Why Now? The A Cappella Movement and Popular Music in Australia from 1987 to 1995." MA thesis, Monash University, Melbourne.

Elsley, Penny. 2012. Personal comment. *Joining the Dots at the Big Sing,* June 30. http://www.rachelhore.com/blog.

Hore, Rachel. 2009. "Past Projects." *Rachel Hore.* http://www.rachelhore.com/pastproj.html.

———. 2010. Personal communication (e-mails), September 23 and 31, 2010.

———. 2012. Personal comment, "The Narrative Is Bigger than the Music." *Reflections from the Organisers,* June 30. http://www.rachelhore.com/blog.

Hurley, Andrew Wright. 2012. "German-Indigenous Musical Flows at Hermannsburg in the 1960s." Paper presented at Shifting Sounds: Musical Flow, IASPMANZ Annual Conference, Hobart, December 5–7, 2012.

Lambert, Sarah. 2012. Personal comment, "The Big Sing in the Desert 2012," Facebook. https://www.facebook.com/TheBigSingInTheDesert2012?ref=ts&fref=ts.

Masso, Alex. 2013. "Community Choirs in Australia." In *Music in Communities Network Report, Music Council of Australia.* www.musicincommunities.org.au.

Merlan, Francesca. 2005. "Indigenous Movements in Australia." *Annual Review of Anthropology* 34 (1): 473–494. doi:10.1146/annurev.anthro.34.081804.120643.

Murray, Neil. 2008. *Native Born: Songs of Neil Murray.* Camberwell East: One Day Hill.

Myers, Fred. 2010. "All Around Australia and Overseas: Christianity and Indigenous Identities in Central Australia 1988." *The Australian Journal of Anthropology* 21 (1): 110–128. doi:10.1111/j.1757-6547.2010.00070.x.

Nakata, Martin. 2002. "Indigenous Knowledge and the Cultural Interface: Underlying Issues at the Intersection of Knowledge and Information Systems." *IFLA Journal* 28 (5–6): 280–291. doi:10.1177/034003520202800513.

———. 2007. "The Cultural Interface." *The Australian Journal of Indigenous Education* 36 (S1): 7–14. doi:10.1017/S1326011100004646.

Ottosson, Åse. 2006. "Making Aboriginal Men and Music in Central Australia." PhD diss., Canberra: Australian National University.

———. 2010. "Aboriginal Music and Passion: Interculturality and Difference in Australian Desert Towns." *Ethnos* 75 (3): 275–300. doi:10.1080/00141844.2010.503899.

Pybus, Carol Ann. 2012. "'We grew up this place': Ernabella Mission 1937–1974." PhD diss., University of Tasmania.

Radano, Ronald, and Philip V. Bohlman, eds. 2000. *Music and the Racial Imagination*. Chicago and London: University of Chicago Press.

Radke, Doug. n.d. Cover Notes for *Hermannsburg Choir on Tour*.

———. 1967. "Hermannsburg Tour in Retrospective." *The Lutheran* 20: 9.

Rickwood, Julie. 1997. "Liberating Voices: Towards an Ethnography of Women's Community A Cappella Choirs in Australia." MA thesis, Australian National University, Canberra.

———. 1998. "Embodied A Cappella: The Experience of Singing a Displaced Eclectic Repertoire." *Perfect Beat* 3 (4): 68–84. doi:10.1558/prbt.v3i4.28741.

———. 2010. "Taking the Piss?: Australian Blokes and A Cappella Choirs." In *What's It Worth? Value and Popular Music: Selected Papers from the 2009 IASPM Australian New Zealand Conference,* edited by S. D. Brunt and K. Zemke, 55–63. Dunedin: IASPM-ANZ.

———. 2011. "Singing In Between: An Australian Experience of 'Cultural Inter-relatedness' through Community Singing." In *Proceedings SEMPRE Conference "Striking a Chord": Music Health and Wellbeing: A Conference Exploring Current Developments in Research and Practice,* edited by M. Shipton and E. Himonides, 96. Folkestone, UK: Sidney De Haan Research Centre for Arts and Health, Canterbury Christ Church University.

———. 2012. "Reconciliation Made Sound: The Performance of Harmony and Healing in the *Sorry Song*." *Context: A Journal of Music Research* 37: 93–106.

———. 2013a. "Singing In Between? Re-visioning Intercultural Community Singing." *Proceedings of the Musicological Society of Australia/New Zealand Musicological Society Joint Conference Proceedings 2010,* edited by M. Poole, 218–229. Dunedin, NZ: University of Otago.

———. 2013b. "'We are Australian': An Ethnographic Investigation into the Convergence of Community Music and Reconciliation." PhD diss., Interdisciplinary Cross-Cultural Research Program, Research School of Humanities and the Arts, Australian National University, Canberra.

———. 2014a. "The Big Sing in the Desert: An Emphasis on Exchange and Common Ground." *Musicworks* 19 (June): 9–16.

———. 2014b. "Indigenising a Canon: The Entry of 'My Island Home,' 'Baba Waiar' and 'Kulba Yaday' into the Repertoire of Community Choirs." *Perfect Beat* 15 (1): 45–65. doi:10.1558/prbt.v15i1.17145.

———. 2014c. "African Grace in Central Australia: Community Choirs, Reconciliation and Intercultural Performance." *International Journal of Community Music* 7 (3): 343–363. doi:10.1386/ijcm.7.3.343_1.

Rose, Jon. 2003. *Inkat'irbirberintjaka:* Ntaria Aboriginal Ladies Choir/ I worship you here in your dwelling place, Lord: Ntaria Aboriginal Ladies Choir. http://www.abc.net.au/arts/adlib/stories/s904138.htm.

———. 2008. "Listening to History: Some Proposals for Reclaiming the Practice of Live Music." *Leonardo Music Journal* 18: 9–16. doi:10.1162/lmj.2008.18.9.

Schwarz, Carolyn, and Françoise Dussart. 2010. "Christianity in Aboriginal Australia Revisited." *The Australian Journal of Anthropology* 21 (1): 1–13. doi: 10.1111/j.1757–6547.2010.00064.

Smith, Graeme. 2005. *Singing Australia: A History of Folk and Country Music.* North Melbourne: Pluto Press Australia.

———. 2008. "Folk Music: Movements, Scenes and Styles." In *Sounds of Then, Sounds of Now,* edited by S. Homan and T. Mitchell, 151–166. Hobart: ACYS.

Stokes, Martin. 2004. "Music and the Global Order." *Annual Review of Anthropology* 33 (1): 47–72. doi:10.1146/annurev.anthro.33.070203.143916.

Stuart, Morris. 2012. Personal comment, "The Narrative Is Bigger than the Music." *Reflections from the Organisers,* June 30. http://www.rachelhore.com/blog.

———. 2014. Personal communication (e-mail, March 31, 2014).

Subasic, Emina, and Katherine J. Reynolds. 2009. "Beyond 'Practical' Reconciliation: Intergroup Inequality and the Meaning of Non-Indigenous Identity." *Political Psychology* 30 (2): 243–267. doi:10.1111/j.1467-9221.2008.00690.

Westwood, Matthew. 2007. "Religious Choirs a Constant across Desert Generations." *The Australian,* September 14. http://www.theaustralian.com.au/news/arts/religious-choirs-aconstant-across-desert-generations/story-e6frg8n6-1111114413183.

Personal Conversations (Interviews)

Cooper, C. (2010). Personal conversation (Interview 8/1/10).

France, K. (2010). Personal conversation (Interview 9/19/10).

Gunn, P. (2010). Personal conversation (Interview 7/31/10).

Hudson, N. (2010). Personal conversation (Interview 9/19/10).

Jackson, B. (2010). Personal conversation (Interview 7/31/10).

Stuart, B. (2012). Personal conversation (Interview 9/6/12).

Stuart, M. (2012a). Personal conversation (Interview 9/6/12).

CHAPTER 11

Transforming Lives

Exploring Eight Ways of Learning in Arts-based Service Learning with Australian Aboriginal Communities

Anne Power, Brydie-Leigh Bartleet, and Dawn Bennett

Within the fields of community music and community arts in Australia, community service learning is gaining prominence as a key pedagogical strategy that connects community service with structured reflection and learning activities (Siebenaler 2005). Arts-based service learning is increasingly being used to bring together university students and community members to work on community-led projects of cultural significance. This arts focus combines well with the service-learning approach as it promotes what Rendon (2009) calls *sentipensante* (sensing/thinking) pedagogy. *Sentipensante* pedagogy aims to disrupt entrenched belief systems that divide knowing, thinking, and feeling. Such disruption can bring to light experiences that are threshold and transformative. Patricia Cranton, a leading writer on transformative learning, explains that the "elegantly simple" definition of transformative learning includes the idea of people changing the way they interpret their experiences and their interactions with the world (2006). In order to flesh out these ideas further within the Australian context, this chapter draws on the reflections of pre-service teachers and arts students from three universities during and after their experiences participating in arts-based service learning with Aboriginal communities. These reflections center on Yunkaporta's "8 Ways Framework" (2009, 10), a view of Australian Aboriginal cultural competence that allows the inclusion of Aboriginal perspectives and learning techniques. This chapter argues that arts-based service learning can be transformative when participants engage in all the dimensions of the 8 Ways Framework and allow shared knowledge to become wisdom in their lives and practices.

In his doctoral thesis Yunkaporta (2009) highlighted eight ways of learning drawing on Aboriginal worldviews. As he argues, "Aboriginal culture has not been lost—just disrupted. Aboriginal ways of knowing, being, doing, valuing and learning remain in an ancestral framework of knowledge that is still strong" (Yunkaporta 2009, 1). Of relevance to our work across cultures and Aboriginal nations, he draws on Nakata's (2007) idea of shared learning at the cultural interface and on the idea of a dynamic overlap of knowledges from different peoples (Yunkaporta 2009, 3). Similarly, in an earlier document, Marika (1999) used the metaphor of Ganma, where the saltwater and freshwater meet to form a lagoon. Each of these ideas is about the interweaving of knowledge strands that are Aboriginal and Torres Strait Islander with those that are Western, and both provide useful tools for reflecting on the intercultural dynamics of arts-based service learning with Aboriginal communities. The 8 Ways Framework is designed to assist teachers to engage with Aboriginal communities. It is a pedagogy focused on strengthening identity, achieving success, and transforming lives (Bat, Kilgariff, and Doe 2014). Using the lens of the 8 Ways Framework, the students' experiences and reflections hold up a mirror to service learning with Aboriginal communities.

At the heart of this chapter is a collaboration that involved two arts-based service learning projects at Tennant Creek (Northern Territory in Australia) and a third project in the Perth metropolitan area (Western Australia). The collaboration highlights the core value of relationship building in teaching and learning (Butin 2003), and underpinning and supporting this centrality of relationships was the students' use of the 8 Ways Framework.

Context and Approach

This chapter reports on part of a larger nationwide study into arts-based service learning with First Peoples in Australia, involving three universities (see Bartleet et al. 2014). The three ABSL programs involved differing cohorts of students within each of their respective university structures. The program run at the University of Western Sydney was situated within the broader program called Professional Experience 3 (PE3) in the Master of Teaching Secondary Course at the University of Western Sydney (UWS). This program requires pre-service teachers to complete sixty hours of work in a service learning context that directly addresses social disadvantage.

The pre-service teachers reported here (Nick, Victoria, Blake, Corinne, Lisa, Paul, and Sharni) had successfully applied to participate in the PE3 program known as Community Action Support, located in Tennant Creek in Australia's Northern Territory. Approximately ten students per year are selected from a rigorous application and interview process that considers attributes such as teaching competency, maturity, and self-awareness (Jameson, Clayton, and Jaeger 2010). These attributes are important, because in any intercultural setting it matters not only what is done but also how and with whom (Sandmann, Moore, and Quinn 2012). These seven pre-service teachers participated in the program between 2011 and 2013 and were selected from the pool of some forty participants because their reflections on the 8 Ways Framework have encompassed different Aboriginal perspectives.

First Peoples students form 80 percent of the high school population in Tennant Creek. The majority of students come from the Warumungu people, the traditional custodians of the land, along with Warlpiri and Kalkadoon peoples and non–First Nations students. The UWS partner in Tennant Creek is the Australian Literacy and Numeracy Foundation (ALNF). Since 2009, ALNF has supported pre-service teachers in Tennant Creek placements and, most recently, in a school at Elliott. The service-learning experience (developed in partnership with ALNF and the Papulu Aparr-Kari Language Centre) focuses attention on First Nations educational outcomes in remote Australia.

Before the four-week service learning experience, the pre-service teachers engage in a training week, including cultural training with the Aunties at the Papulu Aparr-Kari Language Centre. In Aboriginal culture, Aunties are wise women who are guardians of respect and rules of behavior (Robertson, Demosthenous, and Demosthenous 2005). During the week of training, there is consultation with the community about the projects to be undertaken during the summer placement. This consultation is undertaken with community members such as the high school executive and the elders at the Language Centre. At the Language Centre, pre-service teachers learn about skin relationships and receive a skin name. In so doing, they come to understand how skin names relate to the organization of First Nations society, from marriage to all the circumstances of daily life, including their responsibilities to each other. Such responsibilities remain a way of managing life and ensure that there are common understandings about obligations to the land. During the Tennant Creek placement, Papulu Aparr-Kari provides other connections for pre-service teachers—for example, translating song lyrics and providing insights into the 8 Ways Framework, to which the pre-service teachers have been exposed in their teacher education.

The second program run by Queensland Conservatorium Griffith University (QCGU), called the Winanjjikari Service Learning Program, has involved a small group of university students (approximately five to eight) and staff travelling from Brisbane to Tennant Creek for approximately two weeks to take part in this program every year since 2009. To date this program has directly benefited over thirty-five university students in undergraduate programs, as well as hundreds of community members. The aims of the program are twofold: (1) to enhance the way in which Aboriginal content is embedded in arts-based curricula at Griffith University; and (2), to develop Griffith's relationships and connections with Aboriginal communities. A defining feature of the work has been the desire to place the responsibility for deciding about activities and approaches in the hands of community members. In order to enact this approach, Griffith has developed a strong partnership with the regional arts organization Barkly Regional Arts and with local Aboriginal musicians and sound engineers at the Winanjjikari Music Centre in Tennant Creek. The program has differed from year to year in response to community needs. The first year involved setting up a recording studio; the second year aligned with the Desert Harmony Festival; and in the third year of the pilot project students worked on song writing and recording projects. In the later years, students worked and performed at the Desert Harmony Festival.

Despite such varied activities, three key phases have been shared across each year of the project. First, students receive intercultural training. Where possible, this commences prior to the program and includes a brief cross-cultural orientation session. Once in the community, students attend classes on language and culture with respected Warumungu Elders. Second, students collaborate with Aboriginal artists at Winanjjikari Music Centre in artistic tasks. Third, all students engage in three reflective activities, which form their assessment and provide important data for the program's ongoing research. Students produce field diaries that document their learning processes; they reflect on the intercultural competencies developed through this work; they participate in an interview about the learning process and the implications of this for Aboriginal content in the curriculum; and they create a five-minute digital story about the experience using footage from their trip. Lastly, students communicate their experiences to the university and broader Brisbane community via digital stories, workshops, and presentations.

The third program worked with Wadjuk Noongar people, who are the traditional custodians of metropolitan Perth. Noongar people are "the only Aboriginal people in Western Australia to have seen a metropolis rise on their traditional lands, and while they were the first in the state to face the brunt of colonialism, major elements of their traditional culture remain" (Thomson et al. 2015). The project involved four academics and thirteen students who were undertaking online journalism, journalism feature writing, and film and television units. Students responded to a call for expressions of interest and enrolled in a semester-long unit.

The projects, suggested by local indigenous organizations, included partnerships with Noongar Radio (an Aboriginal community radio station), the Langford Aboriginal Association (which runs programs related to culture, health, and well-being), Indigenous Community Engagement and Awareness (a youth-run reconciliation and community awareness foundation), Kart Koort Wiern (an Aboriginal reconciliation and cultural awareness training consultancy), and the Wirrpanda Foundation (which aims to build capacity among Aboriginal people). Students worked with their community partners over a twelve-week period, during which time the project team emphasized the need to establish relationships of trust by taking the time to listen and interact. During the first month, four three-hour workshops introduced the students to action research, service learning, and Noongar culture and history. The project team involved all participants in regular readings and guided reflections.

Ethical approval was granted for all elements of data collection and reporting at each of the collaborating universities. Students, teacher-supervisors at the schools, and Aboriginal community members all completed consent forms. By interviewing pre-service teachers, it was possible to assess whether the service learning prepared them to organize, manage, and prepare their classrooms in ways that improved outcomes for Aboriginal students. Similarly, arts students responded to interviews and guided reflections; some created digital stories. Questions elicited ideas exploring what they had learned from each other collegially and their commitment to enhancing Aboriginal arts and culture in the future. We have followed a thematic approach to analyzing this data that draws on the 8 Ways Framework in order to further flesh out the ways in which such arts-based service learning programs with First Peoples can lead to transformative learning experiences for all involved.

Using and Observing the 8 Ways Framework in Arts-based Service Learning

Story Sharing

The symbol in figure 11.1 indicates story sharing (Yunkaporta 2009). He explains that the killer boomerang symbol is a narrative model: "Your story starts with normal life (handle end) then builds to a climax (boomerang elbow), but at the end (boomerang tip) when things calm down and return to 'normal,' life is never the same. It's at a higher place than before because new knowledge has come" (Yunkaporta 2009, 4). The importance of storytelling in service learning is also something Guffey (2008) reiterates, in that people come to know themselves in this world: "through the inter-relationship of storytelling and service-learning. Think of storytelling as a needle and service-learning as the thread. The story makes an impression and creates an opening, then service-learning follows. Together they draw the fabric of life: people, places and nature together in new experiences. Connecting the power of storytelling with each generation . . . takes real-life encounters in the form of service-learning."

In the UWS service learning program, it was exemplified by the stories that Nick, a pre-service teacher, and Joseph, a Year Ten Warlpiri young man, shared. Nick had considerable experience in bands and had toured in several states. He told about his experience touring and about what he had studied to be where he was in starting his teaching career. In turn, Joseph told "about bush tucker . . . about going out bush, what he does when he goes there, where he gets water from, what they hunt, how they kill it, why they go bush" (Nick, UWS, journal).

This relationship produced a trusting cultural interchange. Each of the participants spoke about the benefits of such reciprocal learning and how much they valued the collaborative aspects of their time together. They valued supporting each other musically as well as intellectually collaborating in problem solving. Their learning was enhanced in the togetherness of

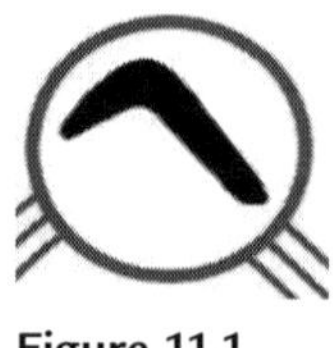

Figure 11.1

the activity. Whether this was expressed as developing autonomy, enjoying learning together, or becoming a genuine ensemble, the essence underlying each of these different learning contexts was reciprocity. For Joseph, it was about developing as a young musician, strengthening his ability to spontaneously improvise on rhythmic and melodic ideas initiated by one member of an ensemble and passed on to another. For Nick, it was formative to his teaching style and to the ways he interacted with students in a class group because he had a deeper awareness of the ability and life of each individual.

Initially, the Curtin students were concerned that their lack of awareness might make it difficult to gather and share stories respectfully within an indigenous context. One of the lecturers noted this concern in his reflections: "I am concerned primarily with the issue of appropriating Aboriginal stories. At the Week 1 class I asked the Noongar presenter if appropriation was a big concern of his. He replied that he thought it was not too much of a problem 'as long as [the reporter] engaged sincerely with the [Aboriginal] community'" (Graham, Curtin). Several students reflected on the need to learn a new way of working. Maddie anticipated that her practice would need to change even before she met community resistance. She later documented the transition to a new way of working and the effectiveness of a more sensitive approach:

> I learned that if you want to talk to indigenous people about a story, you have to get to know them first and let them trust you and stuff beforehand. . . . I first got so much resistance, and I knew that certain lines were going to get taken out because they were too deep and personal—which I got upset about because that was the interesting part of the story. . . . So it's the second piece I did where I actually sat down with about four of the other ladies, . . . That was where it flowed a lot more naturally because the members do actually want to have a chat and tell you what they're thinking and . . . finding a story was much better once I got to talk to the community members themselves. (Maddie, Curtin)

For some students, including Maddie, this new way of doing things meant working around nonindigenous "gate keepers" in order to hear from community members directly. Having slowed down in order to establish relationships of trust with their community partners, students described the different nature of story sharing in this context and the change of focus from *finding* a story to the *story* itself. Rachel experienced this "slowing down" as a new way of working that involved simply being with her community: "So I spent three weekends out there just talking to people and being involved with them and trying to find a story from that. Before that, I would look for the story. I would have a group of people where I'm just trying to find a story from that group of people instead of focused on the story itself" (Rachel, Curtin).

Once they had learned to listen, students found people far more likely to share stories. This illustrates how essential developing relationships of trust is. Having seen the impact of the cultural awareness training, together with a great deal of "being with" community, students began to imagine how, as media professionals, they might play a personal role in issues such as reconciliation: "the ladies . . . never cease to inspire. As future journalists, it was interesting to note how enthusiastic people were to work with us—recognising the power of the media and the often-inaccurate representation of Aboriginal people" (Rachel, Curtin).

At times, story sharing was unexpected. A diary error stranded an indigenous community partner and a journalist student, Jessica Cummins, three and a half hours away from Perth with no event to cover. Instead they headed to a local café to have lunch. Jessica later recounted some of this story, sharing it in an online article (Cummins 2013), from which this is an excerpt:

> figures from a 2012 Reconciliation Australia and Australian Youth Affairs Council report (Reconciliation Australia, 2012) . . . found that 81 per cent of young people think students should learn more about Aboriginal and Torres Strait Island history and culture in schools. As I relay these statistics to Ingrid while we sit in the shade of the alfresco area, she stares off into the distance before speaking. "The gap is there because Indigenous education has not been made mandatory yet. Just ask yourself, if the majority of people have never had an ongoing interaction and understanding of Indigenous culture, then where the hell have they been learning about it?" The question leaves me stumped. Here we are, two strangers eating lunch together . . . and I have learned more about Indigenous culture and history from one conversation than I ever did during the four years I attended high school in Australia.

The conversation exemplifies the attitude of many Aboriginal Australians, who acknowledge the ignorance of non-Aboriginal people and yet, rather than lay blame, focus on the need for change.

Likewise for the Griffith students, they discovered that when they took the time to listen to the stories being shared, community members were incredibly generous with the knowledge they shared with them. Knowledge about country, culture, and customs were exchanged, as described by QCGU student Jeff:

> He [local elder] was telling us [QCGU students] about different ways to hunt and how he goes out to get kangaroos and he was explaining the two sets of boomerangs that we got from him, which he'd had for over a year and a half and he used them in traditional ceremonies. So he used them in one of the songs that we performed, when the elders played them as clap sticks. How . . . they were one of his most precious things and he was giving them away as a symbol to us, which was really something. (Jeff, QCGU, 2012)

These lessons would be very hard to teach within the formal walls of a university classroom, where a connection to country is so often not appropriately communicated. These insights point towards the importance of acknowledging country, whether in a remote location or one's own metropolitan city, and the tremendously rich and important lessons that come from sitting down with elders and Aboriginal artists and respectfully listening to their stories that flow from sitting on country and then sharing stories in response.

Learning Maps

Yunkaporta points out that learning maps "help students to see where they are and where they are going on their learning journey" (2009, 5). Signifying learning maps, the symbol in figure 11.2 represents a way of learning that pre-service teacher Victoria realized was important. She came to understand that the Aboriginal students with whom she worked needed to picture how they might successfully complete a task, so she created models for them to observe, saying: "Certainly they engage quickly with practical activities. They just came in, saw what they had to do, looked at a couple of pictures and thought, 'Yes, I can do that.' It was a source of great excitement, because they could see success written in the process" (Victoria's journal).

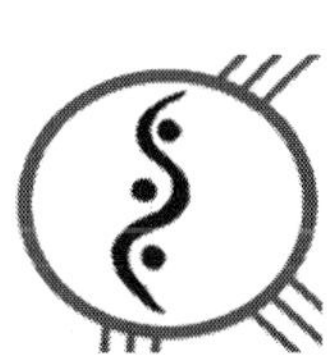

Figure 11.2

The embodied experience of participating can prompt tertiary students to engage in deeply reflective examinations of their subjectivities as well as their perceptions of the world around them. A key element in the process has been the use of guided critical reflection (through field diaries, focus group interviews, and informal group debriefings). These aspects of critical reflection also provide valuable insights about the depth of the learning experiences. As Swords and Kiely (2010, 151) contend, "the most powerful transformative learning experiences stem from intentionally structuring . . . activities before, during, and after the program to engage students in critically reflective learning and contextual, emotional, visceral, and connected forms of learning."

As Yunkaporta (2009) explains, these learning journeys can be drawn as a map, with points of understanding indicated along the way rather than at the end: "Learning journeys never take a straight path but wind, zig-zag, or go around" (2009, 5). For the QCGU students, as with tertiary students in the other programs, relationship building and task sharing have to be prioritized if the students hope to accomplish anything. This meant their learning journeys had a particular rhythm that was distinct from what they were accustomed to in their university classrooms. As James reveals:

> At times it has felt like things have been moving quite slowly and we might not be achieving as much as was expected of us. However upon reflecting on our first week I have realised some of this slow-going has actually been a necessary and ideal way to settle in to the new environment, acclimatise and become familiar with who we are working with. . . . I don't think it would have been advisable for us as guests in a new environment to begin in any other way. . . . Taking the time to acclimatise and allow the people of Tennant Creek a chance to get to know us and feel comfortable with us in their town has been a very necessary aspect of this trip (James, QCGU, 2009).

Nonverbal Learning

The symbol of the hand in figure 11.3 represents all knowledge that can be understood or acquired without words, including gestures, inference, expressions, eye movement, kinesthetic learning, images, and revealed knowledge (for example, dreams, insight, inspiration, reflection) (Yunkaporta 2009, 5). Music provides a powerful medium for this nonverbal communication. The QCGU students have often reflected on the act of jamming as the most appropriate and direct form of intercultural communication, describing the nature

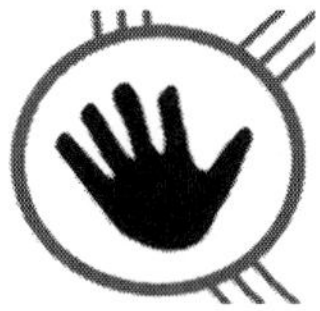

Figure 11.3

and benefits of these experiences through reference to discourses of music as a "universal" or "common language." As Amie said to one of the project team:

> I've sort of reflected on the fact that music is just that common language that's sort of being able to bridge a lot of the boundaries between us. That very first thing we all kind of got in and had a listen to each other's music and had a jam and it sort of started to flow from there. Whereas if you were stuck in a room and were just chatting to each other for a few hours, you could go out and we'd still be sitting in the room next time you come in. So I think it was good to have that common link from the get go. (Amie, QCGU, 2009)

A further example of the use of the above symbol for nonverbal communication was UWS pre-service teacher Blake's affirmation of the high school students when they had played through their nervousness and successfully performed at the Open Mic night. He recalled a student who "came up to me and said 'I'm just going to go home, I can't play it.' I was with him for about ten minutes, encouraging him and saying that, if he started the song, half-way through he'd feel incredible. At the end he didn't say much but he was smiling. You could tell. Nick and I ran down the path to give them a high 5 at the end" (Blake, UWS). Blake did not need to say a lot to convey his admiration of the student's efforts, his appreciation that this was a major challenge that had been met and overcome. Everything was conveyed nonverbally.

A concept that has reverberated throughout all aspects of this research has been the importance of relationship building. Chupp and Joseph (2010) concur that service-learning projects such as this one hinge on the development of mutually beneficial relationships between pre-service teachers, their students, and local community members. As the pre-service teachers in this case study came to realize, by taking the time to nurture a sense of trust and connection with their school students, they were able to feel a stronger connectedness to the community and, in turn, make a "safe space" for creative experimentation, cultural exchange, and personal growth. While the duration of these relationships was only four weeks, the experiences provided a powerful catalyst for the pre-service teachers to reflect on their own teaching practice. Through their relationships with the high school students the pre-service teachers came to appreciate the importance of giving encouragement, critiquing the cultural politics of their own educational experiences, showing vulnerability in the classroom, and connecting with other teachers and musicians outside the school gate.

Symbols and Images

Part of what the students absorbed in their service learning projects was that objects, images, and metaphors were a way of sharing culture, as shown in the symbol in figure 11.4 (Yunkaporta 2009, 5). UWS pre-service teacher Corinne was a keen observer of Aboriginal teaching styles. When she watched Auntie Heather teach about the topic of the Overland Telegraph Line, she noticed the simple drawing of one pole supporting the line. Auntie Heather explained that she wanted her students "to understand that when they started they only had one pole for the wire. Our people used to call it the wire trail then" (interview with Auntie Heather). Yunkaporta confirmed that Aboriginal thinking is often done in images or shapes rather than words (2009, 5).

Working in the urban environment, it was an image that first alerted film and television student Lisa to differences between the radio broadcasting studios of her Aboriginal partners and those she had experienced elsewhere:

> One of the things that stood out to me most at Noongar Radio was the wallpaper we had in one of the recording booths . . . at first I wasn't quite sure why I was so interested in this room, but looking back I think it was the point where I realised that there was so much more dimension to Aboriginal community media than mainstream media. It also reflects the biggest thing I learned in this unit, which is that there's so much room for discussion of Aboriginal culture in so many areas of life, not just for Aboriginal people but [for] non-Aboriginal people. (Lisa, Curtin)

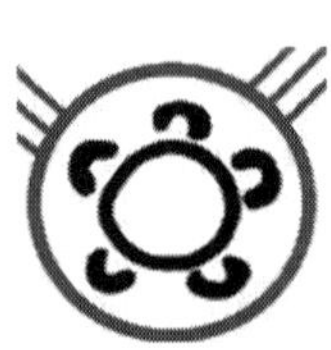

Figure 11.4

Land Links

The symbol in figure 11.5 indicates place-based learning. As Yunkaporta explains, this symbol represents a river. All the animals, plants, and geographic forms in land and water contain deep knowledge. "They also provide metaphors for concepts. Knowledge of local land and place is central to Indigenous ways of knowing" (2009, 6). It was UWS pre-service teacher Lisa who tried to articulate something of the teaching that the place enabled when she said:

> I don't know whether it's possible to capture a lot of it as so much is interpersonal. So much is about building relationships with students in school and then seeing them in the community. The place puts a stamp on what you teach. It's so different—physically, teaching is different. . . . It would be good to show the way kids react to teaching, such as the amazing things you see in the music room. It would be good to show the way kids behave differently—there's an entirely different culture. I think the language to describe it is really limited. (Lisa's journal)

In their reflections, the pre-service teachers struggled to find the words to explain what they were learning and becoming. They observed the different participation of the school students and the ways in which students stepped between traditional and contemporary culture.

Given that the WA projects all occurred within a familiar urban environment, the WA team did not expect students to rethink their relationship with place. However, their changing perspective came into view when Noongar elder and Curtin University elder in residence Associate Professor Simon Forest led a one-day excursion to the township of Pinjarra, eighty-six kilometers south of Perth. Students and lecturers traced the steps of the 1834 punitive expedition led by Governor James Stirling, who led the massacre of Binjarab Noongar men, women, and children. Simon described the massacre as a watershed moment in the shared history of Noongar people and people of European descent.

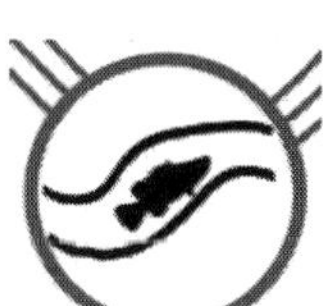

Figure 11.5

Asked to imagine familiar places at a different time in history, students began to question their understanding of not only the places seen that day but places with which in some cases they had had been familiar since they were children:

> The fact that this site was so "normal"—in fact all of today's places were—makes me realise I drive, walk and live daily life in places I don't understand. I need to learn much more about these places and I need to make sure my children, grandchildren learn about it and to respect Aboriginal culture and people. I'm not sure how to do this. . . . I wonder how much more of our history is unknown, not understood, ignored. I now feel more anxious about the need for change and reconciliation than ever before. (Aaron, Curtin)

This embodied and emplaced experiential learning, however, also reflects the very deep connections that many participants experienced in an unprompted manner during their ABSL trips. For example, Sarah, a Torres Strait Islander "salt water" UQ (QCGU guest) student, spoke at length about her journey to firestick country (the desert).

> My first thought was we're not in Kansas anymore, Toto. . . . I guess every time you go to a country or a different person's country, the physical environment is always going to impact on you in a very different way. . . . It's the desert. . . . It's a really harsh environment out here. . . . Just going through this smoking landscape that had recently had a bushfire, and everything was vibrant red and black and charred and burnt, and just rocks—red rocks, spinifex grass. . . . Then realising how much of life and bush medicine and food is actually available, if you know the right things to do. . . . Then when I went to the centre today, and found out that the basis of ceremony here is all fire and smoking things out. Then when somebody lit that fire last night, just randomly, it just—that summed it up for me. I was like yes, this is fire country. Then if you are confronting that along with a bunch of other people as well—it's just something to do with heat. Tempers fray, people get tired, people get worn out. . . . It's like a resonating theme seems to be burn out. I just—there's all these fire analogies, there's all these things associated. . . . But in terms of the problems that each different community or country has, they're so individual. One is never like the other. (Sarah, QCGU, 2011)

Sarah's reflections show not only a deep sensitivity towards the harshness and unforgiving nature of this land, being a saltwater person, but also the ways in which the nature of this firestick country pervades *everything*. It influences how people relate to one another, how they relate to their own inner worlds, and the endurance they have for their work.

Nonlinear Processes

Nonlinear learning, indicated by the symbol in figure 11.6, is involved in the adaptability that is inherent in the creation of new knowledge. Yunkaporta (2009, 6) explains that the symbol represents circular logic at the center, and the lines on either side show the interface between opposites. In Aboriginal worldviews, opposites meet to create something new, with the concepts of symmetry and balance valued above oppositional thinking. Pre-service teachers Nick and Blake encouraged lateral ways of thinking when they worked with Year Twelve students to refine their compositions. Shaenee's composition "Being Here" was one that evolved. She had the bass line and could sing the melody she wanted to unfold over the top of that. Her first thought was to have a driving tempo, but Nick, Blake, and her classmates encouraged her to experiment with relaxing the tempo into a ballad-like style. Thinking differently about the tempo let Shaenee begin to hear the kind of keyboard sound that could provide the inner texture of the music. Her music was transformed and she found a new self-confidence in her work.

It is neither easy for students to compose nor for pre-service teachers to critique and advise in composition. Both are challenging. There needs to be an open dialogue that is respectful, in which the creative act can flourish in an environment that allows experimentation and the acknowledgment that errors are learning opportunities. Shaenee's work became strong and individual through trialing suggestions that were respectfully made. Here, by thinking laterally, Shaenee was able to blend her original idea with suggestions that came from Nick and Blake and from her peers. That learning space permitted new ways of understanding and being. It was what Jaworski (1997, 382)

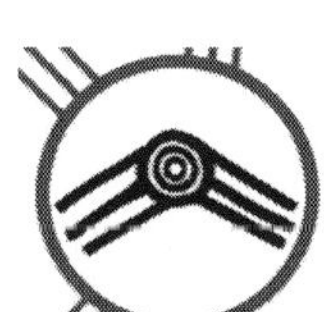

Figure 11.6

describes as "a communicative resource whose manifestations go well beyond the mere absence of speech."

In a similar vein, Griffith community partner Jeff McLaughlin (former manager of WMC) described the difference in the "white fella" fast pace, and how this was not always appropriate: "Let's be honest, normally when you get people who've never come out, you get a thing called a white snowstorm, where you get all these people imposing stuff, but I don't know what you've been telling them [because] they've come in just absolutely the right way. Where you're not imposing, 'I'm from the East Coast' . . . and they've just got it" (Jeff, QCGU, 2010).

Deconstruct/Reconstruct

The symbol in figure 11.7 represents deconstructing and reconstructing. For the students in Western Australia, working with indigenous people in their home city of Perth led them to question, and in some cases begin to reconstruct, their understanding of media reporting, Australian history, their previous education, and their relationship with familiar places.

Students were shocked to realize that their prior education, both at school and during university, had neglected indigenous cultural awareness and non-colonial tellings of Australian history:

> How little I knew about the history. It shocked me when listening to [indigenous visitors] speak to me about racism and the way Indigenous people were treated, because I realised that there were a lot of significant things I knew nothing about. (Jody, Curtin)

> Aboriginals in today's society still hold a lot of anger but little power. I think there is an overwhelmingly large amount of non-Aboriginal Australians who are ignorant (as I was) about the violent past of "settlement." These stories have been passed down through generations of Aboriginal people but more should be exposed to all Australians. (Phil, Curtin)

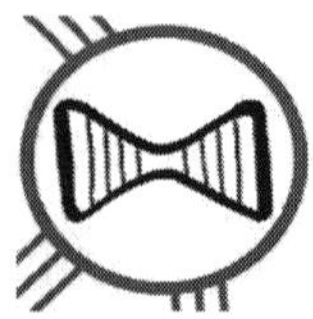

Figure 11.7

As prejudices fell away, several students began to align their new way of thinking with their future professional practice. This was particularly evident among the journalism students:

> I think it did make me identify the power we have as journalists. I'm much more critical of news . . . because it's just small decisions that if you don't know better, can shape the whole way a person interprets a story. That . . . might just be a crime story or something. But as soon as you make it about another culture, it changes that whole view. It shouldn't be an issue of what colour the person's skin was. (Rachel, Curtin)

Deconstructing and reconstructing was also part of the process when preservice teacher Paul assisted a group of cross-generational students, called the Stronger Sisters, to move from the initial lines of a song to the completed lyric. There were immediate past students of the high school as well as students from Years Eight to Eleven. The students were motivated to write about their life in Tennant Creek. When they began, they had the hook line "Tennant Creek where we belong" to express an intense connection to the place. Eventually, they collaboratively wrote a verse and chorus:

> Love is sometimes hard in this red desert land
> We sing from the heart so you understand
> Music is a part, the fire in our voice
> The music is within us, the music is our choice.
> We're the Tennant Creek girls, come and follow my beat
> We play football Stronger Sisters' team
> Listen and learn. Follow our dreams.
> Music takes us high, come and touch the sky
> Listen to your heart, it tells you when to stop
> Tennant Creek where we belong.
>
> We know where we come from, we know where we stand
> We come here together, hand in hand.
> Finding our path, we're taking our way.
> We're making a future, creating a change.

This group of young women saw their role as facilitating change, of speaking publicly and positively about their town. They were so proud of their heritage, their town, and their community.

Community Links

Bringing new information home to the community, represented by the symbol in figure 11.8, was something to which Sharni was deeply committed. She provided her Year Ten class with the "mission" of making a statement through dance and song about a community issue. The students chose the issue of the impact of alcohol in communities. As Wickett (2007) observed, remote communities have difficulty reacting to messages from government sources but are open to messages that have been generated within the community. The Year Ten class came to understand the power of what they were creating through reflecting on what they expressed artistically. Their dance was about the need to build self-esteem and pride in their traditions and abilities, and the lyrics of the chorus ran: "Hard fact, hard life. You don't need grog to have a fun night." A vital aspect of the collaboration was the input of the Pupula Aparr-Kari Language and Cultural Centre (one of only six language centers mentioned in the House of Representatives Standing Committee 2012). The ladies at the center translated the song words created by the student community into Warumungu. Sharni, working with the student community, presented the video to the local Council of Elders. In this way, the elders and the workers at the language center could also provide a channel for the message in the song and dance project and consider how they might diffuse this among the communities. At every stage of creation, this project aligned with a key goal of service learning: building the capacity of academic and community partners to sustainably address community needs and work for social justice (Vogel, Seifer, and Gelmon 2010).

The WA students were part of a learning community that involved their lecturers, community partners, and visiting guests. Though the concept of a learning community was not explicitly discussed with the students, they quickly felt an affinity with their peers. The following comment, for example, was made only three weeks into the program: "I'm sensing greater understanding as a group, and also perhaps a slight sense of solidarity, being a small group" (Ben, Curtin).

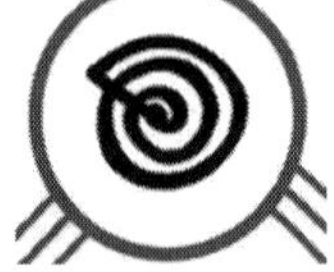

Figure 11.8

Community partners expressed synergies between the project and their experiences elsewhere. In line with the reciprocal learning aspect of service learning, some community members also expressed changing attitudes that led to changing practices: "This experience has been a real eye-opener. . . . It reminded me of a time when I was up in the Kimberley . . . and one of the elders said to me: 'it's all about looking, listening, learning but also engaging.' And I think sometimes, [people] look, listen and they learn but they don't have that opportunity to engage" (Tim, Curtin).

A continuity of those community links has been an important aspect of the QCGU program. For instance, students have returned under their own steam and now work for Barkly Regional Arts. Others have made a commitment to music education in the broader Northern Territory and have taken up teaching positions in the NT. The community has welcomed this ongoing commitment, as Alan (BRA executive officer) explained: "People who do take that extra leap to come back, without any expectations even; there will be a place somewhere in the region for them to land, especially if they have come through this program. It carries a little bit of a badge now, of acceptance. They're the folk who become friends of the region forever. That's a badge of honour itself because that's not an easy thing to happen" (Alan, QCGU, 2011).

Transformations at the Cultural Interface

All project participants reported transformations in their personal and professional thinking. Some students wrote that they might have previously been unaware of their own personal cultural biases:

> Definitely made me more culturally aware, not even just with Indigenous people, but with everyone. I've always been accepting of other people, I'm sure my friends would say the same thing. I'm never one to turn away from someone just because they're of a different culture. But it's definitely made me more aware of the things that you don't see right in front of you in terms of culture. (Louise, Curtin)

For others, the learning was articulated in terms of the personal potential to create broader change:

> So far in my course I've only been taught in *theory* how to report *on* Indigenous people in the media, but to have the opportunity to experience actually working alongside an Indigenous community is something

> not every journalist has the opportunity to do, especially when still at university. (Phil, student's italics; Curtin)

The shared storying of Nick and Joseph grew out of their recognition of each other as musicians and their curiosity about each other's learning journey. They shared stories of what they valued, and, as they performed together, other teachers saw that the sharing "increased a hunger for music" (Teacher W's interview). Nick saw the potential for Joseph to develop professionally: "He's got a set that he could support someone coming through town. He could follow them on the road and tour with them." He wanted to encourage this potential: "When he starts rapping, making it up while he's playing drums, that blows me away" (Nick's journal, UWS).

Victoria became engrossed with learning maps as symbols of the learning process. At one time, the students were to look for a picture of a type of fish. One student found a picture of a carp, and Victoria realized that she seemed to know a lot about animals and fish.

> I got the sense that it was cultural knowledge as she knew their language names. When I said I came from the Blue Mountains and that I lived in the bush, we became best buddies, because I lived somewhere there were animals, I wasn't just a person from the city. It was interesting the way she seemed to be operating within a taxonomy. I don't know how to explain it or what to call it yet. There was some "thing" she was drawing on. If I can know something about how to connect with [the students] and what sort of things they're interested in, then it makes their life easier and my life easier. Everything goes in a way that's much more productive. I hit a trigger with her. In another context I may not be able to operate that trigger, but I saw what happened when it worked. (Victoria's journal, UWS)

Victoria watched the transformation that took place for the student. At the same time, her own learning process was about trying to identify what it was that connected with the student and captured her interest.

For both Nick and Victoria, the lens of the 8 Ways Framework enabled them to focus on their teaching and assess its impact with Aboriginal learners. For them, striking up cross-cultural dialogue involved shared storying and learning maps. For Corinne, watching Auntie Heather and observing her use of an iconic image was an object lesson in incorporating cultural knowledge.

As a teacher Auntie Heather prepares thoroughly: "Doing this topic of the Overland Telegraph Line is a new thing for me and the students as well. I spent a lot of time reading information about how they brought the Line through the territory, made their way across" (Auntie Heather interview, UWS).

For Lisa, her experience was about the way the place impacted on learning. It meant appreciating the way the school bus picked students up in the morning, the way the elders interacted with the school community, the way the natural environment is incorporated into the curriculum, from the birdlife out at the dam to the colors in the late afternoon at Karlu Karlu (The Devil's Marbles). Lisa knew that she was still working on differentiating her lesson material: "I'm still struggling to crack it . . . but I have more trouble engaging the Aboriginal kids in my class. In part I think it's because I don't know when to push and when to hold back. Intuitively with the other kids I know where those boundaries are. I've been on the other side of that seat" (Lisa's journal, UWS).

Nick and Blake, as they worked with Year Twelve students in composing, had the students describe where they found their composition ideas and how they developed them. Shaenee had been listening to children's game programs, such as Super Mario. She created a minor-sounding phrase and developed it through repetition. Then she created a new section and a return of the first section. Her fleshing out of this simple structure had the benefit of Nick and Blake, along with her classmates, with whom to try out chord progressions and instrumental colors. Paul was keen to work with students on song lyrics. With a group that included different ages, he encouraged lyrics that caught the essence of the town and what it meant to the people who had grown up there.

Beyond the interaction of Sharni and the students, other teachers talked of the full participation of the class:

> Engagement has been through a simple dance, and it got them instantly involved. So it wasn't a confronting introduction. It's really working. There isn't a student who's not participated. Sharni has linked it in with a community message. She has discreetly been in touch with the Council of Elders. In class, she had three of our Indigenous young men who are ESL speakers and who participate in ceremony, right next to her. They were talking full on about mental health issues. She was able to cross quite a few boundaries there. It was magic to see. It's a dance and with it they're learning about mental health. (Teacher M's interview, UWS)

In the experiences of the students reported here, Cranton's definition can be seen in action. The 8 Ways Framework was critical to the reinterpretation of their experiences with Australian Aboriginal communities. The students grew professionally and personally because they knew they were on a learning journey alongside their community partners and the students they were teaching. They were open to adjusting their thinking to accommodate a more accurate or expanded understanding. The practical insights shared in this chapter point towards the potential of arts-based service learning to act as a transformative experience in intercultural settings and as a powerful pedagogical tool in the fields of community music and community arts in Australia, and indeed more broadly in the Asia Pacific.

References

Bartleet, Brydie-Leigh, Dawn Bennett, Kathryn Marsh, Anne Power, and Naomi Sutherland. 2014. "Reconciliation and transformation through mutual learning: Outlining a framework for arts based service learning with Indigenous communities in Australia." *International Journal of Education and the Arts* 15(8). http://www.ijea.org.

Bat, Melodie, Claire Kilgariff, and Tina Doe. 2014. "Indigenous tertiary education—we are all learning: Both-ways pedagogy in the Northern Territory of Australia." *Higher Education Research and Development* 33 (5): 871–886. doi:10.1080/07294360.2014.890575.

Butin, Dan W. 2003. "Of what use is it? Multiple conceptualizations of service learning in education." *Teachers College Record* 105 (9): 1674–1692. doi:10.1046/j.1467-9620.2003.00305.x.

Chupp, Mark G., and Mark L. Joseph. 2010. "Getting the most out of service learning: Maximizing student, university and community impact." *Journal of Community Practice* 18 (2–3): 190–212. doi:10.1080/10705422.2010.487045.

Cranton, Patricia. 2006. *Understanding and Promoting Transformative Learning.* 2nd ed. San Francisco, CA: Jossey-Bass.

Cummins, Jessica. 2013. "Connecting to culture." *Inkwire,* June 18, 2013: n.p. Retrieved from http://inkwirenews.com.au/2013/06/18/ingrid-cumming.

Guffey, J. 2008. "Embracing an Indigenous Understanding of Service-Learning." Keynote Address presented at the NWIC Second Summit on Indigenous Service-Learning, North West Indian College, Bellingham, WA, USA. Retrieved from http://www.servicelearning.org/library/resource/7938.

House of Representatives Standing Committee on Aboriginal and Torres Strait Islander Affairs. 2012. *Our Land, Our Languages.* Canberra: Commonwealth of Australia.

Jameson, Jessica, Patti Clayton, and Audrey Jaeger. 2010. "Community Engaged Scholarship as Mutually Transformative Partnerships." In *Participatory Partnerships for Social Action and Research,* edited by L. Hater, J. Hamel-Lambert, and J. Milleson, 259–277. Dubuque, IA: Kendall Hunt.

Jaworski, Adam. 1997. "'White and White': Metacommunicative and Metaphorical Silences." In *Silence: Interdisciplinary Perspectives,* edited by A. Jaworski, 381–402. Berlin: Mouton de Gruyter.

Marika, Raymattja. 1999. "Milthun latju wanga romgu Yolngu: Valuing Yolngu knowledge in the education system." *Ngoonjook: A Journal of Australian Indigenous Issues* 16 (December): 107–120.

Nakata, Martin. 2002. "Indigenous knowledge and the cultural interface: Underlying issues at the intersection of knowledge and information systems." *IFLA Journal* 28 (5–6): 280–291. doi:10.1177/034003520202800513.

Reconciliation Australia. 2012. *Yarn about Youth.* Sydney: Australian Youth Affairs Coalition.

Rendon, Laura. 2009. *Sentipensante Pedagogy.* Sterling, VA: Stylus.

Robertson, Boni, Catherine Demosthenous, and Hellene Demosthenous. 2005. "Stories from the Aboriginal women of the yarning circle: When cultures collide." *Hecate* 31 (2): 34–44, 178, 180.

Sandmann, Lorilee R., Tami L. Moore, and Jocey Quinn. 2012. "Center and Periphery in Service Learning and Community Engagement." In *Understanding Service Learning and Community Engagement,* edited by J. Hatcher and R. Bringle, 25–46. Charlotte, NC: Information Age Publishing.

Siebenaler, Dennis. 2005. "Music and service learning: A case study." *Journal of Music Teacher Education* Fall (15): 23–30. doi:10.1177/10570837050150010105.

Swords, Alicia C. S., and Richard Kiely. 2010. "Beyond pedagogy: Service learning and movement building in Higher Education." *Journal of Community Practice* 18 (2): 148–170. doi:10.1080/10705422.2010.487253.

Thomson, Chris, Dawn Bennett, Michelle Johnston, and Bonita Mason. (2015). "Why the where matters: A sense of place imperative for teaching better Indigenous affairs reporting." *Pacific Journalism Review* 21 (2): 141–161.

Vogel, Amanda L., Sarena D. Seifer, and Sherril B. Gelmon. 2010. "What influences the long-term sustainability of service-learning? Lessons from early adopters." *Michigan Journal of Community Service Learning* 17 (1): 59–74.

Wickett, Elizabeth. 2007. "Visual anthropology and development: Video as critique, praxis and process." *Visual Anthropology Review* 23 (1): 69–75. doi:10.1525/var.2007.23.1.69.

Yunkaporta, T. 2009. "Aboriginal pedagogies at the cultural interface." PhD diss., James Cook University, Townsville. Retrieved from http://eprints.jcu.edu.au/10974/4/04Bookchapter.pdf.

Yunkaporta, Tyson, and Melissa Kirby. 2011. "Yarning up Indigenous Pedagogies: A Dialogue about Eight Aboriginal Ways of Learning." In *Two Way Teaching and Learning: Toward Culturally Reflective and Relevant Education,* edited by R. Bell, G. Milgate, and N. Purdie, 205–213. Camberwell, Vic.: ACER Press.

CHAPTER 12

Emergence, Care, and Sustainability

A Community Arts Project in Early Childhood Education

David Lines

MAPS, or Move, Act, Play, Sing,[1] was a community-inspired early childhood project based in Auckland, Aotearoa–New Zealand. The main idea behind the project was to build meaningful arts learning experiences through community artist interventions for the young children, teachers, and parents in three early childhood education centers within the greater Auckland region. The project involved three performing arts: music, dance, and drama, and sought to broaden early childhood education knowledge about performing arts education, in other words, how performing arts education could be thought about, planned for, and enacted with and by young children in normal, everyday community settings. The project was also influenced, in part, by the Italian-based pedagogy Reggio Emilia, which through its notion of "100 languages" and other key concepts (Dahlberg and Moss 2006; Rinaldi 2001; Mawson 2010) brought to the project a way of thinking about children learning through community and through multiple modes of inquiry, including music.

The MAPS project was built around the idea of fostering a constructed, research-informed learning community. It developed partly from preparation and planning and partly from careful responses to circumstances that arose through practice. The community grew organically from the initial research team to include three Auckland-based early childhood centers, the center teachers, children, and parents, and a group of junior researchers (research assistants) who actively participated in center observations and group research discussions. Key to the formation of the research community was the collective vision of the research team who actively sought to build and include other participants in the research experience and draw from their collective input. In this sense it was a practice-based research project that was inspired by the idea of "community."

Prior to developing the project the research team prepared a written paper that was critical of the detached forms of music learning often experienced in institutional music education (Lines and Naughton 2009). This detachment, it was posited, arose in many areas of music education (from university right down to early childhood) and led to music often being taught in piecemeal ways, as tidbits of knowledge, or as sets of skills (skill-sets) to be learned rather than as meaningful music learning sourced from and by the group. Problems arose when music teachers and students/children actively separated the processes of music learning and engagement from the cultural meaning music had for their lives as active and participatory human beings. Addressing this problem as endemic to music education and its associated atomistic curricula and instrumental modes of operation meant constructing a different kind of pedagogical model based on the idea of community. We wanted time to explore the spaces of learning that were often neglected or bypassed in music and other arts learning with children. It was suggested that these spaces could be found in the life-affirming culture of a community of learning provided the nature and value of that community itself was affirmed. Given that two of the research team worked in the field of early childhood, the group decided that the early childhood education area would be an interesting place to start reconstructing performing arts pedagogical experiences that were imbued with meaningful aspects of community, as opposed to the individualistic and adult-centered forms of arts knowing. As a past teacher educator in music, I viewed this move as also a kind of self-critique arising from dissatisfaction with my own prior instrumental forms of music teacher education, which in the past had focused on "skills" rather than on social and community meaning. As principal investigator in the project I was keen to develop a more sustainable and culturally appropriate model of performing arts teaching and learning that could be shared with others.

The project also took inspiration from the New Zealand curriculum *Te Whāriki: He Te Whāriki matauranga mo nga mokopuna o Aotearoa/Early Childhood Curriculum* (Ministry of Education 1996), which as a bicultural document had some thoughtful, community-minded notions of teaching and learning through the following themes: *Mana Atua* (well-being), *Mana*

Whenua (belonging), *Mana Reo* (communication), *Mana Tangata* (contribution), and *Mana Aotūroa* (exploration). With this innovative curriculum already in place, it seemed sensible and culturally appropriate to explore how those principles could be applied in the performing arts in the specific contexts of early childhood center communities.

An ethnographic, qualitative, practice-based research project was designed and put into action. Three very different early childhood centers agreed to be part of the project: a semirural center, an inner-city private center, and a Māori immersion center that worked primarily in Te Reo (Māori language). Early childhood teachers in the three case-study centers worked with the research team over a period of eighteen months on performing arts–focused activities. In addition they concentrated on building performing arts experiences with their children in their centers. Each center initially took on a music, dance, or drama focus for a term (three months) at a time, rotating regularly, so that over the course of a year they had a variety of experiences in different performing arts modes. The centers each completed the project with a specific "community event" that was designed to bring parents and other members of the community into the learning and sharing experience with the teachers and children. The teachers were aided in their journey through regular weekend workshops where all of them met together and established their own learning community of sorts. In addition, community artists helped them through co-teaching as they developed confidence in their performing arts engagement. The research team recorded material for analysis in various forms: video evidence, photographic evidence, audio interviews, and written journal notes. Interviews were commonly held in groups, with teachers and artists sharing views of their immediate performing arts experiences as the project unfolded. An online Moodle (Internet blog designed for educational use) also assisted in data gathering, and all teachers were encouraged to share thoughts of the project with the other teacher-participators through this digital medium in addition to face-to-face interviews.

Cluster days were set up every three months on Saturday where the research team met with teachers, community artists, and other interested community members to workshop music, dance, and drama practices, and talk and reflect on the MAPS ideas and what participants thought about them. This coming together as a whole group became very important to the research and to the participants. The community artists reported that bringing the larger group together in this way "enabled them to see their role in the bigger project"—as part of this research community. The "playfulness" of this day was important too, as it was about becoming more relaxed and having fun. In short we started to feel we were a community.

The community artists brought the notion of community into performing arts experiences with teachers and children. We employed three kinds of community artists in the project—one each to represent music, dance, and drama. We were keen to employ people who worked as artists in the community and who had a passion for their community work not necessarily "teacher-educators," because it was important to inject into the project the idea of the artist who works with people and the cultural environment of the community first and foremost; these community artists were not preconditioned to follow set criteria or curricula from specific educational institutions or paradigms. The point was not to "consume" a curriculum outcome or create an arts "product" in the first instance, but rather to lead the teachers and children through a series of collective, meaningful performing experiences that simultaneously involved them in developing their own arts skills and knowledge through each experience. This direction was very important to the research team, as underlying the project was a sense of the need to restore performing arts experiences and learning through meaningful and connected ways of being.

Sustainability, Emergence, and Care

The MAPS project, then, was about bringing a real sense of community into arts education for young children, and the heightened focus on community put certain key concerns about early childhood performing arts education into relief. One of the main purposes of this chapter is to show how the themes of sustainability, emergence, and care came to underpin this community-focused project, in both a critical and a positive, constructive sense. These themes collectively helped frame the project, enable new ways of pedagogical thinking, and move the participants into more community-minded expressions of performing arts learning.

Communities need to be *sustainable* in order to survive. Built into the function of a healthy community are the practices of community members who sustain a level of community practice and well-being over time. Further, the notion of sustainability has become an increasingly important factor in early childhood research. From an early childhood arts perspective this means that teachers, along with parents and children, need to find ways in which meaningful arts practices can be maintained and nurtured over time using potential resources and participants. In sharp contrast to this ideal was a concern felt by the researchers that arts education provision in early childhood was actually unsustainable in its present form due to limited opportunities for teachers and children to develop arts ideas in their center communities. This problem was seen both as an awareness and as a training issue and resulted in a disconnect between the performing arts and the community. Arts teacher professional development is often exercised through one-off workshops from experts with little sustained buy-in from teachers. The MAPS project team wanted to encourage a more connected form of arts teaching and learning that fed off interactions and connections that could be fostered—were they real, virtual, imaginary, spiritual, or technological. The sustaining and nurturing of meaningful community connections through the performing arts would help performing arts teaching and learning become a more regular and community-minded daily experience in centers.

Key to the sustainability of this project was the proviso that each center would create a community event that celebrated the performing arts. Each center thought very carefully about how they would do this event and who would participate in it. One decided they would ask parents to combine with teachers in music-making activities with the children. Parents were also included at another center, which created a special inclusive event in the local town hall based on a range of creative activities and experiences triggered by a children's story the center teachers liked. A third center wanted to express their community event from a Māori perspective. They invited parents, teachers, and children to take a journey up a local "mountain," or *maunga,* to experience dance, drama, and music in an environment that reflected their spiritual and community-held beliefs. These special community events were not "staged" performing arts performances as such; rather, they focused on inclusiveness and what was meaningful to each group. In this way these experiences sustained the ongoing life of the individual center.

Recent early childhood music education research has been challenging in terms of honoring the child as a musical being in teaching/learning and play contexts (de Vries 2006; Knudsen 2008; Marsh 2008; Barrett 2006; Young 1995). Breaking free from teacher-centered contexts of music teaching and learning, these expressions of musicality and learning have centered on the child as initiator and constructor of music through play, spontaneous vocalizations, and improvised, emergent social contexts. In this project we responded to this new awareness of the child by becoming interested in more emergent ways of learning through play, child exploration, and child interest. This also had a link with Green's (2008) concept of informal learning in music, which was based on an enabling pedagogy built on children working in groups on musical projects of their own interest. Emergence, then, became a key theme in the project. It meant that, from a pedagogical point of view, community artists, teachers, parents, and other helpers would try to listen carefully and observe forms of expression and interest in the center community. A consequence of this approach is that they experienced their performing arts in a more improvisatory way, through careful listening to and watching the ideas that children brought to each class or experience, in contrast to more structured, curriculum-driven type approaches that focused more tightly on set learning structures and paradigms. The emergent ideas that came from the children—and the meaningful community connections that inspired them—allowed a more open pedagogy and arts community practice to evolve.

Taking this approach on board, the community artists who worked on the project began to initiate experiences with the teachers and children that invited them to participate freely with their own sounds, physical gestures, and stories. This required a particular kind of pedagogical approach, which started with simple structures that enabled ideas to flow, and then invited responses and the creation of new performing arts forms and means of expression. It was perhaps the dance sessions that provided opportunity for improvised responses in a most immediate way. The free and open yet inclusive approach of the dance community artist—Adrian—encouraged spontaneous ideas and suggestions from teachers and children. Animal gestures, for instance, were called for in the group, and actions and movements were accepted and developed, offering subtle opportunities for social interaction and the possibility for movements to be further developed through suggestions from the children—A crazy rhino! A huge rhino!

Adrian (dance) said that his pedagogy had evolved from a responsive improvisation toolkit he had developed through improv dance and through his work with a disabilities dance group. He also noted that having his own child kindled his desire to develop playful dance ideas. For Molly, the drama community artist, emergent practice came from "talking it through" and "getting others' interpretations." This required a kind of pedagogy of listening (Young 1995) or developing a real sensitivity to the collective expressiveness of the children. She used process-drama techniques, but with a special kind of understanding that invited children to explore their own interests. Kirsten, the music community artist, also had a very open and responsive style of engagement with the teachers and children. "We're going see where the sound takes us today," she would say. Her lessons were very interactive and became a series of imaginative sonic discoveries through narrative, costume, song, and sound exploration. These actions cared for both the children and the artistic openness of the world of sound and music in which they became interested through her sessions.

This kind of emergent pedagogy began to be adopted by the teachers themselves—in one center especially in drama and storytelling. Teachers reported that improvised storytelling with the children allowed them to "let go" and become children themselves, thus entering more authentically into a constructive relationship with their pupils. Other teachers described this as a "ripple effect," wherein the act of jumping in (metaphorically) set off expanding ripples that influenced others and gave them permission to be themselves and enjoy expressive games and experiences with the children. Emergence in this sense became a very democratic and enabling community process that recognized, not only the importance of the relationality of the community, but the individual differences that came through in a way that was accepted by all.

The research group agreed with the contemporary critique of child development theory that positioned the child in an objective, individualistic way (Dahlberg and Moss 2006). The worrying process of individualization in education is further intensified through the need to comply with educational measurement and assessment and through neoliberal conceptions of the educated child. As a result, modern-day institutional music and arts education can be an "uncaring" environment for the child where the needs, desires, interests, and community relationships are ignored. An ethic of care, in contrast, honors the subjective and relational learning acts that arise in learning communities with others through the arts.

An ethic of care was regarded as an essential component of the project; this was particularly important for a community project in the performing arts because many teachers and parents had previously experienced feelings of separation and detachment from music, dance, and drama. These arts had, in some cases, generated feelings of uselessness. This was particularly noticeable in music with teachers who shied away from singing with the children because they felt they themselves could not sing. It became important, then, that we approach the performing arts in a caring way, a way that accepted the teachers as they were. Indeed, caring meant looking at both teachers and children in new ways—for instance, as musical beings who had rhythm in their language and play, or as dancing beings who expressed themselves daily through physical gestures. A caring ethic enabled each center community to come to the performing arts on their own terms and not from feelings of inadequacy or fear.

Implications for Community Music

One thing that stood out in the MAPS project was that embracing all the performing arts broadened the possibilities for new experiences and learning. The multidimensional aspect of the performing arts allowed individual teachers and individual students to shine depending on their specific interests and desires. Not only that, but the combination of the arts, as experienced in the final community events, offered more powerful outcomes for the children, parents, and teachers. Community music programs to date (as reported in many research or practice journals) have tended not to engage in other art forms beyond the sphere of music. From an ethical and community point of view, a more multimodal approach to community music—a broadening to community arts—would potentially offer children and youth more opportunities for expression.

Another important aspect that stood out in the MAPS project was the notion of community as a very powerful tool for addressing specific needs in institutional education. Although it should be said that early childhood centers tend to be less structured and in many ways are more innovative than other education institutions like schools and universities, the impact of the community model was hard to ignore. Music and the performing arts more generally tend to be taught through carefully designed performative structures in educational institutions, and often through staged performances and a variety of skills and knowledge tests and examinations. While these forms of learning and assessment can be instructive, the absence of community-mindedness and an uncaring ethic can, as argued earlier, elicit a sense of disconnection and nihilism. This disconnect is well known and has in fact led to the community music movement transporting itself away from institutional education to a place where it can have more impact, away from the "hang-ups" of institutional music education. What the MAPS project demonstrated, however, was that a strong sense of community and meaningful relationships have an important role to play in the reform and sustainability of performing arts education in schools and early childhood centers, and that community music can play a part in this reform.

Finally, the MAPS project offered an interesting pedagogical model that had a certain synergy with how community music is often taught through workshops and improvisatory contexts. Closer investigation of how the community artists worked with teachers and children showed how an open and inclusive pedagogical stance often led to productive, child-centered interest points and a heightened sense of interest and desire in the group. There is considerable potential here for further exploring how improvisatory pedagogies work in different contexts, through sensitive and exploratory approaches to teaching and learning, in both community music and more formalized early childhood settings like those experienced in MAPS.

Note

1 The MAPS project report can be found on the Teaching and Learning Research Initiative website at http://www.tlri.org.nz/tlri-research/research-completed/ece-sector/move-act-play-and-sing-maps-exploring-early-childhood. I would like to acknowledge all the authors of the final project report who in some way played a part in the collective research experience, namely, David Lines, Chris Naughton, John Roder, Jacoba Matapo, Marjolein Whyte, and Tiffany Liao.

References

Barrett, Margaret. 2006. "Inventing songs, inventing worlds: The 'genesis' of creative thought and activity in young children's lives." *International Journal of Early Years Education* 14 (3): 201–220. doi:10.1080/09669760600879920.

Dahlberg, Gunilla, and Peter Moss. 2006. "Introduction: Our Reggio Emilia." In *In Dialogue with Reggio Emilia: Listening, Researching and Learning,* edited by C. Rinaldi, 1–22. London and New York: Routledge.

de Vries, Peter. 2006. "Being there: Creating music-making opportunities in a childcare centre." *International Journal of Music Education* 24 (3): 255–270. doi:10.1177/0255761406069661.

Green, Lucy. 2008. *Music, Informal Learning and the School: A New Classroom Pedagogy.* London: Ashgate.

Knudsen, Jan. 2008. "Children's improvised vocabularies: Learning communication and technology of the self." *Contemporary Issues in Early Childhood* 9 (4): 287–296. doi:10.2304/ciec.2008.9.4.287.

Lines, David, and C. Naughton. 2009. "Changing Places: Openness, Pedagogy and Heidegger." Paper presented at the Philosophy of Education Society of Australasia Annual Conference, The East–West Center, University of Hawai'i, December 3–6, 2009.

Marsh, Kathryn. 2008. *The Musical Playground: Global Tradition and Change in Children's Songs and Games.* New York: Oxford University Press.

Mawson, Brent. 2010. "Finding our way: Interpreting Reggio in the New Zealand context." *Early Childhood Folio* 14 (1): 18–22.

Ministry of Education. 1996. *Te Whaariki: He Whaariki matauranga mo nag mokopuna o Aotearo/Early Childhood Curriculum*. Wellington: Learning Media.

Rinaldi, Carlina. 2001. "A pedagogy of listening." *Children of Europe* 1: 2–5.

Young, Susan. 1995. "Listening to the music of early childhood." *British Journal of Music Education* 12 (1): 52–58. doi:10.1017/s0265051700002394.

PART III

Connecting Community Music to Teaching and Learning Contexts

CHAPTER 13

Step Outside and Bring in the World

A Wealth of Community Musics at Your Doorstep

Jennifer Walden

International schools are generally made up of students from forty to sixty different countries, including some students from the host country. Students typically attend an international school because one or both of their parents are working in the host country as expatriates. In most cases, schools are located somewhere in or on the outskirts of a city, with teachers and families living in the city and commuting to school. Characteristic of these settings is the fact that the school exists within a host-country culture that is potentially very different from the home cultures of its students. This in essence makes every local cultural event a possible learning experience for students and families. In many international schools teachers follow a prescribed curriculum (predominantly British or American), and to varying degrees include aspects of the surrounding culture. Some teachers have the flexibility, coupled with the desire, to enhance programs and design entire units based on events occurring in the community. These teachers embrace the culture, its festivals, customs, and traditions, and do their best to organize firsthand experiences for students.

In my years of living overseas as an international school music teacher, I have often felt there are many cultural experiences occurring virtually on our doorsteps: experiences that are integral to understanding the host country's culture and its people; experiences that can enrich learning in our student's lives as well as our own. Educators are facilitators of learning opportunities and, for some, traditional cultural displays occurring within the area can be formulated, with proper facilitation, into connections between students and culture bearers or, from a larger view, school with community. These connections require thought, time, and planning, but are well worth the effort.

As an international school educator, I share my observations through an autoethnographic approach about discovery, investigation, learning, organizing, and sharing. Often a novice with respect to many cultural phenomena, I found myself in partnership with students, taking the plunge along with them into discovery and understanding. In the following narratives and case studies I will highlight components leading toward successful school–community relationships. Themes integral to connecting host culture music and schools will be illuminated throughout each section.

Taiwan

My journey through Asia as an international school music teacher began in Taiwan in 1981. Taipei American School (TAS) is a large international school for expatriates situated in a suburban community. Teaching and support staff includes expatriates along with locally hired teachers. I began my work at TAS as a student teacher in the music program, which ran elementary general music classes and band and choir at the middle- and high-school levels.

The first step toward building school–community relationships for music making is searching out what is available in the community and the school itself. In Taipei, events occur every few weeks in the city's communities. They are usually advertised on radio, the Internet, or posters (in the local language). More often, community members know of events and spread the word to friends, which is usually the case with teachers at international schools: much of the time, colleagues who are from the host country inform teachers of upcoming cultural events. In addition, expatriate teachers and families who are acquainted with community members through sports, music, art, dance, religion, and other recreational activities find out and share information about upcoming events. As a teacher eager to learn about events occurring in the area, I frequently asked my local colleagues and growing circle of local friends about upcoming concerts, presentations, and performances. In addition, I spent time exploring the country by train, bus, and on foot, and was lucky enough to come upon the occasional event just by chance, such as funeral processions (musicians, mourners, professional wailers), the opening of a new business (lion dance, fireworks), festivals in rural towns (an ocean celebration in Tamsui that occurs only every nine years was a highlight), lantern festivals, and temple celebrations, to name a few. To me, even the rhythmic chantings of Taiwanese paper collectors, soup vendors, and portable food-stall owners held their own distinct musical identities.

The second step is to initiate communication. Often, local colleagues or friends who know about particular events are happy to help with initial introductions between teachers and community members, providing translations when/if needed. Conversely, if a local colleague or friend is not available, language may be the first obstacle. Certainly in my experience learning the language of each host country has been invaluable, but it cannot be expected that everyone will have the opportunity to study the local language. Therefore, at times, just being bold is what is required to establish initial contact. This means throwing inhibitions aside, preparing what needs to be asked, calculating an opportune moment, and approaching a performer or person involved in an event. Often if they do not understand what is being asked, they will find someone who does.

In my first few months in Taiwan I attended many cultural events, determined to try to make connections with musicians, and usually finding success. From my perspective, musicians were often surprised at first, not only because I was an obvious foreigner, but also because I was a foreigner interested in their music (this surprise was even more evident when I became the foreigner interested in their music who also spoke their language). Sometimes they seemed a little embarrassed and would smile and laugh, but when they realized I was genuinely interested, they would do their best to communicate or find someone who could.

Dynamics changed when I was able to speak enough Mandarin to (1) make introductions, (2) talk about their music with them, (3) ask about bringing students to rehearsals, and (4) arrange for musicians to possibly visit the school. No longer did everything have to be translated through a third person, saving time and giving me a firsthand picture of what the musicians were saying about their music. Some musicians were eager to have me try playing their instruments, and some were very shy and stood back to watch.

Problems with cultural differences were few. Perhaps the initial issue in some cases was that of validity. Often I sensed that it was strange to the musicians with whom I spoke that this tall, Caucasian, Mandarin-speaking foreigner was seriously interested in their music. It seemed to take a few minutes of conversation to get over this first hurdle. Furthermore, sometimes I suspected the musicians were saying "yes" to my requests because it was what they felt I wanted to hear. It initially took more than one visit from me for the musicians to be convinced that I was earnest in my pursuit. When the musicians realized I was serious about learning and sharing their music with my students, conversation would turn to the possibility of visits, discussing schedules, and dates. Often musicians had daytime jobs as well, making it more difficult for them to visit the school, but the idea of students visiting them was usually well received. The most difficult element at this point was not cultural but technological: maintaining connection before the time of cell phones, e-mail, and fax machines was a challenge. Phone calls began with a few minutes of confusion, followed by repetition of times and dates for arranged visits. These had to be repeated a few times before engagements just to make sure details were secure. Sometimes taking a few students to a rehearsal was all that resulted, but this in itself was a rich experience for the students: to be in the rehearsal atmosphere, watching the dynamics of the group, hearing the sonorities, and making their own connections to the event.

Chinese New Year, one of the biggest events of the year in Taiwan, is a spectacle of music, dance, theater, decorations, food, clothing, fireworks, and family traditions. It is also an opportune time to have community musicians come into the school and share with students the features that identify the holiday. This was approached in a number of ways at TAS and included all or a combination of the following:

- Guests work with students in classrooms on activities such as calligraphy, lanterns, *hong bao* (red, decorated envelopes in which money is placed to give to children), and typical decorations for the season. Teachers organize schedules for visitors and delegate age-appropriate activities to different grade levels: younger students make paper-cut lanterns; middle- and upper-school students create red posters adorned with traditional Chinese New Year characters painted during calligraphy classes and decorate *hong bao* in Chinese brush painting styles. Teachers assist with setup and materials, and those who can do the calligraphy collaborate with the guest to ensure that students are getting the most out of the activity.
- Special sessions are organized for food demonstrations for teachers and students. These are often led by TAS parents who are Chinese American, who work with students in their homerooms to create red-bean New Year sticky-rice cakes. Foods that require more preparation are brought in by Chinese families and shared as samples.

- Presentations given on family traditions and customs. TAS family members give talks to middle- and upper-school classes on what occurs in their households as Chinese New Year approaches. These presentations are scheduled into regular class times, taking about forty minutes and covering clothing, fireworks, decorations, and family gatherings.
- Traditional Chinese New Year songs taught by visiting musicians in collaboration with Taipei American School music teachers. These musicians are often family members or TAS friends who visit scheduled music classes.
- Lion- and dragon-dance troupes perform outside (at separate times), offering all students the opportunity to see and hear the combination of drums, gongs, and cymbals as musicians accompany movement. These dances take place outside, usually in the afternoon when other activities are complete.
- Students travel with teachers off school campus to attend community lion- and/or dragon-dance performances.

Each year activities vary, depending on availability of community artists and funding. Guests are always provided with a schedule, food and drinks, and are paid for their time.

As much as most school–community events are successful, there are naturally occasions upon which plans fall through and/or ideas about experiences conflict. Occasionally culture bearers, earnest as their intentions are to share their art, do not have experience working with students and are not prepared for the educational dimension of their visit. Musicians are not necessarily teachers; with this in mind, if a visitor is unsure how to proceed, teachers can employ techniques to maintain student engagement. With some pre-planning, the teacher and visitor can coordinate age-relevant sessions, explanations, possibility of stories, and question-inspired dialogue to pave the way for connections with students and help make experiences meaningful. If there is a failure to connect, learning is minimal, or worse, the experience has a negative impact. Another issue is that of time. If the organizer interprets a given time as precise and the guest interprets it as a relative guideline, or vice versa, complications may occur. Disappointment may also occur if the organizer has a vision about what the experience will be like and this changes unexpectedly in the actual session with no opportunity to rectify it. To summarize, it is vital that each party have a clear idea of what is expected and is also prepared for that expectation to deviate somewhat. As teachers, thorough preparation can avoid disappointment.

From this first experience in an overseas school, I learned aspects of school–community relations that would carry through my career as an overseas teacher.

- Often those organizing liaisons are the teachers who are passionate about student awareness of their host country's culture.
- Most people in the host country are happy to share cultural traditions.
- Building relationships requires asking questions, following leads, organizing, graciously welcoming guests from the community into the school, and taking students to community events.
- It is important to be prepared for schedule changes, misunderstandings, and inconsistencies in what you envision the experience to be and what it actually turns out to be.
- By facilitating questions and dialogue between an otherwise inexperienced guest artist and students, a potentially negative experience can be turned into a positive one.
- Learning the local language and music augments experiences in learning about the culture and also contributes to more efficient communication with potential guest artists.

Outside of work with TAS, my fascination with Chinese music and culture grew. I spent evenings at the Taipei Chinese opera house, observing, listening, and trying to absorb as much as I could. In the teahouses of Taipei I listened to musicians play the multistringed zither (*gu-zheng*), and I was keen to learn to play one. This came to fruition on the next stop on my Asian journey.

Upon completion of my work in Taipei, I was hired to teach music and grade one at a large Chinese/American school (National Experimental High School) in the town of Hsin Chu, eighty kilometers southwest of Taipei. The Chinese portion of the school catered to children of Taiwanese employees of the large nearby industrial park. With a few Americans also employed at the park, the school offered a curriculum in English to the American children (about eighty students at the time). Outside of the school, I had a whole new town to explore and ended up in a local music store, where I was able to locate a *gu-zheng* teacher. I took weekly lessons at the music store, and through my teacher (who, coincidentally, also worked at the same school as I did but in the

Chinese portion) I was able to meet more musicians in the community. Some of these musicians played percussion for a Chinese martial arts lion-dance troupe, which I regularly observed, keen to learn the music and movement. With the combination of the unique timbres of Chinese ensemble music, the movement and music of the lion dance, and the sounds, instruments, costumes, makeup, and movements of Chinese opera, I found myself again formulating how such amazing and varied phenomena could be shared with students. This was not to be realized until a few years later.

Malaysia

The next stop on my Asian journey as an international school music teacher was in Kuala Lumpur, Malaysia, in 1991. I was hired at the International School of Kuala Lumpur (ISKL) to teach general music grades kindergarten to five and beginning band.

Kuala Lumpur, Malaysia's capital city, is a fascinating mix of three major cultures: Malay, Chinese, and Indian. ISKL has two campuses (soon to relocate as one), with a student population of more than sixteen hundred. Teaching and support staff includes expatriates along with locals representing all three host cultures. As a result of those three dominant cultures many various cultural events take place within the same city, thus providing many opportunities to make school–community connections.

During my time at ISKL, music and art teachers were dedicated to bringing Malaysia's cultural features into the school's classrooms to facilitate cross-cultural experiences. Many resources were "at our fingertips," with a large number of expatriate and local staff already involved to varying degrees in the arts and culture of the region, including *bharatanatyam* (Indian classical dance), *salwar kameez* design (a traditional style of east Indian clothes), *batik* (wax-resistant dyeing of cloth), Chinese brush painting, and *Thaipusam* devotees (Hindu festival). In addition, teachers in the music department pursued instruction in local cultural traditions, sourcing community musicians and arranging instructional sessions in Malaysian and Indonesian *gamelan* (traditional percussive instruments from Southeast Asia), *kompang* (traditional Southeast Asian frame drums played in groups for celebrations and social occasions), *silat* (north Malaysian music/martial arts combination), *dikir barat* (vocal style sung in groups, usually on the topic of current social and political issues, accompanied by gongs and non-pitched percussion instruments), and Chinese festival drumming. Between the cultural resources already in place at ISKL and the additional resources pursued by the music and art teachers, a highly useful and varied resource bank of community musicians was established–one that is still used today.

Connecting with the Malay Community

The first experiences students at ISKL had with Malaysian gamelan instruments were at the Malaysian Cultural Centre, where authentic gamelan instruments were housed. The center made the instruments available to school groups for scheduled periods of time, and for three years running we took students for a half-day excursion. Students played Orff instruments at school in preparation. Musicians at the center provided a short demonstration on the instruments along with dancers, after which students were given the opportunity to play under our instruction. Over the years we came to recognize musicians at the center who were always gracious and happy to see students eager to play the instruments. Through this relationship we were able to locate a set of gamelan instruments for sale and bought a set for ISKL. To this day, the instruments are housed in their own room and every student in grades kindergarten through six has the opportunity to learn to play.

Kompang (fourteen-inch shallow frame drums) are used in celebrations, festivals, athletic events, and weddings throughout Southeast Asia. With some investigation by ISKL music teachers, a musician specializing in *kompang* was located and hired to give a workshop at the school. We were able to buy class sets of *kompang* at a small shop in an old district of the city (Ahmad Toko Antik); this connection remained strong for the five years that I was in Malaysia; the proprietor had gongs, *angklung* (pitched bamboo tubes suspended in frames, shaken to make a sound), *gendang* (drums), *suling* (a type of bamboo flute), single gamelan instruments, *wayang kulit* and *wayang golek* (shadow puppets and solid wood puppets), and many other instruments and artifacts from the area. He played a significant role in helping us locate musicians, instruments, and cultural events in Kuala Lumpur.

When Hari Raya Puasa (celebration of the end of the fasting month of Ramadan) is under way, it is an excellent time to access community members to bring their traditions into the classroom. With many Muslims working at ISKL, these connections were seamless, with members of extended families offering their time and expertise. Guests led activities in making the following:

- *Ketupat:* a rice dumpling traditionally packed inside a woven palm-leaf pouch. The pouch itself is very distinct; replicas of the pouch alone are made, in bright ribbon and other synthetic materials. Art teachers invite *ketupat* makers into regularly scheduled art classes, assisting and facilitating engagement as needed.

- *Baju kurung, baju kebaya* (traditional Malaysian Muslim outfits for women) and *baju melayu* (for men). Students and staff are encouraged to bring their Hari Raya clothes to school to share the different styles, colors, and accessories. Often these sessions take place in music classes.
- *Kuih lapis* (sweet layered dessert) and *bandung* drink (rose water and milk) are brought in by families for students to sample. Classroom teachers organize community members to bring samples.

Guests were gracious, happy to share their customs, and treated with respect by students. Because many were members of ISKL families, students were able to make more direct connections with them, meeting the parents, aunts, uncles, and so on, of their classmates.

Perhaps the most impactful school–community music experience attended by ISKL was the music camp organized and hosted by Medan International School, Medan, Indonesia. Students attending the camp spent four to five days in workshops led by local Indonesian musicians, studying Javanese, Sundanese, and Balinese *gamelan, anklung, gordang sembilan* (a set of nine large drums played in a row), *suling,* and *tingklik* (a bamboo gamelan instrument of eleven hollow bamboo tubes suspended with string over a wooden frame). Community musicians were hired each year to teach participating students. Chaperoning teachers were assigned to groups of students, attending workshops with them and helping out when needed. Students fortunate enough to attend for one or more years formed friendships with students from other participating schools and with the musicians leading the workshops.

Because music and art teachers at ISKL continued to have the positive results of bringing Malaysia's culture into the classroom, establishing connections with the community, and taking students to work with community musicians, the administration maintained funding for it to continue. Students were excited about meeting community musicians, being welcomed into different environments, hosting guest musicians, and playing instruments and music of the region; some students became skilled in more difficult techniques and were highlighted in concerts, assemblies, and classroom presentations.

Connecting with the Indian Community

Exploration into Indian music began with my fascination with the Indian sitar. Turning to my Indian colleagues as first resources, I was directed to the

Temple of Fine Arts, a center for Indian music, dance, yoga, and martial arts. My visit resulted in my finding a sitar teacher, who then became a valuable connection for the school when festivals of India were being recognized.

In the autumn, Deepavali, also called Diwali or Divali, is a festival of lights celebrated by Hindus, Sikhs, and Jains. Included in the celebrations are music, dance, decorations, food, traditional clothing, lights, and family traditions. Art and music presentations were arranged to lead students in a variety of Deepavali traditions, including the following:

- Art classes led by guests in *rangoli* (patterns created at entrances, on living-room floors, or in courtyards) using materials such as colored rice, dry flour, colored sand, or flower petals and meant as sacred welcoming places for Hindu deities. Students fill in pre-made symmetrical designs or create their own patterns and fill them in. Some designs were on hallway floors, typical of the tradition.
- Clay oil lamp (*diya, divaa, deepa, deepam,* or *deepak*) building and decorating, under the guidance of community artists and school family members
- Guest musicians (with the help of my sitar teacher and the Temple of Fine Arts) demonstrating instruments in music classes, culminating in an assembly for the entire school (often a north Indian sitar and tabla performance)
- Dance specialists (including staff members) presenting traditional and modern versions of Indian dance
- Relatives of staff members presenting their *salvar kameez* fashion designs
- Hindu families attending ISKL sharing traditional foods and presenting preparation methods to select classes
- Henna, or *mehndi* (plant-based dye used for decorating hands and nails) demonstrations carried out by ISKL family members

Similarly to what I had experienced in Taiwan, locating community musicians and artists required time and effort. To reiterate, ISKL already had a pool of specialists within its own walls who were excellent resources. They were able to connect us with communities outside of the school, which we then visited and investigated possibilities for school–community events. Most Indians living in Malaysia speak English as well as Tamil, making communication manageable and eliminating the need for an interpreter. Logistically it was easier to have guests come to the school rather than taking students out of school for the day, because (1) out-of-school trips take music teachers away for an entire day of instruction, (2) substitutes are required to cover music classes, and (3) transportation must be organized long before the event takes place. Often musicians were happy to be guests at the school.

Because the Hindu festival of Thaipusam occurs not far from ISKL's elementary campus (Batu Caves), students heard about it and often were curious to learn what it is about. The festival is limited to only two locations in the world, and we felt fortunate to have an account from someone directly involved. One of ISKL's local staff, a devotee for a few years, agreed to help reveal some the mysteries of the event. He graciously offered his time and knowledge, providing insightful information on devotees' activities leading up to the festival (cleansing themselves through prayer, focusing only on their devotion, and fasting for approximately forty-eight days prior to the event). He described the dances performed by *kavadi* bearers (*kavadi* is both a dance and an apparatus carried by devotees) and the instruments played (to accompany trance and movement as devotees make their 272-step journey up to the caves). Before discussing the festival with students, difficult aspects of the event had to be negotiated (piercing, trances, self-inflicted discomfort), with respect to age appropriateness. As opposed to sensationalizing the event, the goal was to promote understanding of traditions and why devotees carry out each ritual. In addition to creating a basis for understanding for students this also deterred stereotyping and dispelled rumors. Teachers did not take students to the festival; any students who attended were accompanied by their parents.

To facilitate such a varied array of activities at ISKL, music and art teachers worked together on schedules, budget, and the organization of guest visitors. Most activities took place during already scheduled music and art classes. The advantage of such scheduling was that it made it possible for music and art teachers to attend each session, at the ready to assist in facilitating optimum student participation, general management, and clear communication. As guests revisited the school over the years, they became accustomed to what worked best and adjusted their presentations accordingly. These community members have been longtime "associates" with ISKL and are welcomed warmly by staff and students upon each visit. Rarely did misunderstandings occur, and if they did, it was usually over time. As stressed earlier in this chapter, time is regarded differently from one culture to the next, and this must be taken into consideration when organizing school–community events.

Connecting with the Chinese Community

As 30 percent of Malaysia's population is of Chinese ancestry, there are many opportunities for exploring Chinese music. Kuala Lumpur hosts a large range of Chinese musical organizations, which can be found through festivals, cultural events, and traditional music shops.

Chinese New Year is a widely celebrated festival in Malaysia and certainly was not overlooked by ISKL. The ever-popular lion-dance visit is organized through connections maintained by ISKL staff. Students love hearing the sounds of the big drum approaching through the hallways, following one and sometimes two lions to the gym for the performance. Usually troupes present a traditional dance, during which lions move characteristically to the drum rhythms, working their way around the audience, pretending to eat mandarin oranges and throwing the peels out at them. One year's performance brought a surprise when, instead of throwing mandarin peels, the lion dancers shook pop cans and sprayed students with Fanta and Coke—a good reminder to teachers always to have an idea of what visitors are planning. With live examples to emulate, students are inspired to play traditional rhythms on classroom percussion instruments after presentations. For my first two years at ISKL, music students played Chinese lion-dance rhythms on substituted drums. From our connections with musicians in the Chinese community we soon had culturally traditional *da gu* (large drum) and *luo* (cymbals) for the students to play.

This brings to light the issue of substitute versus culturally traditional instruments. In conversations over the years, a number of community musicians have voiced their curiosity regarding how students in my classes played the music without "the instruments." In my experience, students generally do not care about the authenticity of the instruments they are playing as long as they are making music. However, I have also observed if students *do* play culturally traditional instruments, and are then given the choice between these and substitutes, they prefer the culturally traditional.

Similar to activities at the school in Taipei during Chinese New Year, the following are popular among students at ISKL:

- Demonstrations of traditional foods (including samples from the ISKL Chinese community)
- Calligraphy demonstrations with opportunities to participate, often carried out in scheduled art classes

- ISKL family members sharing stories, decorations, and traditions organized in classrooms through collaboration with teachers and parents
- Lion and dragon-dance musicians working with students, teaching patterns and playing technique (when time permits, usually in scheduled music classes)

Connections with ISKL Chinese families grew over the years as these families became a regular part of Chinese New Year celebrations.

Chinese opera specialists took some time to locate. After weeks of following leads, speaking with artists, and attending events that included Chinese opera, I established connection with a singer able to run sessions in Chinese opera makeup, movement, and vocal technique. I met her during a Chinese festival in Kuala Lumpur when I made my way backstage at a Chinese opera, asking to observe the actors putting on their makeup and costumes. I had a clear idea of what I felt would work best for students, and found the perfect candidate. She was an accomplished Chinese opera singer who spoke English and was intrigued with the idea of sharing her profession with students. She was hired to work with grade four students and do a short presentation for the entire school at the end of her daylong visit. To ensure that the day would go smoothly, it was important to establish the following:

- Time of arrival (transportation paid for)
- Time and duration of each class
- Breaks scheduled, including food and drinks
- Expectations for each class, broken down to time allotted for makeup (two students selected to have their faces painted while others watch), movement (focused on battle-scene choreography), and singing techniques (both with the entire class)
- Order of events at the presentation: time and expectations
- Amount being paid for the guest's visit

With these guidelines in place for visiting artists, little is left up to chance, therefore facilitating a successful visit. The only obstacle that came up with our Chinese opera guest was her preference to have a person sing *to* for the presentation. This was quickly rectified with a request to one of ISKL's local Chinese staff who had studied enough Chinese opera to pose opposite the professional and create more authentic staging.

As a contrast to the loud music of the Chinese lion dance and Chinese opera battle scene, students experienced the quieter genre of the *gu-zheng* (Chinese zither). Although a guest specialist could not be organized, my work with Chinese *gu-zheng* players in Taiwan made it possible for me to lead activities experimenting with sounds of the instrument and accompanying instruments (*muyu,* a woodblock carved in the shape of a fish and struck with a wooden mallet; *Xiaobo,* small cymbals). In their encounters with these instruments, students not only created new sound combinations but also learned that Chinese music is not limited only to loud, historically outdoor genres.

Like all forms of art, music changes as musicians try new ideas, blend different sonorities, and create new sounds. Through community connections, ISKL music teachers came to know a young music teacher at a Chinese Malaysian school. He invited us to see the work he was doing with *da gu* (meaning "large drum" in Mandarin; Chinese drum used for lion and dragon dance). He had about fifty Chinese teenage musicians playing the *da gu* using traditional mallets and playing technique, but infused the choreography of *taiko* drumming (also "large drum" in Japanese, utilizing distinct movement while playing drums) into the piece, including visual effects with long rolls of colored silk creating "waves" in between the drum lines. The spectacle was a tremendous array of audio and visual artistry, the leader being strict and precise in his vision and directions to students. Although our own students were not able to experience the performance, the ideas we gathered from it and the relationship we had with the Chinese musician afforded us many inspiring concepts to share with our own students and provided connections that led toward acquiring our own Chinese lion dance drums. This same musician is now the artistic director of Hands Percussion, an organization based in Kuala Lumpur (est. 1997) that performs worldwide and also runs community outreach programs that afford students all over Malaysia the chance to learn to play a variety of percussion instruments.

From these first steps of getting to know staff and faculty at ISKL and their respective areas of expertise, researching what occurs in the local culture to resourcing musicians, learning from them, taking students to visit them, and inviting them to the school, strong ties with community are created that last for years.

Singapore

From Malaysia, my Asian journey took me a few hundred kilometers southeast to live in Singapore in 1996. Singapore American School (SAS) is a large international school with a diverse population (now four thousand students) and a strongly supported arts programs. My teaching position was elementary general music kindergarten to grade four, with beginning orchestral strings in grade five. Already familiar with the three dominant cultures of the area (Malay, Chinese, and Indian), I was interested in learning how SAS approaches building relationships with community musicians. Although it came to my attention that few connections had been established as yet, my new colleagues were committed to the idea and we became allies in our endeavors to explore what was available.

When school began in August 1996, the new SAS campus was not completely finished and therefore building company employees were still present when classes began. One construction worker who seemed particularly interested in music activities turned out to be a dance instructor who ran a dance school in India. We invited him to teach basic *bharatanatyam* steps to our students when possible. He was a great asset to our classes and clearly preferred dancing to laying cement. In addition, from the many SAS teaching assistants who were from the region we sought help in making decorations and learning local songs for UN Day celebrations. Owners of local food stalls and Housing Development Board (HDB) shops contributed their expertise in *kompang*, traditional clothing, festival foods, and live lion-dance performances.

Chinese Music

I turn our attention again to Chinese New Year, as one of the images that prevails is flatbed trucks whizzing through the city, loaded with drummers and lion dancers on the back in full costume (including someone clutching the lion's head), playing the large drum and cymbals with enthusiasm and volume that could not be ignored. Usually one hears them before seeing them, the drum resonating above the traffic mayhem. In fact, this is a method of advertisement, and it works: my connection with a lion-dance troupe began with their truck passing near my neighborhood. I heard the drums, and fortunately, shortly after passing by they stopped at a local food stall and I was able to catch up with them. The leader and I discussed schedules and cost, and I was able to hire the troupe for the last day of Chinese New Year (the festival goes on for two weeks). We arranged for them to do a performance in the community in which I was living, enabling SAS students and friends to attend the presentation. Afterwards the performers, some of whom could communicate in English, were happy to talk to students about their work and demonstrate their instruments and lion-dance choreography. I had a lengthy conversation with the troupe leader, discussing how he teaches his new students and what he finds works best with young learners. As an added bonus, the impressive lion's head and tail were on my doorstep the following morning with a note saying, "I hope you are able to continue teaching lion dance to your students, now with this real Chinese lion." With the acquisition of the lion's head and tail, students at SAS were given insight into a more culturally traditional experience, learning how to operate the large mask and how to work together to make the lion look "real." As a collaborative project, the Mandarin classes at SAS accompanied the student lion dancers as they went from classroom to classroom before Chinese New Year. The lion made its way once around the room as drums and cymbals played, at which point music stopped while Mandarin students recited traditional Chinese New Year phrases. Over the years, with the resources of a local shop ("Eng Tan Huat," on River Valley Road), SAS has furnished music classrooms with Chinese lions, dragons, drums, cymbals, and gongs.

Malay/Indonesian Music

Gamelan music had its inception in the SAS music program through activities played on Orff metallophones. In researching where to find a set of gamelan instruments in Singapore, music teachers were lead to LASALLE-SIA College of the Arts, an institute that has since grown into a thriving arts and media school. Because of the success of the "gamelan visit" program in Kuala Lumpur, I was ready to try replicating this with SAS students. This began with a Saturday morning visit to the college with a few interested students, whose parents thought it a good idea and were happy to provide transportation. I had arranged with the college to have use of the instruments for an hour. Employees of the college were very helpful, letting students explore and also helping out when they tried playing the pieces they knew from lessons at SAS. The event grew to a half-day excursion occurring on a school day during which full classes of music students travelled by bus to the college, played gamelan instruments, learned about the history and instruments of gamelan, and watched a short video on gamelan. SAS music teachers led the experience, preparing students first in music classes and facilitating the transfer to authentic gamelan instruments at the college. Students of the college were at the ready to assist when needed, which made for a mutually collaborative event: SAS teachers and students meeting with and learning from college students, and college students learning from SAS teachers about engaged teaching methods. This relationship with LASALLE-SIA College of the Arts brought about further learning for SAS music teachers, as they joined an evening gamelan group at the college.

Because there had been little incorporation of local musical genres prior to my arrival at SAS, the administration was open to the idea but slightly skeptical. Upon recognizing the positive outcomes of the gamelan experience, they suggested investigating a gamelan purchase for the school. Acquisition of SAS's own gamelan instruments was made possible through funding from the Parent Teacher's Association. It has since been given its own home and is a featured part of the walk-by route for new or prospective parents, who are always fascinated and enthusiastic that their children will have the opportunity to learn these beautiful instruments. All students have nine weeks of lessons each year and the opportunity to perform for the school and parents.

In each of my Asian locations as an international school music educator I was able to find not only community musicians willing and happy to share their art but also colleagues just as driven as I to tap into local communities and learn about their activities in music. We learned (through unfailing determination) the importance of

- being aware of the expertise of one's own colleagues, local and expatriate;
- keeping one's ears and eyes open to cultural events occurring in surrounding communities;
- the nuances of making initial contact and beginning communication (sensitivity to cultural values and expectations);
- being clear from both parties about times, scheduling, and expectations;
- making sure guests feel welcomed, appreciated, and held in high esteem; and
- paying artists an amount that reflects respect for their expertise.

The outcomes, so frequently positive, warranted the time and effort required to make connections and establish relationships. While students find reward in these experiences through listening, playing, observing, and sharing, there are less tangible benefits as well: namely, developing empathy and understanding, making connections, and acquiring pride in their own cultures and in knowing about other cultures.

CHAPTER 14

Shuo Chang as Burdens in Song

Xinyao *and Education Communities of Practice in Singapore*

Eugene Dairianathan and Chee Hoo Lum

The April 2014 issue of STAR-POST (an e-publication of the Singapore Teachers' Academy of the Arts [STAR] of the Ministry of Education [MOE]), revealed how the academy's music master teachers (MTTs) and music program managers (PMs) had been conducting fieldwork research on a recent initiative for schools:

> We have been learning at workshops and dialogue sessions with various arts practitioners, conducting interviews with pioneers in various music genres, designing and trialing lessons with colleagues at the Arts Education Branch (AEB) and our STAR Associate teachers, and been in conversation with our partners at the National Library Board (NLB) and the National Arts Council (NAC). These have guided STAR's design of a unique professional development curriculum for teaching living music traditions in Singapore and to support schools in the implementation of the revised syllabus for General Music from 2015. Our curriculum, entitled *Teaching Living Legends,* distinctively develops participants in their music *practice, pedagogy* and *perspective.* (MOE 2014, 2; emphasis in original)

The message went on to publicize the launch of a teaching seminar in July 2014 with a view to developing a pedagogical resource kit "rich with pedagogical ideas and multimedia resources" to be made available to seminar participants in order to "further support our teachers in applying their learning" (MOE 2014, 2). The musical practice of *Xinyao* was included among the many local musical practices such as *Dikir Barat* (Lee 2008), Indian Orchestra, Malay Rhythms, the National Anthem, Singapore Songs, and Singapore Composers.

The curriculum package came replete with suggestions of teaching plans based on a selection of well-known *Xinyao* songs, interviews with creators, performers, and participants' views of the musical practice and a resource package that included background information about the practice sourced from newspaper articles in both English and Mandarin.

The inclusion of Malay folk traditions, Indian Orchestra, the National Anthem of Singapore, and Singapore Songs would have been "givens." Malay folk traditions speak to a sense of indigeneity, considering the existence of a Malay community before the founding of Singapore by Stamford Raffles in 1819 as part of the East India Company and later a British colony (Phan 2004, 18–20). *Dikir Barat,* while being of East Malaysian ascription (Lee 2008), is legitimized as Malay music and culture in Singapore. The national anthem "Majulah Singapura" alongside Singapore songs, fund and fuel National Education in Singapore based on constructed paradigm of a Singaporean identity that transcends ascriptions and allegiances of politics, language, religion, and culture and represents the nation's four major communities—Chinese, Malay, Indian, and Other (hereafter CMIO)—purportedly constituting Singaporean-ness. This CMIO construct continues to affect National Education through its shaping of the use of music in Singapore's public school system. For instance, in writing music textbooks for Singaporean classrooms, one must not only be cognizant of, but also clearly reflect the CMIO construct in discussions of musical practices, introducing songs appropriate to this context in a category called National Education Songs that exhort political and communal stability and promise the sustainability of Singapore's economic success (Dairianathan and Lum 2012). The inclusion of local composers speaks to the indigenization of global practice, in this case the inclusion of the Euro-American art music tradition, but now by local composers.

The Singapore Indian Orchestra[1] emerged out of two initiatives: the People's Association (hereafter PA), which initiated the Singapore Indian Orchestra and Choir; and a much earlier consolidation that identified with the Indian community noted for the promulgation of north and south Indian classical and folk traditions, including dance and theater forms in the entity of the Singapore Indian Fine Arts Association (hereafter SIFAS).[2] Koh points out that the PA was "the community development arm of the Prime Minister's Office" (1989, 885), and by 1985 the Ministry of Community Development was created, incorporating the Cultural Affairs Division of the Ministry of Culture and the PA, which by Koh's accounts represented "a logical development" (719). That the Singapore Indian Orchestra (formerly Singapore Indian Orchestra and Choir) should have been seen as consolidation of practice by a community by PA may be seen as legitimization at the national level of a musical practice, albeit one experimental in its soundscapes.

It should therefore not surprise us to see *Dikir Barat,* Malay rhythms, the national anthem, and Singapore songs and the Indian Orchestra exuding National Education imperatives. But what of the curating of *Xinyao?* What is this musical practice? What and who does it speak of and for? What is its relationship with those who were sensuously imbibed in this practice? When did it begin and how did it proliferate and permeate? Who did this practice speak to, and in what ways? What are the resonances that make the association of the practice with National Education initiatives, if it did or does?

When *Xinyao* is included in the curatorial practice (Peers and Brown 2003) of an agency of the Ministry of Education in Singapore[3]—the single most influential service provider for educational needs for its residents from early childhood through higher education—one is prompted to ask how *Xinyao* connects with indigeneity, indigenization, local cultivation of global musical practices, and its co-opting into a national/ist agenda.

This chapter seeks to explore the musical practice of *Xinyao* as one full of a sense of genealogy and tradition, practice/s, principal protagonists and repertoire, correlations as a community and among other communities' ubiquity, connections with government/ality, and continuity. This exploration will serve to examine critically the nature, role, and identity of *Xinyao* as a musical practice with subscription towards a consolidation of community of practice. Finally, this chapter reflects on *Xinyao* as a journey/ing of reliving (contra reviving) a musical practice, particularly in the curatorship of an agency of an educational agenda of the Singapore government.

A Brief Chronology

Much of this account is drawn from Dairianathan and Chia (2007, 149–150). Students from junior colleges and polytechnics formed groups and performed their own "ballads" and songs from broadcast media in their schools and on their campuses, predating newspaper articles and newly minted terminology that became *Xinyao.* The first reported *Xinyao* concerts graced the period

1983–1985. In the same period, local broadcast media featured creators-as-performers on a half-hour radio program. A singing competition (better known as the Talentime Series) organized by local Chinese (read Mandarin-language) broadcast media introduced an amateur vocal group category in 1983. *San Ren Dui* 三人队 became the first *Xinyao* group to win this section of the singing contest in 1984. The release of the first *Xinyao* compilation album in 1984, *21 Tomorrow*, generated sales of twenty thousand copies and aroused considerable interest in print and broadcast media. *Xinyao* songs like "Chance Meeting" by Eric Moo gained entry to the Singapore Chinese billboard charts. Thomas Teo, Dawn Gan, and Eric Moo later became the first *Xinyao* singers to successfully release solo recordings, encouraging the Chinese talent-time series to introduce a "local compositions" category. The inaugural two-night Xinyao festival was held in 1985, fuelling the formation of the Young Songwriters Society in May 1986, whose aim was to promote *Xinyao* artistes and activities. By 1987, the annual festival featured "newcomers" such as strobe lights, back-up dancers, four-piece bands, performers' outstanding outfits, and slick presentation. Towards the end of the 1980s, prominent *Xinyao* songwriters took to singing their own songs, Liang Wern Fook and Loy Fei Huei being the most notable.

The 1990 annual *Xinyao* festival, however, was "reduced to a school concert playing to a half-empty hall," and the 1990 Sing Music Awards was scrapped because "too few *Xinyao* albums were submitted for nomination." On the other hand, *Xinyao* gained greater interest from consumption through the public and media. In 1993, a venue for *Xinyao* enthusiasts and aspirants to sing and present their songs became possible with the opening of The Ark Lounge (based on a well-known lounge chain in Taiwan bearing the same name but not amounting to a franchise). Other lounges followed suit, like one called The Fifties. Chin Soo Feng (1994) drew attention to a radio program called *Station of Music*—launched through the joint efforts of a local radio station, "Radio 100.3FM," and a *Xinyao* organization called Feeling Associates—which aired a *Xinyao* selection to introduce "the better songs to overseas record companies. Hongkong, for example, is greatly in need of songs for its many stars."

Into the millennium, a "Xing Pop" concert of Singapore Chinese pop music from "yesterday till today" as one of the opening celebrations at the Esplanade in 2002, a two-night sold-out concert featuring *Xinyao* and Taiwanese *Mingge* 民歌 practitioners, a COMPASS (local performing rights group) press-release in 2002 of a resurgent *Xinyao* festival in mid-2003, a

Xinyao Reunion Concert on March 22, 2003, featuring Eric Moo and Friends 2004 witnessed the launch of a book and CD-anthology (Han 2004) and another edited by Liang entitled *Xin Yao: Wo Men De Ge Zai Zhe Li* 新谣: 我们的歌在这里.

A Mandarin print media article (Chen 2010) attempted to stimulate interest in *Xinyao* among a wider and younger audience drawn to prominent practitioners like Liang Wern Fook, Loi Fei Huay, and Xing Cheng Hua. This article highlighted results of a questionnaire about what *Xinyao* was or could be defined as and took on board a brief account of its prominence. A larger question loomed in the article pertaining to continuation—what it meant to have continuation, what about *Xinyao* might be continued, who might be identified in the continuation, and the ways in which such continuation might take place. While Wern Fook suggested that "continuation" might be too onerous a term, he deferred towards finding ways to maintain the vitality and energy *Xinyao* brought through its prominence and practice as well as its advocacy and accessibility to a younger and larger audience who might not know of its coruscating past or its impact on Mandarin-language popular music in Singapore. In the same year, Liang was awarded the Cultural Medallion, Singapore's highest national honor for contributions to the arts.

The release of a film *That Girl in Pinafore* (我的朋友, 我的同学, 我爱过的一切)[4] in August 2013 had *Xinyao* as one thematic feature as well as *Xinyao* repertoire, notably for Liang, his version of *Sparrow with Bamboo Twigs,* which drew on *Xinyao* and familial and metaphorical connections.[5] Prior to STAR's 2014 public promotion of *Xinyao* as one of their curatorial practices, a group of students at Hwa Chong Institution had set up an internet resource for research, education, and repositioning the practice of *Xinyao.*[6]

A brief chronology such as this accepts a revisionist disposition given that what is written sometimes clarifies and qualifies written discourse when encountering more recent oral accounts. These recent interviews also help with an understanding of alternative views of and about the practice of *Xinyao* that results in an evolving narrative. This can only have more positive bearings on a more comprehensive view of *Xinyao,* its creators, performers, and consumers, while also illuminating aspects of its practice and the community it attracted and their motivations.

Xinyao as Youth-based Creative Community

Fundamentally, *Xinyao* emerged as a shortened term for *xin jia po nian qin[g] ren chuang zuo de ge yao* (the songs composed by Singapore youths), an aphorism based on the first and last romanized syllables of a longer description. Oral interviews suggest that *Xinyao* was a term that emerged from and through the Mandarin mass-print media. An entry on *Xinyao* in Singapore describes it as a Mandarin vocal genre accompanied by guitars, which began in the early 1980s among teenage students (Lee 2001). Practitioners in this niche community of youth were known for their *use* of Mandarin as a live/lived language and for whom Mandarin informed their lives as first language. Little is explained about the role of the guitar in this phenomenon called *Xinyao,* and the practice is identified more with language and linguistics rather than musical form. Oral accounts observe how *Xinyao* was already present in events organized by Chinese literary and drama societies in secondary schools and junior colleges that had Chinese language and literature as their predominant focus. Personal interviews and anecdotal accounts reveal that many students, particularly from secondary schools and junior colleges (age group thirteen to eighteen years), formed groups and performed their own "ballads" in their schools well before this musical practice appeared in newspaper articles (Dairianathan and Chia 2007, 149–150). Oral accounts refer to the practice of amateur music making by students, but without a specific name or label affixed to this practice. According to Lin (2004), oral and aural modes of communication and transmission distinguished this practice, which was rooted in the everyday experience. Lyrics were available via cipher notation and cassette tape recordings, while tunes were sung by students who were able to recall what they had listened to and disseminated it. Transmission of repertoire took place through school exchange programs like a concert, with the lead singer using guitars or other portable instruments as accompaniment. Concerts of this nature in schools were likely to have been organized by the Chinese (Mandarin) Literary and Dramatic Society.

Although the term *Xinyao* had not yet appeared, its practice had been advertised through concerts featuring students' own compositions. Second, their songs indicate a predilection for secondary processes of music as the primary motivation for appropriating musical structures to suit their usage. Given their informality of learning through oral and aural transmission, choice of simple constructions, simple chords, and memorable melodic lines, *Xinyao* practitioners were able to be effective in creating and performing their own songs. At the level of language, a predilection for Chinese language and literature contextualizes the implications of a change to the use of English as mandatory lingua franca, even in schools that had in the past relied on Mandarin, Malay, and Tamil as their first languages of instruction.[7] Mandarin, as well as

Malay and Tamil, would then become equal (contra first) language options alongside English. Moreover, language was not only seen as a medium of grammar and syntax but also understood as a language of live/d performances of literature and culture—in this case Chinese/ness. Therefore, it would make sense to practitioners of Chinese language and literature to focus on elements of Chinese history and culture rather than music.

Xinyao as Glocal Musical Community

At the musical level, there were other sources of influence. Liang's recollections mirror the creative pathways of many like him who studied Mandarin as a first language and who engaged with and consumed music of similar influences. He referred to songs sung by his parents and their contemporaries, lullabies as well as his own ABRSM (understood in the local context as the Associated Board of the Royal Schools of Music syndicated examination system) training (Liang 2003), which drew on influences from both art song and entertainment songs but were distinguished by a more sophisticated understanding and use of Mandarin as prosaic and poetic language, and were motivated by the power of their collective experience and facilitated by directness of musical material. *Xinyao* practitioners recalled that the local Mandarin radio station broadcast a selection of college campus songs from Taiwan known as *Mingge* (民歌). Benjamin Ng's study of Japanese popular music in Singapore observes how Taiwanese songs of popular culture and mass entertainment prior to *Mingge* (民歌) "were Mandarin covers of Japanese enka (urban nostalgic and emotive songs) or kayokyoku (early Japanese pop)" (Ng 2002, 1–2). This explains *Mingge* practitioners' aversion to a popular/ized culture not entirely of their ownership despite the provenance. The predilection for college campus songs therefore represented a repertoire with which Taiwanese could identify and call their own in terms of music creating, performing, and listening. But in interviews recently conducted by STAR (MOE) researchers, it was the Japanese soundscape that provided subtle influences for the songs by some *Xinyao* practitioners fuelled by songs sung at the Japanese Red and White Festival.[8] Influence, at a more local level, included the musical practice of "poetry and music" (*Shiyue* 诗乐) by students from the former Nanyang University (today Nanyang Technological University). For Liang, *Shiyue* was very refreshing and different and had a strong influence and impact on him because songs in *Shiyue* placed emphasis on literary themes espoused in Mandarin poetry. This also goes some way to explaining why *Xinyao* was described less as a musical but more as a lyrical practice (Dairianathan and Chia 2010).

Musically, the use of electronic keyboards, guitars, and harmonicas draws on much more than Chineseness, not to mention global influences in chord progressions and the symbolism of instrumental resources. Oral interviews with *Xinyao* practitioners revealed influences of individual expression in song, fuelled by American folk artists like Don Maclean, Bob Dylan, and Peter, Paul and Mary (Koh Nam Seng 2003). This makes for an intriguing association of *Xinyao* with songs of American contemporary folk and protest culture even though the lyrical content of *Xinyao* made no connection with such protest culture agendas. Almost paradoxically, *Xinyao* opens experience to potentials and potentialities but does not necessarily prescribe. This point is made when practitioners reveal their attraction for the *secondary processes of music* of protest—songs as the *primary* motivation for appropriating musical structures to suit their usage. As with the range of social forces and processes prevalent in local and global cultures, *Xinyao* retains consonance with syncretic processes in contemporary cultures that have use and user values, with music as vehicular access.

Students, particularly from secondary schools, junior colleges, and even polytechnics, formed groups and performed their own "ballads" in their schools as well as songs from broadcast media. Given their early beginnings in school classrooms or campus spaces, much of this extra/musical learning began with the use of language. Many who came to participate in *Xinyao* were conversant with Mandarin either as a native language or as a subject in a school where it was a niche mode of lived experience. Themes in *Xinyao* songs included reminiscing about the departure of childhood, school life, the excitement of special moments, the camaraderie shared around campfires, friendships, and the laughter and tears of innocence; protests against the pressures to achieve academic excellence and material comfort; the plight and inner struggle of teenage victims of an education streaming system and broken families during the 1980s; infatuation, falling in love, naïve optimism, true tests of friendship, being lost in the process of growing up, the ever-changing identity in the lived experiences of a shopping-mall teenage protagonist called Ah Ben; and even a song exhorting the Singapore brand (Dairianathan 2004, 254–257). Many of the first songs in the musical practice of *Xinyao* resonate with Liang's accounts of his days of self-discovery and "apprenticeship" in music and text understood in the processes of writing *through* music.

Xinyao as Mandarin-conversant Community

Xinyao's rise to prominence in the 1980s in Singapore coincided with a national "Speak Mandarin Campaign" initiated in 1978 that resulted in the use of Mandarin in official communication, extending to commercial endeavor and eventually affecting the use of Chinese dialects among family and friends. For a niche community steeped in Mandarin and *live/d* practice, this would have made no difference *to* or *for* them, except for their interactions among non-Mandarin conversant communities in Singapore (Dairianathan and Chia 2010).

Public concerts of *Xinyao* helped "with" and "in" the construction of identity among Mandarin-speaking youth and the empowerment of youth communities in its early stage of development (Kong 1996, 115). Sufficient interest was created for the then Singapore Broadcasting Corporation (Mediacorp today) to run a half-hour radio program introducing *Xinyao* singers and songwriters. Other important events included the Chinese talent-time series in 1985, which introduced a "Local Compositions" category. The Boon Lay Community Centre Readers Club organized the first two-night *Xinyao* festival held at the World Trade Centre Auditorium and oversaw the formation of the Young Songwriters Society in May 1986. These activities had promoted *Xinyao* and its artistes. It is instructive that broadcast media in Singapore, in adopting Mandarin as its lingua franca for Chinese communities there, began their forays into developing Mandarin drama serials shortly after the Speak Mandarin Campaign. The rise of *Xinyao* also enabled the single local media broadcaster (SBC/TCS and Mediacorp today) to ride on *Xinyao*'s prominence towards cultivating an infrastructure to enable potential singer/songwriters to compose and sing theme songs for television drama serials as well as act in them. In this way, *Xinyao* expanded from a community of students into spheres of endeavor that eventually associated its practice with public, broadcast, and even popular culture.

Xinyao as Community-club Music

Xinyao did not go unnoticed in community music circles either. The first community center–organized *Xinyao* concert was held at the Hong Lim community center in 1984, apparently coinciding with the formation of a *Xinyao* performing group. In 1986, the PA organized a concert for young music enthusiasts from fourteen community centers in the hope that young people in other community centers would form their own *Xinyao* groups as a healthy and creative activity to express their feelings, regardless of the theme. In an article by Low Mei Mei (*Straits Times,* June 10, 1986), the PA, which in 1986 had twenty-four such groups under its aegis, hoped to popularize local ballads by working with *Xinyao* performing artists and those who had made their mark with celebrated *Xinyao* hits. With a view of *Xinyao* as the medium of expression for locally composed music, the role of the PA emerged as facilitator and coordinator to create more opportunities for *Xinyao* enthusiasts to perform, exchange, and grow through activities like concerts and competition and music camps, as well as providing technical support in management, production, and administration while performing artists concentrated on their work creating and performing music. Meanwhile, Tang Guan Seng, the parliamentary secretary (of education), stated at the closing ceremony of an inaugural *Xinyao* music camp that students would benefit more from *Xinyao* if they discussed the songs with musicians, artists, and writers of literature, adding that experienced and accomplished senior musicians would give the youngsters not only spiritual support but also practical guidance, which would help raise the standard of *Xinyao.* Subsequently, more than seventy *Xinyao* enthusiasts from community centers took part in a PA-organized three-day *Xinyao* music camp. Veterans and professionals like Eric Moo, Billy Koh, and Dawn Gan were invited to give tips and share their experiences. At that time, it was also hoped that *Xinyao* would attract participation from the local English-educated Chinese communities.

Xinyao as Commercial-based Community

It was at this *Xinyao* music camp that Billy Koh, a *Xinyao* pioneer from the group The Straw, suggested how the PA could help popularize *Xinyao* at the grassroots level while professionals concentrated on trying to get their songs onto the local chart-topping list. Billy Koh's suggestion alluded to a separation of *Xinyao*—as student-initiated community—into amateur and professional endeavors. Successes with the first *Xinyao* compilation album in 1984, *21 Tomorrow,* as well as the entry of *Xinyao* songs into Singapore Chinese Billboard charts, meant that prominent *Xinyao* practitioners were considering the machinery of popular culture to gain wider dissemination and were prepared to negotiate commercial recording industry expectations with creative endeavor and ideals. A forum in August 1987 precipitated the view that songwriters' creativity should not be hampered by the term *Xinyao* (Dairianathan and Chia 2007, 149–150).

Such processes had their own ramifications. The early 1990s seem to have been marked by an ebbing of interest in the movement. The *Xinyao* Festival, according to a 1994 newspaper article, was reduced to a school concert playing to a half-empty hall in 1990. In the same year, the *Sing Music Awards* was scrapped because too few *Xinyao* albums were submitted for nomination. The better part of the 1990s had been concerned with sustaining interest in *Xinyao,* but mainly as a community of consumption: for examples, the opening in 1993 of The Ark Lounge, based on a well-known lounge chain in Taiwan; and a radio program called *Station of Music* launched in 1994 through the joint efforts of Radio 100.3 FM and a *Xinyao* organization called Feeling Associates (reportedly initiated in 1989) with a membership of ten thousand, including those from Malaysia. It was instructive that the aim in this instance was to introduce promising songs to overseas record companies, for example Hongkong, for further commercial adventures (Dairianathan and Chia 2007, 149–150).

Xinyao as Co-curricular Education Community

Data in the 1990s emerges from the Co-curricular Activities (today the Arts Education branch of MOE) about participation in *Xinyao* activities in Singapore schools (Leow 1998), more poignantly, their declining popularity. What is evident from this data is a newly negotiated tension in a community supporting *Xinyao* between creator as sociocultural author and a musical role and function in broadcast media and popular culture. First, should we be surprised at the diminishing support for school-based activities? What is left for the aspiring creator of *Xinyao* who just wants to be heard among friends or in more intimate sessions when *Xinyao* has acquired currency as a commercial endeavor? Second, none of the prominent *Xinyao* practitioners have been accorded superstar status, unlike their colleagues in popular culture. Many *Xinyao* reunion concerts, though professionally put together, are events where the audience sings along with their "stars" without detracting from the overall amplified effect. This understanding of community sees the interwoven creators, performers, and audiences as an autered collective, with the principal protagonists singing *Xinyao* songs as communal rather than individual intellectual property, albeit not in the legal sense.

Xinyao: The Various Senses of Communities

Throughout its emergence and prominence, *Xinyao* has acquired currency and identification, with

- Community representing school youth-based creative endeavor, including informal teaching and learning;
- Community representing Mandarin as first language speakers and users;
- Community representing music as vehicular access to sophistication of language use, in this instance Mandarin;
- Community emergent through public broadcast and even local televised drama culture;
- Community of creative endeavor in popular culture in Mandarin popular music, notably its principal protagonists who transited into Mandarin popular music;
- Community-club music via the Peoples Association, a branch of the People's Action Party (PAP), the single dominant political party in Singapore;
- Community representing Mandarin as national and constitutional language support;
- Community representing a past educational system—Mandarin as first language medium of instruction;
- Community representing national heritage and therefore National Education; and
- Community as a web-based community resource.

Given their early beginnings in classrooms or campus spaces, much of this *extra/musical* learning began with the *use of language through music.* Many who came to participate in *Xinyao* were either Mandarin conversant or studied in a school where Mandarin was the main language of instruction. Ironically, *Xinyao*'s rise to prominence in the 1980s in Singapore seemed to coincide with the relinquishing of Mandarin as first-language medium of instruction, while the national Speak Mandarin Campaign initiated in 1978 rendered the use of Mandarin as lingua franca among the various Chinese dialect-based communities and, into the 1990s, prominent *Xinyao* practitioners like Cai Li Lian became "spokespersons" for the Speak Mandarin Campaign (e-mail correspondence with Tan Wei Ping, June 2003).

Nevertheless, it is through this niche community of Mandarin-conversant students in Singapore schools that *Xinyao* acquired iconic value through creative, sociocultural, political, and commercial adventures, transcending the iconicity of the situation and context and transforming its practice into sacrosanct spaces in time, even transcending time. Presently, *Xinyao* is carried on and sustained by communities marked by difference and time, meaning and function, for enthusiasts of and enquirers about *Xinyao* alike. *Xinyao* appears as a topic on local musical practices in MOE-approved secondary school music textbooks (Stead and Dairianathan 2008). It is also relied on as an exemplar for present-day Mandarin-language teaching and learning in some Singaporean schools. In addition, *Xinyao* is available as a web-based resource.[9]

Xinyao as Continuity of Community

Chen Ying Zhen's newspaper article (2010) rekindled the 1987 question of *Xinyao*'s identity and future but curiously let emerge a quintessential characteristic of *Xinyao* through Liang's treatment of texts. 新谣 *Xinyao* was *read* as 歌谣 Gey*ao* (new ballad) and even 谣言 *Yaoyan* (new rumor). *Xinyao* is now understood not only as an instance of local creative endeavor but also as a reminder of their unique double play—musical and linguistic homophony (Dairianathan and Chia 2010). These later signifiers—新谣 / 歌谣 / 谣言—are not frivolous language games; they are revelations of a changing and evolving identification of and with *Xinyao*.

Xinyao emerged in schools where Mandarin was the medium of instruction and was supported by its own community of practice. This positions *Xinyao* and the school between a distant and abstract memory so strongly desired that it is again mapped on both to other incongruent spaces that are themselves subject to the perils of profit margins or altered ideals and to a curatorial practice based on rueful recollections of how things used to be. It is instructive that STAR has been seen to act as agent and agency to support this endeavor by advocating for its teaching fraternity. If one views the *Teaching Living Legends* initiative by STAR, MOE (Ministry of Education 2014), then one sees curatorship of *Xinyao* from an originary point—the school in the present, including formal (read literary) and informal (read music) pedagogies evident in its practice. Perhaps it is in the space of a school supported by the Ministry of Education, Singapore—as singular source of educational capital—that *Xinyao* can be more meaningfully relived (rather than revived) as a community of creative communal endeavor, in and through music.

Notes

1 https://www.facebook.com/SingaporeIndianOrchestraandChoir.
2 http://www.sifas.org/briefhistory.html.
3 http://www.moe.gov.sg/education.

4 http://incinemas.sg/blog/883/That_Girl_in_Pinafore_Aims_to_Bring _Back_Xinyao _Music.aspx.
5 https://www.facebook.com/girlinpinafore/posts/490720354352798.
6 http://Xinyao 2014.weebly.com.
7 http://www.moe.gov.sg/initiatives/compulsory-education/files/ce-report.pdf.
8 http://www.nhk.or.jp/digitalmuseum/nhk50years_en/categories/p54.
9 http://Xinyao organisationsingapore.blogspot.sg/p/introduction-to-Xinyao .html.

References

Chen, Y. (陈映蓁). (2010). "*Xinyao:* At the Crossroads." *Lian He Zao Pao* (联合早报), February 17.

Dairianathan, Eugene. 2004. "Shuo Chang, the Essence of the Songs of Liang Wern Fook." In *Write You a Song* (写一首给你歌), edited by L. Han, 254–257. Singapore: World Scientific Publishing.

Dairianathan, Eugene, and Chee Hoo Lum. 2012. "Soundscapes of a Nation/alism: Perspectives from Singapore." In *Patriotism and Nationalism in Music Education,* edited by David Hebert and Alexandra Kertz-Welzel, 111–129. Farnham, UK: Ashgate.

Dairianathan, Eugene, and Ming Yen Phan. 2005. "A Narrative History of Music in Singapore 1819 to the Present." Technical report submitted to the National Arts Council, Singapore.

Dairianathan, Eugene, and Wei Khuan Chia. 2007. "*Xinyao*: Questions of Culture (戴有均、蔡慧琨 新谣：文化的定位)." In Quah Sy Ren (柯思仁) and Song Geng (宋耕), eds., *Beyond Boundaries* (超越疆界), 147–162. Singapore: Global Publishing. http://hdl.handle.net/10497/981.

———. 2010. "*Shuo Chang* (说唱): Giving Voice to and through *Xinyao* (新谣), a Musical Practice in Singapore." *Journal of Multi-Disciplinary Research in the Arts* 2 (1): 1–19.

Koh Nam Seng. 2003. Interview with Eugene Dairianathan, Singapore, December 11.

Koh, Tai Ann. 1989. "Culture and the Arts." In *Management of Success: The Moulding of Modern Singapore,* edited by Kernial Singh Sandhu and Paul Wheatley, 710–748. Singapore: Institute of South East Asian Studies.

Kong, Lily. 1996. "Making Music at the Margins? A Social and Cultural Analysis of *Xinyao* in Singapore." *Asian Studies Review* 19 (3): 100–124.

Lee, Tong Soon. 2001. "Singapore." In *The New Grove Dictionary of Music and Musicians: Vol. 23,* edited by Stanley Sadie and Jim Tyrrell, 421–423. New York: Macmillan.

———. 2008. "Singapore." In *The Garland Handbook of Southeast Asian Music,* edited by Terry E. Miller and Sean Williams, 291–294. New York: Routledge.

Leow, Wah Ping Amy. 1998. "Music and Gender in Singapore." Academic exercise, Department of Sociology, Faculty of Arts and Social Sciences, National University of Singapore.

Liang Wern Fook. 2003. Interview with Eugene Dairianathan, Singapore, June 17.

———. 1990. *Sparrow with Bamboo Twigs.* Retrieved from https://www.facebook.com/girlinpinafore/posts/490720354352798.

———. 2004. *Write a Song for You: Liang Wern Fook Anthology of Lyrics* Xie Yi Shou Ge Gei Ni: Liang Wen Fu Ci Qu Xuan Ji (写一首歌给你：梁文福词曲选集). Edited by Han Lao Da (韩劳达). Singapore: Global Publishing (八方文化创作室).

Lin, Wan Ying Mindy. 2004. An Analysis of Selected Singapore Ballads (*Xinyao*), 1980–1990. Academic exercise (BA Hons.), National Institute of Education, Nanyang Technological University.

Ministry of Education (MOE). 2014. "STAR post" April. Retrieved from http://www.star.moe.edu.sg/star/slot/u1131465/STARPost-2014-04-April.pdf.

———. 2015. "Compulsory Education." Retrieved from http://www.moe.gov.sg/initiatives/compulsory-education/files/ce-report.pdf.

National Arts Council. "Traditional Arts Sector Plan." Retrieved from https://www.nac.gov.sg/docs/ . . . /6-annex-e—-traditional-arts-sector-plan.p.

Ng, Wai-ming Benjamin. 2002. "Japanese Popular Music in Singapore and the Hybridisation of Asian Music." *Asian Music* 34 (1): 1–18.

Peers, Laura, and Alison K. Brown, eds. 2003. *Museums and Source Communities: A Routledge Reader.* London. New York: Routledge.

Phan, Ming Yen. 2004. "Music in Empire: Western Music in 19th Century Singapore through a Study of Selected Texts." Master's thesis, National Institute of Education, Nanyang Technological University, Singapore.

Stead, Peter, and Eugene Dairianathan. 2008. *Joy of Music, Secondary One Textbook.* Singapore: Star Publishing.

Tan, Wei Ping. 2003a. Personal communication (e-mail), June 26.

———. 2003b. *Xinyao (Singapore Ballads) and the Construction of Singaporean Identities.* Academic exercise (BA Hons.), National Institute of Education, Nanyang Technological University.

"That Girl in Pinafore" (我的朋友, 我的同学, 我爱过的一切). Retrieved from http://incinemas.sg/blog/883/That_Girl_in_Pinafore_Aims_to_Bring_Back_Xinyao _Music.aspx.

We Did the Dream, We Sang Songs (我们做过的梦, 我们唱过的歌). Retrieved from http://Xinyao 2014.weebly.com.

Xinyao Singapore. n.d. "Introduction to Xinyao." Retrieved from http://Xinyaoorganisationsingapore.blogspot.sg/p/introduction-to-Xinyao.html.

CHAPTER 15

The Community Band Experience in Singapore through Two Lenses

The Local and the Expatriate

Leonard Tan and Melissa Cain

Singapore, a Southeast Asian city-state located at the southern tip of the Malay Peninsula, was originally a Malay fishing village. In 1819, it became a British colony and a key trading post of the British East India Company. The increase in trade attracted immigrants from many different parts of the world, primarily China, India, and the Malay Archipelago. On August 31, 1963, Singapore gained independence from Britain and joined the Federation of Malaysia. It broke away from the Federation on August 9, 1965, and became an independent state, the Republic of Singapore (Abshire 2011; Freer and Tan 2014).

During the colonial period, there were already wind bands in Singapore. These bands played an important role in the social life of the European community, in particular, the British (Cameron 1965). They performed to mark the king's birthday, accompanied theatrical performances and orchestral concerts, and entertained audiences in outdoor performances. During the early part of the twentieth century, the Second Straits Settlement Police Band was formed via an audition of players in India and subsequently served as a source of Western music to the public. The various Chinese clan associations were also supporters of bands in Singapore during this period, aiding the formation of groups such as the Yeung Chin and Ai Tong Primary School Bands. Band activities continued during the Japanese occupation (Dairianathan 2006).

In 1965—the year of Singapore's independence—then Prime Minister Lee Kwan Yew initiated the school band project as a matter of "high priority" (P. Tan 1998, 63). Launched as an extracurricular activity in primary and secondary schools, the rationale of the band project was to build social values like group discipline and esprit de corps and foster a sense of national identity, educate the general public, and develop culture and the arts (L. Tan 2012a, 2015; Dairianathan 2006). To this end, twelve directors from the Royal British Air Force and Navy bands were invited to Singapore to begin groundwork in school band training (P. Tan 1998). After that time, school bands mushroomed all over the city-state, generously supported by governmental funding. By the turn of the century, school band members comprised a significant proportion of students who took part in after school musical activities (known as performing arts "co-curricular activities," or CCA for short). School band concerts—often featuring a wide and eclectic range of repertoire—were popular among concertgoers and formed an important part of Singapore's cultural and artistic landscape (Dairianathan 2006).

Along with the proliferation of school bands came a vibrant community band movement—one that has enabled thousands of school band musicians to pursue their passion and learning well beyond their school years. In 1977, with the support of Yamaha Music (Asia), the National Theatre Symphonic Band (NTSB) was formed by the National Theatre Trust; this band was renamed the Singapore Wind Symphony (SWS) in 1992. In addition, the community band movement received a significant boost in 1990 when then senior minister of state for education, Tay Eng Soon, noted the need for community centers to form bands, as it was noted that an estimated less than 10 percent of school band members continue to participate in band activities upon school graduation. Following Tay's recommendations, five community bands were formed: Kim Seng Wind Symphony, Moulmein Wind Ensemble, West Winds, Sembawang Wind Orchestra, and Audio Image Wind Ensemble. Alumni bands also increased in numbers, as did wind bands with religious affiliations such as the Singapore SOKA (Buddhist) Association Symphonic Band (P. Tan 1998). After the turn of the millennium, community bands continued to grow at a rapid rate, as attested by the formation of groups such as the Philharmonic Winds (Singapore).

Despite the vibrancy of the community band scene in Singapore, there is, as far as can be determined, not a single study that investigates how it relates to the school band; this parallels the paucity of research worldwide that investigates relationships between music making in schools and later in life (Mantie and Tucker 2008). Furthermore, there is no research that examines the nature of community band participation in Singapore, either from the perspective of locals who have been trained through local school bands or from the lived experience of expatriates who learned through school bands in their native countries. Both emic and etic lenses are crucial, as the local sees the Singaporean community band as a cultural "insider," whereas the expatriate experiences it very differently as a cultural "outsider." An overview of the Singaporean community band movement viewed through the lenses of both local *and* expatriate participants illuminates the nature of participation in the Singaporean community band scene—and how it relates to music making in schools, Singapore, and the world at large—more comprehensively and efficaciously than if either is used alone.

Purpose and Methodology

The purpose of this chapter, therefore, is to provide insights into the community band experience in Singapore from two perspectives: the local and the expatriate. The research questions in this study were: (1) What is the nature of participation in a Singaporean community band? (2) What is the role and place of formally organized community music activities in creating a sense of collective identity and purpose? and (3) How do accounts of participation from the local and the expatriate highlight themes of similarity and contrast? As the authors themselves were active members of community bands in Singapore, the autobiographical accounts of their involvement in them serve as the primary sources of data in this "collaborative autoethnography" (Chang, Ngunjiri, and Hernandez 2012). The first author, a male Chinese Singaporean, began his musical journey with school bands in Singapore, participated in the Singapore Wind Symphony while still in school, and went on to assume music directorship of the Philharmonic Winds (Singapore). The second author, a female Australian, actively performed with the Singapore Wind Symphony while living in Singapore for twenty years as an expatriate. Given the vastly different backgrounds and perspectives that the two researcher-participants bring to this study, the combination of their voices creates "a unique musical piece" (Chang, Ngunjiri, and Hernandez 2012, 24).

Like other autoethnographies in music education (e.g., Bartleet 2008; Harrison 2012; Schippers 2010; D. Taylor 2014; Thompson 2014), the autoethnographic approach in this study values subjectivity and researcher-participant intersubjectivity (Foster, McAllister, and O'Brien 2006). Through the process of "writing from the heart" (Denzin 2009, 209), authors analyze themselves, their personal lives, and innermost private thoughts (Chang, Ngunjiri, and Hernandez 2012). The musical stories—"data on the self" (Chang, Ngunjiri, and Hernandez 2012, 18)—are particularly relevant to social inquiry of this nature. As Ellis (2004, 194–196) argues, "there is nothing more theoretical or analytic than a good story . . . when people tell their stories, they employ analytic techniques to interpret their world," further adding that "stories are themselves analytic" as "their goal is to evoke a situation the author has been in or studied" (see also Lapadat 2009; Muncey 2005).

In what follows, the authors recount their stories with community bands in Singapore via two separate autobiographical accounts written independently. The accounts were then analyzed according to procedures described by Chang and colleagues (2012), which include data review, segmentation, categorization, and regrouping, identification of themes, and reconnection of themes with the data. Following a discussion of themes that emerged from the data, implications for community music and music education are proffered.

The Local: Leonard's Story

A native of Singapore, I was born to working-class Singaporean Chinese parents, themselves children of immigrants from China who had braved a long and arduous sea journey in search of a better life. Right from a young age, life was pretty hard. Needless to say, private music lessons at home were way out of our league. On one rather uneventful day, when I was in Primary Three, my "best friend" chirped rather excitedly that his mum was going to enroll him in the school band. Lured by the prospect of learning to play a musical instrument for free, I happily tagged along. Little did I realize that joining the primary-school band would change my life and shape my personal and professional identity forever.

As he did with all students, my primary-school band director started me off on the cornet. After a year, seeing that I looked rather plump, he persuaded me to switch to the tuba, as "it's the most expensive instrument in the entire band!" Although I felt "special" at being entrusted with such a pricey instrument, I was not very happy about playing the tuba by the time I reached secondary school—it was a marching band and I had to march with it on the field under the hot sun. Furthermore, I was playing tonic-dominant notes most of the time. In 1994, when I was in Secondary Four, another "best friend" told me he had just been accepted into the Singapore Wind Symphony, Singapore's oldest community band. Frustrated by the lack of musical stimulation in the school marching band, I gave the audition a shot. They must have needed tubas then; I did not have a very secure technique but a relatively decent sound, and so the Dutch conductor, an oboist with the Singapore Symphony Orchestra, accepted me into the band.

What a shock the first rehearsal was! I was suddenly a rookie—everyone around me played "way better." I saw notes in the music that were way out of my range on both ends of the spectrum and was frankly embarrassed that I had to fake my way through many passages. I was seated in between two much older tuba players. On my left was a Singaporean Chinese, a working professional who rather proudly whispered into my ear that musicians in the band did not really need to use tuners, as they "listen to one another." On my right was a Caucasian junior college lecturer from the UK who showed me his large collection of band CDs. My "best friend" and I remember feeling rather lost and inadequate; paradoxically, though, we felt rather proud that we were two of the few school students who were accepted into this ensemble. Although the music seemed hard at first, we got the hang of things after a few weeks; it was really quite easy to learn by "osmosis" when everyone else was so good. By the time of the concert, I was playing quite correctly (or so I thought). Much as I enjoyed playing with the SWS, I had to leave the group to focus on my studies. Nonetheless, the skills I learned were invaluable, and I was able to share them with my peers back in my school band.

After serving the two and a half years of National Service required of all male Singaporeans, I began my tertiary music education at a local arts college that housed a newly formed community band: the Philharmonic Winds of Singapore (affectionately known as Phil Winds). Having heard an audio clip of this group play Stravinsky's *The Firebird Suite,* I was duly impressed and joined the band immediately. The Belgium-born artistic director of the band at that time was my conducting teacher at the arts college, who told the musicians right at the outset that he wanted to develop a group that would make the pushing of artistic boundaries its primary raison d'être. Even though the group is technically a community band, the artistic director boldly programmed challenging works by European, American, and Asian composers that were seldom or never performed in Singapore. In addition, the band performed the artistic director's own compositions, which fused Western wind orchestra with Chinese instruments and Indonesian gamelan, dedicated entire concerts to works by Singaporean composers, and also included the avant-garde works of Edgard Varèse.

Notwithstanding the band's quest for artistic excellence, it seeks to relate to the Singaporean community at large. To this end, it regularly performs during festive seasons such as Chinese New Year, Christmas, and also Singapore's National Day. The pieces performed in these outdoor, casual events centered on music that the community could relate to, and include arrangements of *Xinyao* (Singaporean Mandarin popular music), Christmas favorites, and Chinese New Year hits. As several musicians were school band directors, we also sought to connect with the school band program. One particularly effective strategy was to serve as the "demonstration band" of the school bands' adjudication pieces. Given the competitive nature of many school bands, this drew many school students to our performances. After a few years of outreach programs, we built up a fairly strong following among school students. As many of them wanted but were not yet ready to join the group, we formed "The Philharmonic Youth Winds" to provide an avenue for young musicians to learn from musicians of the band with the eventual goal of preparing and enculturating them to join the adult group. Many of the musicians in Phil Winds today were former members of its youth wing.

As the artistic director's sole conducting student, I was soon tasked to rehearse the band for my teacher and guest conductors. I was rather hesitant at first—the musicians were around my age if not older, and it was hard to make the switch from playing in the ensemble to conducting it. Although I had by that time already begun conducting school bands, I had never conducted an adult ensemble. Still, I had to do what I was tasked. At the first rehearsal, I remember feeling something like I had during my first rehearsal as a tuba player in the SWS—everything moved so quickly. While I frequently had to stop to correct wrong notes with my school ensembles, this band seemed to do so many things automatically, and I had to function and lead at a higher level. I was stretched—in a very good way.

Despite receiving positive reviews from members of the audience and the press regarding the performance standard of the ensemble, there was nonetheless a desire to "prove" ourselves and make Singapore proud in the international arena. In 2005, the band journeyed to Kerkrade, the Netherlands, to participate in the 15th World Music Contest. Although daily rehearsals in the Netherlands were intense, we were thrilled to be awarded the "Gold with Distinction." The group has since travelled to many other countries, including Hamamatsu, Japan, for the "Japan Band Clinic"; Chiayi City, Taiwan, for the "World Association of Symphonic Bands and Ensembles Conference"; and Valencia, Spain, for the "Certamen Internacional de Bandas de Musica." While the group reaches out to the international community by travelling, it also does so by inviting guest musicians from overseas. Interestingly, when guests visit, they often attend post-rehearsal suppers with us, almost as if they had become a part of our community.

In 2008, following the departure of the founding artistic director, I became the music director of the ensemble. As music director, I led the group through performances of works such as Karel Husa's *Music for Prague,* Igor Stravinsky's *Symphonies for Wind Instruments,* Vincent Persichetti's *Symphony for Band,* and John Corigliano's *Circus Maximus.* I also commissioned Spanish composer Luis Alarcón to write a tone poem that fuses Chinese instruments with the Western wind orchestra. Through conducting these pieces, I grew immensely as a musician and a conductor.

While pursuing my doctoral studies in the United States, I was often asked how a community group could program such demanding works. I can think of three possible reasons. First, the intrinsic rewards of performing great works of art make the experience worthwhile in and of itself. Second, due to the rising performance standard of the school band and the increasing number of music graduates there is a healthy supply of technically competent wind and percussion players. Third, given Singapore's love for eating together as a social event, suppers after rehearsals are a must, binding the musicians together as a family. These three factors, I think, enable the group to pull things together for demanding programs. Although perfect attendance during rehearsals is never possible in a nonpaid ensemble ("real work" always takes precedence over rehearsals), those in the room are there, not because they *have* to be there (whether for money or for grades), but because they *want* to be there. This, I think, makes a community group special.

Looking back, my band journey has certainly played an important role in shaping my personal and professional identity. All would not have been possible without the school and community band. Music was beyond my family's financial reach, but it was the school band that started it all, and the community band that enabled me to continue the passion. The SWS stretched me as a young player while I was still in school, while Phil Winds afforded opportunities for me to conduct works I could never have dreamed of doing. The community band has enriched me tremendously—and will continue to do so.

The Expatriate: Melissa's Story

What role does music play in shaping a sense of self, providing an anchor in times of transition, and facilitating integration into a community? As a young

Australian expatriate musician starting my overseas adventure in the bustling city-state of Singapore, I quickly came to learn the importance of being part of a musical community in my new hometown.

In 1991, at the age of twenty-three, I moved from Brisbane to Singapore to teach at an international school. Music had always been a part of my life, and playing in community concert bands was an important part of that experience. I played in bands in primary and high school, in music camps throughout my youth, as a university student, and as an adult. Relocating to Singapore at such a young age was a delightful challenge—new food, new sights, new languages, new sounds, new smells, new friends. As much as I embraced all that Singapore had to offer, however, I soon began searching for the familiar. It was immediately obvious that playing my favorite sport of squash in Singapore was going to be completely unbearable in the 95 percent humidity, so I reached for my trusted companion—the community band experience. The Singapore Wind Symphony began in 1977 and is comprised of musicians from all walks of life. I was welcomed into this musical family as a flautist, the only Caucasian in the group. At that time, the ethnic makeup of the group mimicked Singapore's: mostly Chinese, with a few Malay and Indian musicians. Shortly after, another British oboist joined, allowing us to make up the band's fourth cultural group, colloquially but affectionately known as the "others."

There were many traditions that made me feel at home and mirrored my experiences in Australia. Right from the start it was comforting to be playing challenging music of my favorite conductors such as Robert W. Smith, Phillip Sparke, Johan De Meij, and Jan Van der Roost, but also have the opportunity to learn the region's best-known folk songs ("Chan Mali Chan," "Bengawan Solo," "Di Tanjong Katong," and "Rasa Sayang"). Familiarity also extended to the rehearsal routine; players arrived, chatted among themselves, warmed up, and finally took their seats. Music was practiced in sections, with solos being passed around so that all had a chance to shine. Laughter was common. One thing I never quite got used to, however, was the Singaporean habit of going out for late-night "supper" sessions after rehearsal. Despite the allure of the delectable local cuisine, I couldn't possibly sustain this important group bonding experience beginning at 10 p.m. and arrive at work the next day in reasonable shape. Thus, more often than not, I was forced to forgo this ritual.

It was, however, my visual literacy skills that were particularly tested in my initial years with the band. For the first time in my life, I couldn't understand what my Chinese conductor was saying! Despite having studied Mandarin in high school, I was barely able to participate in the conversation that accompanied the rehearsal, missing out on jokes and important contextual information. Even the two Malay musicians in the group had enough "second language" to get by. Nevertheless, my fellow flautists filled me in, and I maintained an eagle eye on our leader so as not to miss any musical cues. Our conductor's movements were precise and clear; signaling his intentions just as band conductors all around the world do.

I complemented this familiar experience with something new by learning to play Javanese gamelan music at the same institution where SWS rehearsed. Moving between these two musical traditions emphasized the diversity of sound colors, and particularly the enjoyment of sonic exploration, which has been my research area for many years. Reflections on the different transmission systems were just as fascinating: in one case a variety of wind and percussion musicians attentively adhering to a prescribed score, conducted by a leader at the front of the group who directed the finer details, versus a group of metallophone and gong players moving from one instrument to another depending on their skill and interest level; the music being facilitated by a drummer in the midst of a musical journey based on a skeleton framework with no predetermined duration or ending. These insights made me a better musician in both contexts and opened my eyes and ears to the cultural nuances of what makes a musician and an audience member within the community context.

SWS offered frequent opportunities for performances in concert halls and parks, at formal functions and competitions. All were incredibly well attended. This was due to the diligent efforts of the organizing committee, who went out of their way to promote the band at many levels, to sell tickets, and to organize tours. SWS has always had a strong tradition of high-quality local and expatiate conductors, supplemented by guest artists and guest conductors. With Singapore being in the heart of Asia and a stopping-off point for many artistic groups, SWS musicians benefited greatly from having access to such a diverse selection of visitors. SWS has also been the recipient of many commissioned works by local composers such as Zechariah Goh and Johnson Lee and international composers such as Hardy Mertens and John Sharpley.

One thing that struck me early on was the dedication of the regular audience members. This group always included a healthy following of students who played in school and university bands. These audiences were knowledgeable about the repertoire, appreciative of the skill involved, and ultimately supplied the next generation of members for SWS. The well-resourced school band program has always had a strong impact on the band scene in Singapore. An important part of this contribution (and one I have not seen consciously practiced elsewhere) is that music teachers make a concerted effort to educate musicians not just as performers but as audience members as well. This is a particularly shrewd move, as for the most part musical performances only survive if an audience exists to back their efforts. In order for musics to flourish and survive in constantly changing Singapore, they must be supported from a grassroots level.

Perhaps the highlight of my time with SWS was our tour to the Netherlands in 1993 to compete in the World Music Contest in Kerkrade, the biggest global festival for wind music. The dedication of the band prior to our trip was particularly Singaporean. It took the form of long, intense rehearsal sessions, focusing on every minute detail in the music. There was an obvious desire for the musicians to represent their country—the *little red dot*—with pride, to educate audiences about Singapore, and of course, to win. The Singaporean principles of competition and meritocracy shone through during the time leading up to the tour. This contributed to an interesting transformation for me as well. I was not a Singaporean, and yet I felt very much part of the Singaporean musical community through my involvement with the group. This tour played a significant role in molding my musical identity, and I was just as keen for Singapore to be well represented at the competition.

For some of the musicians this was their first long-haul flight and first visit to Europe. I must admit to some surprise seeing the contents of my friends' suitcases on arrival: whole bags packed with essential dietary supplements—chillies, instant noodles, sweet soy sauce, grass jelly and soya bean drinks, Jacob's crackers and Yupi sweets—just in case the local Dutch food proved too unfamiliar or bland. Our time in the Netherlands was spent rehearsing and performing, with some opportunity to play tourist. My oboist friend and I learned an important cultural lesson when "free time" was announced. We had a plan to take in the city sights and a train ride to Maastricht, which we enjoyed immensely. We realized on our return, however, that separating ourselves from the group constituted breaking an unwritten rule. The importance of being part of the group, even when travelling, was paramount, and so the band ate, rehearsed, performed, and entertained themselves together. I was beginning to feel like an honorary Singaporean, until our visit to the Drielanden Labyrinth (the largest outdoor shrub maze in the world). Sixty-five musicians with dark hair collectively bought their tickets and proceeded to enter. As what appeared to be the last of the group made their way into the maze, the "doorman" shut and kept me out, despite my desperate calls of "I'm with them!" After convincing the doorman that I was just an odd-looking

Singaporean, my next challenge was to find the group. Although utterly exhausted by the end of the tour, we were delighted to bring home first prize in our division.

As I reflect on my association with SWS, and in accessing archival documents, I realize the impact that being involved in a community band has on people's musical identities. It was wonderful to learn that more than a handful of players have been involved with SWS since its inception and continue to play with the group today. Their students and children have joined the group, while other members come and go but maintain a connection through attending concerts and visiting rehearsals. While the traditional concert band is essentially a Western-based musical group with many Western traditions, Singapore and Singaporeans have supported this music making alongside the maintenance of local genres and ensembles. SWS has assisted in the development of my sense of self and my transition between cultures. My twenty years living in Singapore was most definitely richer for having been part of the concert band experience.

Findings

After these two accounts were completed, data was coded and analyzed for commonalities and divergences. Four interrelated themes emerged from the analysis: continuity, community, glocality, and identity.

Continuity

Findings in this study suggest that, although conceptually distinct, boundaries between school and community bands are porous. In line with the "continuity thesis" advocated by the American pragmatists (see Shusterman 1989; L. Tan 2012a), the school band and the community band may be seen as Deweyan "working distinctions" (Stroud 2011, 36) that are poles on a continuum rather than two mutually exclusive categories. From the data, the continuity between the school and community bands can be seen in at least four ways.

First, consistent with previous research (e.g., Coffman 2006; Hartz 2003), the community band serves as an extension of the school band and enables its participants to continue their music education. In both accounts, clear connections were made between the authors' school and community band experiences; both also wanted to continue learning and growing musically through the community band (see Augustin 2010; Paterno 2010). Second, school and community bands are so inextricably linked that the latter display characteristics of the former. Both accounts revealed the desire for both the SWS and Phil Winds to "prove" themselves through participation in the World Music Contest, which possibly reflects the rather competitive nature of the Singapore school band (see P. Tan 1998; Lee 2004) and meritocratic ethos of the city-state and its educational system (e.g., Ho 2014). Third, the connection between the school and community band was strengthened by both the SWS and Phil Winds' systematic attempts to connect with school band members. As a cultural "outsider," Melissa was struck by how teachers seek to educate students as audience members; as a cultural "insider," Leonard was part of the driving force in Phil Winds' outreach programs to attract school students to attend the band's concert and, ultimately, to join the group. Fourth, the relationship between the school and community band was symbiotic. The school band trained Leonard and enabled him to play with the SWS; in turn, he brought advanced skills learned in SWS back to his school band. The symbiosis can also be seen in Melissa's account: while school band musicians learned through SWS concerts, they also become the next generation of SWS musicians.

Given the intricate connections described here, it can be seen, therefore, that the labels "school band" and "community band" are indeed "working distinctions." They are more usefully conceived as "soft boundaries" (Detels 1999) that interrelate, interact, and interdepend. Based on the data, the school and community band is one continuous construct.

Community

Four communities emerged from the data: the community band as "a community in itself"; the Singaporean community; the Singaporean band community; and the international band community. These communities interrelate, interact, and are interdependent. Each community is also part of a larger community.

The notion of a community band as a "community in itself" (e.g., Hartz 2003; Paterno 2010) featured prominently in both accounts. Both the SWS and Phil Winds comprise musicians from all walks of life, and the strong social element (e.g., post-rehearsal suppers) evident in their accounts parallels extant research that found that community musicians value both the social and musical aspects of community band participation (e.g., Cavitt 2005; Cope 2005; Palmer 2008; Paterno 2010; D. Taylor 2014). This "community in itself" in turn plays an important role in the Singaporean community by performing in important festive seasons as recounted by Leonard; this is in line with studies that describe how community bands resonate with their local communities (e.g., French 2014). Together with school bands, the community bands form a larger Singaporean "band community" that is inextricably linked to the international band community. This international community can be seen in the "World Music Contest" mentioned in the two accounts, as well as an international array of composers and conductors that both Melissa and Leonard identified. Interestingly, as seen in Leonard's account, when overseas guests attended post-rehearsal suppers with community musicians, the international band community sometimes became a part of the community band itself.

It is clear, then, that the theme "community" that emerged from the data is not a monolithic construct merely connoting the social and communal aspects of the community band; rather, it reveals a dynamic and complex web of relationships between the community band as a "community in itself," the Singaporean community, the Singaporean band community, and the international band community.

Glocality

The term "glocalization" captures the dynamic interplay and coexistence of global and local forces (Meyrowitz 2005), a theme that clearly emerged from the data. Although the Singaporean community band was experienced locally "in Singapore," the people with whom both authors worked and the music they played in their bands were not exclusively Singaporean. Nor were they entirely foreign. Rather, the irresistible forces of globalization intermingled with the local culture in ways that resulted in a uniquely glocalized community band experience.

This is most strikingly evident in the eclectic repertoire of pieces recounted by the two authors. As noted by Melissa, the SWS played pieces that she liked, was familiar with, and made her feel "at home"; at the same time, she relished the opportunity to play Singaporean and Southeast Asian folk songs. Similarly, Leonard recounted that Phil Winds performed works like Persichetti's *Symphony for Band* that are staples in the Western wind band world (see L. Tan 2012b); less commonly performed works; and music related to local cultures, for example, Chinese New Year hits and *Xinyao* (Singaporean Mandarin popular music). In fact, Phil Winds goes so far as to perform works that fuse Western and Asian instruments—a form of interculturalism that enables bands to create new colors and expand their timbral palettes in ways that reflect today's globalized world (see L. Tan 2012a, 278). In addition, both authors noted the commissioning of works (see Rhoden 2008) from a diverse array of composers that included both local and overseas composers; these commissioning projects further added to the glocality of the groups.

As a globalized city-state, Singapore is culturally permeable and attracts people from many different parts of the world. This diversity is seen in the Singaporean community band. The people involved in the band hail from a broad array of countries, including Australia (Melissa), Great Britain (the tuba player in Leonard's account), China (the conductor whom Melissa could not understand), Belgium (the founding conductor of Phil Winds), and Holland (the conductor who auditioned Leonard in SWS). Guest artists from overseas further enrich the diversity. This confluence of people from different parts of the world enabled a rich intermingling of cultural experiences. It must have been the first time Melissa had experienced a band rehearsal conducted in Mandarin (due primarily to the fact that the conductor came from China), and probably one of the few times her fellow flautists had to translate Mandarin for a Caucasian during a rehearsal—in a Singapore accent. Her Singaporean Malay colleagues must have found it rather challenging to understand the Chinese conductor too. Nonetheless, the fact that *all*—regardless of race or nationality—could understand the conductor's gestures attests to the ubiquity and transculturality of the Western classical ensemble tradition (see L. Tan 2012a; 2014). Both global and local forces intersect in Melissa's account.

It can be seen, therefore, that global and local forces interact dynamically in the repertoire and among the musicians who participate in the Singaporean community band. The glocality of the Singaporean community band enables its participants to be "inside and outside at the same time" (Meyrowitz 2005, 23); they are simultaneously in *and* out of Singapore.

Identity

Four notions of identity emerged from the data: individual, ensemble, national, and transnational. With respect to individual identity, it is striking that both authors began the stories of their involvement in the Singaporean community by giving personal accounts of themselves. Leonard told how he could not afford music lessons as a young boy, while Melissa wrote richly about starting a new chapter of her life in Singapore. Clearly, they both saw participating in their respective community bands as being inextricably linked to who they are. This resonates with previous research that found that the community band shapes the personal identity of its participants (e.g., Paterno 2010; P. Taylor 2012).

Ensemble identity—the identity of the individual community band as an ensemble—could also be seen in their accounts. Melissa wrote about how musicians of the SWS always "ate, rehearsed, performed, and entertained themselves together" while the band was in the Netherlands; Leonard described how post-rehearsal suppers bound the musicians of Phil Winds together "as a family." The ensemble identity was also shaped in part by the repertoire. One common word used by both authors to describe the repertoire they played was "challenging." Consistent with previous research (e.g., Hartz 2003; Paterno 2010), the musicians of both the SWS and Phil Winds wanted to be challenged and were willing to invest time and effort to play difficult works that contribute to the identity of their bands as a serious artistic ensemble. They did not see their participation as mere hobby but "serious leisure" (see Coffman 2006; Stebbins 1992; P. Taylor 2012).

National identity also emerged in both accounts. Leonard described how Phil Winds wanted to "make Singapore proud in the international arena." In like vein, Melissa recounted the desire of SWS musicians to want to "represent their country—*the little red dot*—with pride." Of the two accounts, it was the expatriate who wrote more richly about the Singaporean identity. Melissa experienced an "interesting transformation" while participating in the World Music Contest in Holland with the SWS. Although she was not a Singaporean, she "felt very much part of the Singaporean musical community" through her involvement with the group. In fact, the transformation for her was so palpable that she felt like "an honorary Singaporean"—albeit an "odd-looking" one—and was visibly upset when the "doorman" at Drielanden Labyrinth did not regard her as being a part of the Singaporean group. Herein lies the power of music to bind people together as one: the experience of rehearsing with the SWS to "win" a prize for Singapore was such a powerful one that she wanted to be regarded as part of the Singaporean family.

Paradoxically, while national identity emerged from the data, so did transnational identity—the identity associated with being involved in a larger band community that transcends national, political, and cultural divisions. For Melissa, this transnational identity was precisely what grounded her in a new, foreign country. She was thrilled to be in a new environment; yet with so many new experiences she obviously felt the need to go "searching for the familiar"—an urge that playing in the SWS fulfilled. During Leonard's studies in the United States he was asked how his ensemble was able to perform difficult works despite being a community group. Like Melissa, although he was in a foreign country, his identity was grounded on his participation in the community band. Both authors were "foreigners" in terms of nationality but "members" of the larger international band community. They did not have to look to their own native countries, nor did they need to be physically present in them, to find their identities as members of the transnational "community band."

In sum, four themes emerged from an analysis of the data: continuity, community, glocality, and identity. While they have been presented as separate themes, they interact in the lived experiences of Melissa and Leonard in dynamic—even rhizomatic—ways. In the discussion that follows, implications for community music and music education will be presented for each of the four themes in turn.

Discussion

The notion of the school and community band as one continuous construct is a construal that has far-reaching implications for music education. As noted in previous research, music educators can and should encourage and influence participation beyond the school classroom (e.g., Billaud 2014; Busch 2005; Wilhjelm 1998). Although this may seem obvious, how often do band directors work towards awards, festivals, and concerts—and see them as ends in themselves—rather than stress the importance of lifelong learning? More crucially, might an undue focus on performance and competitive goals (e.g., Cain 2011) and some of the ways in which directors teach, actually *discourage* lifelong participation (Mantie and Tucker 2008)? Instead of regarding awards, festivals, and concerts as ends, they may more usefully be construed in terms of what Dewey (1929, 102) calls "ends-in-view," whereby each performance goal is a means of lifelong learning. Although school and community bands may have many "ends-in-view," the final end, or telos, that is of real value, as Dewey would argue, is growth (Savage 2002)—a common theme present in both Leonard's and Melissa's accounts. By focusing on growth as the common telos, and all else as "ends-in-view," both the school and the community band break free from the shackles of excessive performance and competitive pressures. There would also be a common value that cuts through both the school and the community band.

Thinking of community as a dynamic interaction between the various interrelated communities identified (i.e., the community band as "a community in itself," the Singaporean community, the Singaporean band community, and the international band community) also offers several important practical implications. Music educators, students, and conductors should be cognizant of the fact that humans and ensembles do not work in isolation; rather, the communities are interdependent on one another. Close partnerships, then, ought to be fostered between them. For example, school and community bands could work together through joint concerts and performances, the mentoring of school musicians by community musicians, having community groups serve as demonstration bands for school bands, and podium exchange between conductors of school and community groups. The more their awareness of community bands is increased, the more likely students are to participate in them after graduation. School and community bands should also continue to connect with the Singaporean community as well as the international band community. Each community is shaped by and in turn shapes the other communities in the interconnected world of the twenty-first century.

The glocality of the Singaporean community band mirrors the city-state itself: a fast-paced, dynamic, and culturally diverse place that is ever-changing. With its unique blend of local and international repertoire and musicians, the Singaporean community band should continue to seize opportunities and help shape the international band community of tomorrow. Because it has a relatively short history, it is unbounded by tradition and "state lists," rendering it considerable freedom to chart its own future. To this end, the Singaporean community band should look towards the established band traditions of other countries (e.g., the United States, Japan, and Australia) not as blueprints for blind imitation but as sources of inspiration to create its own tradition. It should remain ready to absorb the various cultures and traditions that are *already* in its midst. Furthermore, the commissioning of works that incorporate Asian instruments into the Western wind band may well be one important and significant contribution it can bring to the international band fraternity. At the school level, directors and students may also consider working with musical groups outside the Western classical tradition to truly embrace the intercultural opportunities already inherent in Singapore.

Finally, with respect to identity, music educators and community band directors should place a considerable premium on building strong band cultures with which their participants can identify. Ever so often, it is easy for conductors and administrators to think primarily of the musical and administrative aspects of band while neglecting the fact that the social aspects are just as crucial. In addition, given that musicians in community bands do not necessarily shy away from challenge but instead seem to embrace it, directors should give careful consideration to the music they choose for their community band musicians: it cannot be "too easy." While the practical reality remains that "perfect attendance" is often not possible, the musicians nonetheless need sufficient "pull" factors to draw them into the community band program, of which quality repertoire pegged at the right level of challenge is one (e.g., King 2009; Wilhjelm 1998). It is, after all, not just a hobby, but "serious leisure" that forms a crucial aspect of who they are.

This chapter, to the best of the authors' knowledge, is one of the first studies devoted to the community band experience in Singapore. Future studies might profitably examine more closely each of the four themes identified here. For instance, researchers could probe more deeply into the precise nature of the connection between the school and the community band in Singapore. They could study, not only those who continue their music education in community bands, but also those who choose not to, thereby gaining insights into both the "push" and the "pull" factors associated with community band participation. In order to facilitate the transition from the school to the community band, studies could also be conducted to examine the challenges associated with such a move. Given the vibrancy of the community band movement in Singapore today, further research on this topic can only help to shape the future of lifelong learning in instrumental music education—for the betterment of individuals as well as the local and international band communities.

References

Abshire, Jean. 2011. *The History of Singapore.* Santa Barbara, CA: Greenwood.

Augustin, Cathy. 2010. "A Descriptive Study to Determine the Opinions of Community Band Members regarding the Effectiveness of Comprehensive Musicianship." *International Journal of Community Music* 3 (2): 175–183. doi:10.1386/ijcm.3.2.175_1.

Bartleet, Brydie-Leigh. 2008. "'You're a Woman and Our Orchestra Just Won't Have You': The Politics of Otherness in the Conducting Profession." *Hecate: An Interdisciplinary Journal of Women's Liberation* 34 (1): 6–23.

Billaud, Louise Ann. 2014. "The Case of the Highlands Community Band: Structuration, Self-determination, and the Promotion of Participation beyond the Classroom." DMA diss., Boston University.

Busch, Maria. 2005. "Predictors of Lifelong Learning in Music: A Survey of Individuals Participating in Performing Ensembles at Community Colleges in Illinois." PhD diss., University of Illinois.

Cain, Melissa. 2011. "Philosophy, Policy, Practice: Visions and Realities of Cultural Diversity in Selected Primary Music Classrooms in Brisbane and Singapore." PhD diss., Queensland Conservatorium, Griffith University.

Cameron, John. 1965. *Our Tropical Possessions in India*. Kuala Lumpur: Oxford University Press.

Cavitt, Mary Ellen. 2005. "Factors Influencing Participation in Community Bands." *Journal of Band Research* 41(1): 42–59. Retrieved from http://search.proquest.com.libraryproxy.griffith.edu.au/docview/1092020?accountid=14543.

Chang, Heewon, Faith Ngunjiri, and Kathy-Ann Hernandez. 2012. *Collaborative Autoethnography*. Walnut Creek, CA: Left Coast Press.

Coffman, Don. 2006. "Voices of Experience: Interviews of Adult Community Band Members in Launceston, Tasmania, Australia." *International Journal of Community Music* 23 (1): 37–47.

Cope, Peter. 2005. "Adult Learning in Traditional Music." *British Journal of Music Education* 22 (2): 125–140. doi:10.1017/S0265051705006108.

Dairianathan, Eugene. 2006. "The Wind Ensemble in Singapore: Presence and Practice." *World Association of Symphonic Bands and Ensembles Journal* 13: 31–50.

Denzin, Norman. 2009. *Qualitative Inquiry under Fire*. Walnut Creek, CA: Left Coast Press.

Detels, Claire. 1999. *Soft Boundaries: Re-visioning the Arts and Aesthetics in American Education*. Westport, CT: Bergin and Garvey.

Dewey, John. 1929. *Experience and Nature*. London: George Allen and Unwin.

Ellis, Carolyn. 2004. *The Ethnographic I: A Methodological Novel about Autoethnography*. Walnut Creek, CA: Rowman Altamira.

Foster, Kim, Margaret McAllister, and Louise O'Brien. 2006. "Extending the Boundaries: Autoethnography as an Emergent Method in Mental Health Nursing Research." *International Journal of Mental Health Nursing* 15 (1): 44–53. doi:10.1111/j.1447-0349.2006.00402.x.

Freer, Patrick, and Leonard Tan. 2014. "The Self-Perceptions of Young Men as Singers in Singaporean Pre-University Schools." *Research Studies in Music Education* 36 (2): 165–178. doi:10.1177/1321103x14556575.

French, Gillian. 2014. "Follow the Band: Community Brass Bands in the Scottish Borders." PhD diss., University of Edinburgh.

Harrison, Scott D. 2012. "Letting Go: An Auto-ethnography of Supervising the Research Higher Degree in Music." *International Journal of Music Education* 30 (2): 99–110. doi:10.1177/0255761412439927.

Hartz, Jason M. 2003. "The American Community Band: History and Development." MA thesis, Marshall University.

Ho, Li-Ching. 2014. "Meritocracy, Tracking, and Elitism: Differentiated Citizenship Education in the United States and Singapore." *The Social Studies* 105 (1): 29–35. doi:10.1080/00377996.2013.788473.

King, Tyler C. 2009. "Factors Influencing Adults' Participation in Community Bands of Central Ohio. MA thesis, Ohio State University.

Lapadat, Judith C. 2009. "Writing Our Way into Shared Understanding: Collaborative Autobiographical Writing in the Qualitative Methods Class." *Qualitative Inquiry* 15 (6): 955–979. doi:10.1177/1077800409334185.

Lee, Tian Tee. 2004. "An Analysis of Singapore's Wind Band Music Education System." PhD diss., National Institute of Education, Nanyang Technological University.

Mantie, Roger, and Lynn Tucker. 2008. "Closing the Gap: Does Music-Making Have to Stop upon Graduation?" *International Journal of Community Music* 1 (2): 217–227. doi:10.1386/ijcm.1.2.217/1.

Meyrowitz, Joshua. 2005. "The Rise of Glocality: New Senses of Place and Identity in the Global Village." In *A Sense of Place: The Global and the Local in Mobile Communication,* edited by Kristof Nyili, 21–30. Vienna: Passagen.

Muncey, Tessa. 2005. "Doing Autoethnography." *International Journal of Qualitative Methods* 4(1): 69–86.

Palmer, Roger. 2008. "Questions Arising from the Views of Some Members of Four Amateur Classical Music Organizations." *International Journal of Community Music* 1 (2): 203–215. doi:10.1386/ijcm.1.2.203_1.

Paterno, Christine A. 2010. "The History of the Hanover Wind Symphony: A Closer Look at a Community Band in New Jersey and the Community within the Band." MA thesis, William Paterson University.

Rhoden, Myra King. 2008. "A History of the Tara Wind Community Band." DMA diss., University of Southern Mississippi.

Savage, Daniel M. 2002. *John Dewey's Liberalism—Individual, Community, and Self-Development.* Carbondale and Edwardsville: Southern Illinois University Press.

Schippers, Huib. 2010. *Facing the Music: Shaping Music Education from a Global Perspective.* New York: Oxford University Press.

Shusterman, Richard. 1989. "Why Dewey Now?" *Journal of Aesthetic Education* 23 (3): 60–67. doi: 10.2307/3332763.

Stebbins, Robert. 1992. *Amateurs, Professionals, and Serious Leisure.* Montreal and Kingston, Canada: McGill-Queens University Press.

Stroud, Scott R. 2011. *John Dewey and the Artful Life.* University Park, PA: Pennsylvania State University Press.

Tan, Leonard. 2012a. "Towards a Transcultural Philosophy of Instrumental Music Education." PhD diss., Indiana University.

———. 2012b. "A Comparison of the Sonata forms in Hindemith's and Persichetti's Band Symphonies." *Journal of Band Research* 48 (1): 11–29.

———. 2014. "Towards a Transcultural Theory of Democracy for Instrumental Music Education." *Philosophy of Music Education Review* 22 (1): 61–77. doi:10.2979/philmusieducrevi.22.1.61.

Tan, Penny. 1998. "The Historical Study of Symphonic Bands and Related Ensembles in Singapore." MA thesis, National Institute of Education, Nanyang Technological University.

Taylor, Donald. 2014. "Learning to Sing Again: A Gay Widower's Journey." *Bulletin of the Council for Research in Music Education* (199): 69–86. doi:10.5406/bulcouresmusedu.199.0069.

Taylor, Pamela. 2012. "The Role of Music-making in the Identity Construction of Members of an Adult Community Concert Band." PhD diss., Louisiana State University and Agricultural and Mechanical College.

Wilhjelm, Carl Christian. 1998. "A Case Study of the Ridgewood Concert Band: A New Jersey Community Band Dedicated to Life-long Learning." EdD diss., Teachers College, Columbia University.

CHAPTER 16

How a Music Program Can Build and Sustain a Community

Joanne Ruksenas

This chapter examines the role music can play in building and sustaining a community and is part of a larger study examining the role of active music making in building resilience in preschool-aged children. This group, Aria Angels, represents one of a number of sites in the greater Brisbane region in Queensland, Australia, where this research has been conducted and is ideally suitable for a discussion of how music can build a community. Unlike the other groups in the study, where the goal is to impart musical skills, this church-based group has the primary goal of building community through providing high-quality structured music lessons. I have drawn on my experiences as observer, researcher, and teacher in studio and classroom settings to explore how this group has used music education to achieve the program goal of building a community through music education.

The preschool years are a time of massive neural reorganization and remodeling. The literature from the neurosciences describes the role that music may play in this (Ruksenas 2012; Bryck and Fisher 2012; Hyde et al. 2009). The unlearning hypothesis of absolute pitch indicates that, if we provide quality music education from birth, children will retain this skill for life (Reubart 1985), will be more responsive to active music making, and the music teacher's job will be that much easier. There are a number of well-documented benefits to quality music education at any age. These are described and understood by studies in cognitive psychology and the neurosciences. Though music has always fascinated scientists, the discovery of new neural and glial markers, which led to new understandings of neurogenesis, have also led to new insights into the benefits of active and passive engagement in music for neural development (Motluk 2000; Gould et al. 1999). Many benefits of music have been discovered that have overarching effects that support a number of key areas, including literacy, numeracy, and speech development.

Despite the proliferation of memes and popular science books, which make this research very accessible, the implications and benefits of quality music education do not seem to be making an impact on public education policy. A number of nongovernment schools in Australia have advocated successfully for more frequent music lessons for their students especially from prep—the foundation year of primary school in Australia. In government schools music education is being squeezed out of the curriculum by funding constraints and increased focus on literacy and numeracy (ACARA 2011; Letts 2009). Ironically, research indicates that literacy and numeracy are supported by quality music education (Douglas and Willatts 1994; Habib 2009). High-quality music education in the preschool years has the potential to provide a number of academic and behavioral advantages by simply reinforcing a skill that already exists (Darrow 2008; Geist and Geist 2008; Hallam 2010).

Our Relationship with Music Has Changed

While the ideas of music and community are inseparable in some cultures, this tends not to be the case in Australia. Many factors contribute to this, and it is not to say that we do not enjoy music. The proliferation of music-sharing sites and new technologies means that we have unprecedented access to music from any culture and of any genre. Walk down the street on any day and you can observe people, headphones in ears, absorbed in their own musical worlds. It is the way we engage with music that has changed. In a relatively short time it has become more common for people to be passive consumers of music rather than active music makers (Sacks 2007; Skånland 2013a). The recent adoption of the National Curriculum, which emphasizes literacy and numeracy from the earliest years of schooling, has also seen music incorporated into a single subject—the arts—along with dance, media studies, visual art, and drama (ACARA 2011).

Although these changes have occurred relatively quickly, many parents are less familiar with traditional songs and lullabies that have been passed down for generations (Baker and Mackinlay 2006). The Aria Angels program was designed with this in mind. The idea was that bringing these songs back to families would give both parents and children useful skills that would help them bond. In addition, having the opportunity to meet like-minded families with children of similar ages would encourage a community to form.

Origins

These groups formed in 2010 after the branch of the church associated with community outreach and families identified families with children aged from birth to the first year of school as a potential target for community outreach. While the church offered a wide range of programs, there was nothing in place for families with children of this age outside their baptism program. The concept was to offer a community program based on the Christian ideals of outreach and hospitality. The playgroup format was suggested, but there were a number of these groups in the area already. Although employed by the church, one of the members had a long career in music education, particularly early childhood music and curriculum design. They were also aware of the growing body of research suggesting the benefits of formal music education during development in early childhood (Anvari et al. 2002; Bamberger 2006; Gross, Linden, and Ostermann 2010). Having a music education focus gave the group a point of difference which was very attractive to the families involved in the initial planning and discussions. These families formed the core of the first group and have remained with the program. A music-based program was designed and implemented in three locations in the greater Brisbane region of Queensland.

The program provides a structured, sequential music program for children from birth to school age and their parents or carers. The groups decided to charge a nominal fee per family. This money is used to provide morning tea after the class and a craft activity. Any remaining money is returned to the church at the end of each quarter. Attendance is on a drop-in basis. In the first year, the classes ran throughout the year, with a break for Easter and Christmas. This format has changed each year. From 2015 on, four terms of seven lessons were provided.

The Benefits of Structured Music Lessons

Music and community share a number of characteristics. Music ties us to our history—in time, in place, and with each other—whether we like it or not (Hargreaves and North 1999). Parents participate in the lessons with their children. This gives parents and children the opportunity to bond. It also provides musical skills the families can use away from class. Our changing relationship with music also includes the way parents use music with their children. Over a relatively short time, parents have largely abandoned singing traditional songs and nursery rhymes that were used for generations to soothe and entertain young children in favor of other forms of music, recordings, video, and applications (Baker and Mackinlay 2006).

What children need is to hear their parents' singing voices. Singing helps to facilitate bonding between parent and baby and contributes to the baby's neural, social, and emotional development (de Vries 2005, 2009; Custodero 2006; Bergeson and Trehub 1999; Hanley 2010). Recordings targeted for the baby and preschool markets are often too busy for developing ears to process effectively (Ilari 2009). These classes teach the parents at the same time they are teaching the children, providing them with forgotten skills and methods to sooth and bond with their children and enjoy music themselves (Gudmundsdottir and Gudmundsdottir 2010). Because the repertoire is directed to the children, songs are easy for the parents to learn and use at home. Modeling singing reinforces the idea that singing is natural, which encourages the children to sing (Custodero and Johnson-Green 2003). Because they participate fully in the classes, the parents sing in a supportive environment. This nurtures the many benefits singing has for the parents as well as the children, and gives the parents confidence in their own ability—important in encouraging them to use the skills away from the class.

Organization

The groups are advertised in the weekly church notices and in the newsletters at local church-affiliated schools, but many families learn of the group through word-of-mouth. Each registered family receives a weekly e-mail with news about the previous lesson and upcoming themes. While advertising only in the church and its affiliated schools may seem to run contrary to the original ideal of the program—namely, to run an outreach program for the broader community—demand for this program is very high. By the end of their first year the program had grown from five to more than two hundred families registered across the three centers.

The group where I conduct the majority of my research is located in an area with a number of families who have recently migrated to Australia, primarily from countries in Asia and South America. Their extended families, and on occasion their spouses, remain in their country of origin. For these families, this group is a lifeline of sorts, providing links and contacts with the broader community. It is one thing to be provided with official information, but other parents know which doctor to go to, which is the best kindergarten, the best community services, schools, playgrounds, and shops, and which of these to avoid. This provides invaluable support and friendship for new families (Ungar 2011). Although it may seem problematic that these families first have to attend the church to find out about the group, it is quite common for people who are feeling isolated to reach out to organizations they recognize, the church being an obvious choice. Many of these people have networks with churches in their countries of origin and are introduced to the priest. Once established in the group, they almost invariably bring in other families from their community.

Attendance

Attendance is on a drop-in basis. Each center has a core group of regular attendees, six to twelve families, depending on the center. The ideal number of students in early childhood music classes is no more than twelve children in total. Children who have started kindergarten generally attend once a fortnight. With two hundred families registered, there is clearly a group of families who are well known but attend less frequently. The original site maintains the largest population base and also has the largest physical space. When you consider that a family can consist of parents, extended family, and any number of children, class numbers are generally higher than recommended. Around Christmas and other special occasions, it is common and expected that twenty-five to thirty extended families will be at each class. Because of the high number of registered families, sessions running on a drop-in basis, and the friendships that have evolved, it is also quite normal for numbers to spike unexpectedly to these highs during the year. This can happen simply because one parent has decided to pick up the phone and arrange to meet with others at a lesson. While this is welcome, unexpected fluctuations in class composition and numbers can make planning and teaching quite challenging.

Lesson Planning

Lesson planning follows the three-year rotating structure of the church lectionary. Weekly themes are loosely based on the following Sunday's sermon. For example, in the term approaching the Feast of Saint Francis of Assisi, the patron saint of animals, the theme was "The Circus," each week featuring a different animal. The year 2015 marks the start of the second rotation. The program was designed in this way to appeal to parishioners and non-parishioners alike. Incorporating general themes means the program can be tied to church events, but not so weighed down with dogma that families from outside the church feel confused and alienated.

The teachers have met regularly and workshopped before each term commences to discuss upcoming themes and repertoire, share teaching ideas, and brainstorm solutions to possible problems. A number of revisions to the original format and structure have originated from teacher input at these meetings. While the three groups started with an identical program, these meetings have encouraged discussion and given the teachers confidence to make changes at their own group level. This has helped the facilitators adapt the groups to suit the needs of their own communities while maintaining continuity with the main program.

Class Structure

The classes follow the same format as other immersion-based early childhood music classes, meaning the children and parents learn through singing and movement rather than deliberate instruction. The classes run for thirty-five minutes and feature between twelve and twenty music-based activities. The difference in the number of activities is accounted for by the length of the activity and the level of engagement of the children and families. While these are largely scaffolded and sequential, providing continuity through the term by the repeated use of a piece from lesson to lesson, the lesson plan may also include pieces specific to the weekly theme. These singletons are usually well-known pieces from popular Australian children's repertoire or familiar pieces that the older children learned in previous years. Because their purpose is to illustrate the weekly theme, they are usually not scaffolded and appear for one lesson only. This allows the curriculum to adopt the weekly themes while the structured developmental program flows alongside.

The lessons include a number of different activity types, identified in the literature as beneficial for optimal engagement and musical learning. These are not necessarily included in every lesson. It is important that the children experience them regularly. An effective long-term plan is vital to the success of this, and any, early childhood music program. Young children thrive on familiarity and structure, which captures their attention and solidifies learning (Klinger 1990).

The various activities used in early childhood music lessons have been identified in the literature and are standard in structured early childhood lessons, regardless of methodology, although the terms may not be identical and the emphasis may change. These include bounces, tickles, finger play, games, dramatic play, guided movement to music, free movement to music, untuned percussion, singing, tuned percussion, singing with movement, singing with percussion, movement with percussion, improvisation, singing with movement and percussion, basic ostinato, basic two-part singing, basic note reading, and sung stories. These activities vary in complexity. The first activities on this list—bounces, tickles, and finger play—tend to be performed with an adult and are more suited to babies and very young children. Most of the activities can be used up to the first years of schooling, with the selection of appropriate repertoire. Even so, the outcome for toddlers and preschoolers who perform the same activity will be vastly different, reflecting their progression through physical and cognitive developmental stages.

Recorded music, generally from the Western classical tradition, is used for free movement and music appreciation segments. Using Western classical music allows the children to experience more complex musical structures and sounds. Free movement is generally taught with brightly colored transparent scarves, which provide visual stimulation and help to reinforce and develop the child's proprioception. While a number of different props are used to support learning, scarves are the most versatile. They can also be used for costumes in dramatic play, to throw and catch, and to hide when singing "peek-a-boo" songs, and as markers for circle games.

The classes are singing-based and use songs from the early childhood canon, punctuated by more contemporary composed pieces. The repertoire, like the activities it is used to reinforce, must also reflect the children's developmental and cognitive stages. Ability to speak and sing develops over time, as do the child's memory systems. There are differences in range, length, and rhythmic complexity that set appropriate toddler repertoire apart from preschool pieces. The differences may seem barely noticeable to most adults, but they represent exponentially more complex developmental leaps for children, making repertoire selection a key factor in optimal learning. Age-appropriate, engaging repertoire is easy for the children to learn and remember, important for continuity in a class like this where there are no reinforcing materials like books or recordings. When the children enjoy the repertoire and find it easy to remember, they sing it spontaneously away from the class. This reinforces learning and demonstrates the value of the lessons to the parents and anyone else the child chooses to perform for.

Limiting Factors

Dependence on the Church

This is a church outreach program. It was instituted to provide support and community for families with children too young for school. While the church runs a number of outreach programs, there is no support for parents with young children in the years between baptism and confirmation. Initially, all of the staff in this program were church employees attached to the deaneries where the program is run. This constituted one assistant per deanery to help with the general running of the program and the music teacher, who wrote the program and taught across the three centers. The church also provided the premises, printing costs, and insurance. Around a year into the program the church withdrew funding for the staff. The nominal fee paid by parents meant there was no money in reserve, and certainly no money to pay anybody. Further cuts in support from the church would create the potential to close the program.

Teacher Recruitment and Training

The program facilitator developed this program in a way that it was hoped would be an ideal training round for early career music teachers. Initially, two people were recruited from the church congregations. They had limited training and experience in music teaching in any capacity. This was always going to be problematic, and not just because only one teacher was being paid. These classes do not provide an ideal training environment for early career teachers. The teachers do not write their own lesson plans, meaning they do not pick up the meta-teaching strategies essential for planning success in any other setting. Horizontal planning, understanding how the activities are structured and scaffolded to promote learning across a number of weeks, and how this correlates with the yearly goals being the most obvious of these. Lack of opportunity to reflect on the teaching and to implement changes to the next lesson in response to the needs of the class is possibly the most detrimental, as it does not allow the teacher to cognitively process what has happened and make appropriate changes.

Lesson Structure

The classes are multi-age. Some early childhood music specialists separate early childhood into three distinct groups: babies, toddlers, and preschoolers.

They are dogmatic about the assignment, preferring to have space in a class rather than join classes at different developmental stages. These age groupings are important because they reflect differences in developmental stages and milestones in motor, cognitive, and social skills. Adopting a "take-all-comers" approach as this group does mean the curriculum has to be generic. The teachers cannot easily implement developmental strategies. Nor do they have the opportunity to see the children progress through curriculum designed for specific developmental ages and stages to find out what works and what does not.

Experienced teachers understand the minutiae of the repertoire and can take advantage of these differences to tailor their lessons to meet the needs of the individuals in their classes.

For example, the differences between the folk tunes "Ring a Ring a Rosie" and "Here We Go Round the Mulberry Bush" may not be immediately obvious, but the highly attenuated and repetitive pentatonic tone set of Rosie—la, so, mi, do in moveable sol-fa—is more appropriate to teach toddlers. They are more likely to experience success singing and receive the full benefit of participating in this activity than in singing "Mulberry Bush," which is a longer, diatonic tone set. These differences may sound inconsequential, but to the developing child's mind, these tiny details can be the difference between students experiencing success or failure in these activities—being engaged or disengaged in the lesson (Ostwald 1973). The group's policy of taking all comers and paying on a week-by-week basis means that this level of planning cannot be implemented in these settings.

Lesson Planning

Lesson planning is key to the success of any structured, sequential learning program and is essential for teacher development and enhanced job satisfaction (Prideaux 2003). The lesson plans here are delivered centrally and are designed around a three-year plan based on the lessons in the lectionary, meaning they are not workable for teachers involved with this group. This can create problems in implementation. There is one class per center that caters for all ages. Consider, for example, the simple fact that babies need to be carried. The activities designed for preschoolers are movement-based and are not suitable for this age group. Circle games, in particular, where parents have to sit, stand, and run repeatedly with their infants, somewhat counteract one of the aims of the group, which is to provide a relaxing environment for parents. This is in sharp contrast to the gentle bounces and tickles that dominate the baby and toddler classes. Conversely, the baby-based activities are far from ideal for preschoolers. The children are very aware that these activities are for babies. While they may be fun once in a while, used too often they will lead to behavioral problems, as the older children are not engaged and often recognize them as "baby" games; and bouncing a preschooler on your legs for a lesson proves as stressful for parents as do repeated sitting and standing with an infant. The structure and lesson planning mean the lessons need to be altered "on the fly," which requires highly trained, very experienced teachers with a vast knowledge of repertoire and developmental stages (Campbell and Scott-Kassner 2006).

The lesson plans are not unteachable or inappropriate, but they require highly experienced teachers to implement them successfully. Experienced teachers are able to adapt the activities in the lesson plan to suit the requirements of the different age groups and to accommodate varying individual needs. It is interesting to observe how often experienced music teachers can write a lesson plan and alter it "on the fly," completely unphased, ending the lesson with their lesson goals exactly achieved. Because they know their goals for the class, they are able to respond instantly to the needs of the students. They also tend to reflect extensively on lesson plans after class, so subsequent lesson plans are adapted accordingly (Barrett 2007; Swanwick 2008).

Rapid changes to lesson plans are possible because these teachers have internalized a multidimensional cognitive map of the repertoire. This incorporates at least five variables: developmental stage, presenting behavior, desired outcome, cognitive ability, and prior knowledge. This allows them to instantly recall different pieces with a similar purpose at specific memory nodes and adapt the lesson so the class ends up where they need to be without the teacher becoming stressed and the children becoming disengaged. These are the kind of teachers this group needs to attract, but the way that the groups are structured make this unlikely (Ruksenas 2011). The early career teachers, while trying, are often not able to keep up with the "on the fly" changes needed in this program.

Drop-in Format

The most problematic aspect of the design for early career teachers is the drop-in format, which means there is little to no continuity. Teachers do not know from one week to the next what the population of their class will be, which affects their preparation. This is by far the most stressful aspect affecting the early career teachers. Having the lesson plans provided complicates matters. The lesson plan is simply a list of the pieces without teaching suggestions for different age groups. Early career teachers are more likely to adhere strictly to the lesson plan, lacking the confidence and knowledge of repertoire to understand the purpose for the activities and have access to suitable substitutes from their known repertoire. I have swapped roles and taught the classes on occasion and found this one of the most frustrating aspects because it impacts on planning and development. The teachers' reactions in the classes appear to indicate that this is a source of frustration for them too. For example, they can prepare a class for preschoolers because the same group has been there for the whole term, only to find there are no preschoolers this week, just a room full of babies, so they need to make an immediate mental switch and revise their lesson plans to suit the class. A solution to this could be to design lesson plans with three or four options for each activity, noting the appropriate age alongside. Although this would not solve the problem of multi-age classes, it would provide the teachers with options and a degree of flexibility in their teaching.

Class Numbers

How to find a solution to overcrowded classes is discussed at every teacher meeting. Capping class numbers is commonly tabled but vetoed. The philosophy of the program is not to turn anyone away. Overcrowding is a problem because the children do not receive the same attention from the teacher that they would normally, which can affect their learning and engagement. So, despite their best intentions at the inception of the program, the program cannot afford to advertise more widely with the current structure, for workplace health and safety reasons, if nothing else. This also means that parents have to be involved at every level. A common goal of early childhood classes outside this group is independence. For example, when the children reach preschool age, around three, the parents will leave the room after the first song and return toward the end of the lesson (Belsky and Fearon 2002). This cannot happen here.

A parent fully participating in music lessons with their child beyond the toddler stage is not necessarily negative, particularly in this context. Remembering that the goal for these groups is to form a community, fully participating in these music lessons is a great leveller. There is no activity more nakedly exposed than singing in public unless you are singing about being an elephant with the appropriate and necessary actions, but when everybody is doing it, it becomes an icebreaker (Clift et al. 2011). And it seems easier when the parents are all helping their children to learn. Unexpectedly, the older children often swap parents or choose to participate with another parent. New parents with young babies tend to be very popular, and they do not seem to mind having three or four "adopted" children who help them learn the songs and class routines. This may indicate that the children are reasonably independent and confident despite always participating in a lesson where their parents are present (Masten and Coatsworth 1998).

Links to the Wider Early Childhood Teaching Community

For this program to be successful in its current format, one needed to consult, or at least consider, the existing community of early childhood teachers during the planning phase. The early childhood teaching communities have been working conscientiously to build a strong presence and educate the community about the importance of quality early childhood music education. The structure of the program, level of teacher training, teacher recruitment practices, and price point of this particular program are incompatible with the needs of early childhood education. Failing to consider this has potentially put these groups at odds with this community of experts and their most viable external source of teachers.

Teacher Training and Development

The teachers, although quite experienced now, are missing key steps in their development that would allow them to progress as music teachers in other settings. Training in developmental, sequential lesson planning and reflective practice, key features in any education program, is not available to them through this program (George 2009). Because the lessons run on a three-year rotation based on the lessons from the lectionary, and this is the second rotation, the lessons are all in place and are sent to the teachers before each lesson. If the group manages to recruit new teachers, it appears they will have even less input in the program design and structure in the future.

Of the two original teachers recruited from the parishes as novices, one left the program at the end of 2014, having completed some early childhood music training externally and a formal education degree. This is not in music education, which this teacher decided not to pursue. The second teacher is staying with the program for the time being. The group this teacher is attached to increased the fees specifically to pay her, making her earnings commensurate with early childhood music teachers in day-care settings. There has not been any noticeable decline in family numbers since the fee increase.

The families from this community are generally not from high socioeconomic backgrounds. Responses to interview questions reveal a number of key reasons they attend the program with their children. First, they want the best possible developmental experience for their children and understand the role music can play in this. Second, they recognize that the structured music lessons with a trained music teacher rather than with recorded music set this program apart from other early childhood groups. Third, they see that they are spending quality time with their children, and they value this. And finally, they love their teacher and value what she shares with them, and this is the main reason they "did not bat an eyelid" when the fees were doubled. This is also why the centers continue to thrive as families tell their friends and come to lessons week after week even though the fee structure does not compel them to. Without the music teachers, these groups are like any other play group. There is no reason for them to attend, and there is no community.

The third center is also at a crossroads. This is the center where the principal teacher has always taught, but her ongoing involvement is unclear at this stage. This group has always been fortunate. The group has a mix of recent and established migrant families, but also professional people who attend the church. There has always been a music professional who can take the classes in an emergency. They have chosen to maintain their current fee structure rather than increasing the fees to pay for an early childhood music specialist, anticipating that this trend will continue.

Discussion

There is no doubt that this program has been successful in forming and sustaining a community. Rapid growth from five families to more than two hundred just from advertising within the group exceeded all expectations. There is also little doubt that music is the reason this group formed so quickly with little more than word-of-mouth advertising. Interviews at each of the centers indicate music lessons are the main reason parents bring their children to the groups. The parents understand the developmental benefits of music lessons and recognize that the fact they are provided sets this activity apart from other early childhood activities. They also said they would not continue bringing their children to the program if the music teacher was replaced by a recording, which was suggested to one focus group as a possible solution to teacher recruitment difficulties.

What is also certain is that the program is at a critical juncture. The groups cannot continue in their current format without early childhood music specialists. The program design and funding structure make recruitment of a specialist outside these communities extremely unlikely. From my experience, early childhood music education is often undervalued primarily because its role is misunderstood. Whether this is due to its simple repertoire or play-based learning or to something else entirely is unclear (Kim and Kemple 2011; Lee Nardo et al. 2006). In many ways the issues early childhood music faces are the same problems music education faces: unwillingness to commit funding and resources despite a growing body of literature that indicates the benefits of quality music education to cognitive, social, and behavioral development (Letts 2009). Unlike other areas of music education, the music teaching community, including some early childhood music teachers themselves, openly expresses the belief that anyone can teach these classes. This is far from the truth. Early childhood music education systems point to the need for the very best teachers to teach the very youngest children, and for good reason. Watching an experienced early childhood music teacher teach a class is exhilarating. They are instantly able to alter their lesson plans using their internal multidimensional curriculum to respond to the shifting and often unexpected demands of the class while maintaining musicality. They are skilled artists.

Conclusion

In the light of current research, community-based music programs like these take on a new importance. They have the potential to help level the playing field for disadvantaged families before their children reach school in a supported and caring environment. Because a parent or carer participates with the child, the music learning can be reinforced at home.

With proper funding and structure from the start, and consultation with all stakeholders—including the music-teaching community—groups have been able to attract the teachers they need and build a sustainable program. However, the nominal fee structure of the Aria Angels program in question has left no money in reserve and made it virtually impossible to attract the high-quality teachers the program needs who will stay with it and provide continuity in the long term. The music lessons are what draw families to the program. Parents have indicated that without them this is just like any other play group.

The end of the first three-year curriculum rotation in 2014 has seen many of the original families leaving the program as their children start school. One of the teachers is also leaving the program. Despite the group's increasing weekly fees to fund her position in the last half of 2014, payment depends on attendance and is far below what she could earn teaching in a day-care center or in studio teaching. While she has enjoyed her time teaching with the group, she is not staying in early childhood education. The third center is refusing to pay for a music teacher and is still hopeful that someone from the church will volunteer, possibly a retired music teacher. Whether this person will have the necessary skills to teach these classes remains to be seen.

The provision of music education is the key to the success of this program because the parents understand the value of music education, and attend with their children because they also see that music education sets this program apart from similar early childhood groups. In this context, music has proved very effective in forming and sustaining these communities of families with preschool-aged children. This is reflected in parents' comments during interviews and focus groups and their continuing support for the program despite the organization's giving them every reason not to. The families are not aware of the problems inherent in the design and implementation of the music lessons and the precarious position the program is in without funding. There is a clear demand from the community for this type of program. What is needed is a sound financial plan, whether it is presented to the church or as the basis for a grant application, that pays teachers appropriately according to the level of skill their role demands. Such a plan would allow the program to sustain these communities in the long term and provide access to quality music education that these families, and we, know their children need to support their early learning and development.

A fruitful area for future research would be an examination of how early childhood music is taught and used in other cultures. This might help us to identify areas where support can be provided to maintain cultural identity while also providing impetus for a meeting of musical cultures and ideas.

References

ACARA. 2011. "Shape of the Australian Curriculum: The Arts." Australian Curriculum Assessment and Reporting Authority, Sydney.

Anvari, Sima H., Laurel J. Trainor, Jennifer Woodside, and Betty Ann Levy. 2002. "Relations among musical skills, phonological processing, and early reading ability in preschool children." *Journal of Experimental Child Psychology* 83 (2): 111–130. doi:10.1016/s0022-0965(02)00124-8.

Baker, Felicity, and Elizabeth Mackinlay. 2006. "Sing, soothe and sleep: A lullaby education programme for first-time mothers." *British Journal of Music Education* 23 (2): 147. doi:10.1017/s0265051706006899.

Bamberger, Jeanne. 2006. "What Develops in Musical Development?" In *The Child as Musician: Musical Development from Conception to Adolescence,* edited by Gary E. McPherson, 69–92. New York: Oxford University Press.

Barrett, Janet R. 2007. "Music teachers' lateral knowledge." *Bulletin of the Council for Research in Music Education* 174: 7–23. doi:10.2307/40319476.

Belsky, Jay, and R. M. Pasco Fearon. 2002. "Infant–mother attachment security, contextual risk, and early development: A moderational analysis." *Development and Psychopathology* 14 (2): 293–310. doi: doi:10.1017/S0954579402002067.

Bergeson, Tonya R., and Sandra E. Trehub. 1999. "Mothers' singing to infants and preschool children." *Infant Behavior and Development* 22 (1): 51–64. doi:10.1016/S0163-6383(99)80005-8.

Bryck, Richard L., and Philip A. Fisher. 2012. "Training the brain: Practical applications of neural plasticity from the intersection of cognitive neuroscience, developmental psychology and preventative science." *American Psychologist* 67 (2): 87–100. doi:10.1037/a0024657.

Campbell, Patricia, and Carol Scott-Kassner. 2006. *Music in Childhood.* Belmont, CA: Thomson Schirmer.

Clift, Stephen, Ian Morrison, Trish Vella-Burrows, Grenville Hancox, Elle Caldon, Udi Perry, Penny Holden, Chrissie Parsons-West, Kate Hesketh Moore, Christina Rowland-Jones, and Sam Hayes. 2011. "Singing for Mental Health and Wellbeing: Community Initiatives in England." In *Songs of Resilience,* edited by Andy Brader, 121–144. Newcastle upon Tyne: Cambridge Scholars Publishing.

Custodero, L. A. 2006. "Singing practices in ten families with young children." *Journal of Research in Music Education* 54 (1): 37–56. doi:10.1177/002242940605400104.

Custodero, Lori A., and Elissa A. Johnson-Green. 2003. "Passing the cultural torch: Musical experience and musical parenting of infants." *Journal of Research in Music Education* 51 (2): 102. doi:10.2307/3345844.

Darrow, A. A. 2008. "Music and literacy." *General Music Today* 21 (2): 32–34. doi:10.1177/1048371308316411.

de Vries, Peter. 2005. "Lessons from home: Scaffolding vocal improvisation and song acquisition with a two-year-old." *Early Childhood Education Journal* 32 (5): 307–312. doi: 10.1007/s10643-004-0962-2.

———. 2009. "Music at home with the under fives: What is happening?" *Early Child Development and Care* 179 (4): 395–405. doi:10.1080/03004430802691914.

Douglas, Sheila, and Peter Willatts. 1994. "The relationship between musical ability and literacy skills." *Journal of Research in Reading* 17 (2): 99–107. doi:10.1111/j.1467-9817.1994.tb00057.x.

Geist, K., and E. A. Geist. 2008. "Do re mi, 1–2–3 that's how easy math can be: Using music to support emergent mathematics." *Young Children* 63 (2): 20–25.

George, Judith W. 2009. "Classical curriculum design." *Arts and Humanities in Higher Education* 8 (2): 160–179. doi:10.1177/1474022209102682.

Gould, Elizabeth, Patima Tanapat, Nicholas B. Hastings, and Tracey J. Shors. 1999. "Neurogenesis in adulthood: A possible role in learning." *Trends in Cognitive Sciences* 3 (5):186–192. doi:10.1016/s1364-6613(99)01310-8.

Gross, W., U. Linden, and T. Ostermann. 2010. "Effects of music therapy in the treatment of children with delayed speech development—results of a pilot study." *BMC Complement Altern Med* 10 (1): 39. doi:10.1186/1472-6882-10-39.

Gudmundsdottir, H. R., and D. G. Gudmundsdottir. 2010. "Parent–infant music courses in Iceland: Perceived benefits and mental well-being of mothers." *Music Education Research* 12 (3): 299–309. doi:10.1080/14613808.2010.505644.

Habib, Michel. 2009. "What do music training and musical experience teach us about brain elasticity?" *Music Perception* 26 (3): 279–285. doi:10.1093/cercor/bhn120.

Hallam, Susan. 2010. "The power of music: Its impact on the intellectual, social and personal development of children and young people." *International Journal of Music Education* 28 (3): 269–289. doi:10.1177/0255761410370658.

Hanley, Vivienne Jane. 2010. "The power of song." *Community Practitioner* 83 (5): 38–9.

Hargreaves, David J., and Adrian C. North. 1999. "The functions of music in everyday life: Redefining the social in music psychology." *Psychology of Music* 27 (1): 71–83. doi:10.1177/0305735699271007.

Hyde, K. L., J. Lerch, A. Norton, M. Forgeard, E. Winner, A. C. Evans, and G. Schlaug. 2009. "Musical training shapes structural brain development." *Journal of Neuroscience* 29 (10): 3019–25. doi:10.1523/JNEUROSCI.5118-08.2009.

Ilari, Beatriz. 2009. "Music listening preferences in early life: Infants' responses to accompanied versus unaccompanied singing." *Journal of Research in Music Education* 56 (4): 357–369.

Kim, Hae Kyoung, and Kristen M. Kemple. 2011. "Is music an active developmental tool or simply a supplement? Early childhood preservice teachers' beliefs about music." *Journal of Early Childhood Teacher Education* 32 (2): 135–147. doi:10.1080/10901027.2011.572228.

Klinger, R. 1990. *A Guide to Lesson Planning in a Kodaly Setting.* Oakland, CA: Holy Names College.

Lee Nardo, Rachel, Lori A. Custodero, Diane C. Persellin, and Donna Brink Fox. 2006. "Looking back, looking forward: A report on early childhood music education in accredited American preschools." *Journal of Research in Music Education* 54 (4):278–292. doi:10.1177/002242940605400402.

Letts, Richard. 2009. *The National Curriculum and Strategic Advocacy for Music and the Arts.* Erskineville, NSW: Music Australia.

Masten, Ann S., and J. Douglas Coatsworth. 1998. "The development of competence in favorable and unfavorable environments: Lessons from research on successful children." *American Psychologist* 53 (2): 205–220. doi:10.1037/0003-066x.53.2.205.

Motluk, Alison. 2000. "Grow your own." *New Scientist* 165 (2225): 24.

Ostwald, Peter F. 1973. "Musical behavior in early childhood." *Developmental Medicine and Child Neurology* 15 (3): 367–375. doi:10.1111/j.1469-8749.1973.tb04897.x.

Prideaux, David. 2003. "Curriculum design." *British Medical Journal* 326 (7383): 268–270.

Reubart, Dale. 1985. *Anxiety and Musical Performance: On Playing the Piano from Memory.* New York: DaCapo Press.

Ruksenas, Joanne Christine. 2011. "Why Music Education Needs to Take Itself Very Seriously." Paper presented at International Kodaly Symposium, Brisbane, Australia.

———. 2012. "The benefits of music classes for preschoolers: The ABC of do re mi." *Bulletin of the International Kodaly Society* 12 (1): 19–26.

Sacks, Oliver. 2007. *Musicophilia.* Toronto: Random House.

Skånland, Marie Strand. 2013a. "Music, health, and well-being" *International Journal of Qualitative Studies on Health and Well-being* 8. doi:10.3402/qhw.v8i0.21780.

———. 2013b. "Everyday music listening and affect regulation: The role of MP3 players." *International Journal of Qualitative Studies on Health and Well-being* 8. doi:10.3402/qhw.v8i0.20595.

Swanwick, Keith. 2008. "The 'good-enough' music teacher." *British Journal of Music Education* 25 (1): 9–22. doi:10.1017/s0265051707007693.

Ungar, Michael. 2011. "Community resilience for youth and families: Facilitative physical and social contexts of adversity." *Children and Youth Services Review* 33 (9): 1742–1748. doi:10.1016/j.childyouth.2011.04.027.

CHAPTER 17

Techniques and Tools for Music Learning in Australian Community Choirs

Naomi Cooper

In recent decades, community singing has formed an important part of community music in Australia. Many community choirs formed in the wake of the a cappella movement, which emerged in the mid-to-late 1980s (Rickwood 2010). International a cappella performers such as Frankie Armstrong from the United Kingdom and Sweet Honey in the Rock from the United States played a significant role in bringing a cappella music to Australia through performances and workshops (Rickwood 1997). Similarly, Siphiwo Lubambo, a representative of the African National Congress "who lived in Australia prior to the 1994 election of the Mandela government in South Africa," taught South African songs to many community choirs in Australia (Rickwood 1997, 177). Tony Backhouse played an important role in the dissemination of African American gospel through performing in a cappella quartets, establishing the Café of the Gate of Salvation choir, running workshops, and publishing his book "A cappella: Rehearsing for Heaven: An a cappella Workbook" in 1995. Numbers of community choirs have continued to grow, and the diversity of choirs across the country has rapidly expanded. The Australian National Choral Association (ANCA) stated, "ANCA has over 1000 members Australia wide, with the majority being choirs" (ANCA 2014). There are many more choirs that are not members, including several choirs in this study.

Definitions of "community choirs" are varied, and I have discussed elsewhere the ways in which almost all choirs in Australia can be considered to be community choirs of some sort (Cooper 2014). This is largely due to the fact that very few choirs there are professional in terms of receiving financial remuneration for their work. This wide spectrum of community choirs includes auditioned, non-auditioned, trained, untrained, a cappella, accompanied, men's, women's, children's, homeless people's, prisoners', and church choirs. These groups learn and perform a variety of repertoire, including Western art music, gospel, barbershop, popular, and culturally diverse musics (e.g., African, Welsh, Balkan, Pacific Island, Aboriginal Australian) in venues ranging from the Sydney Opera House to local community halls. A large number of these groups do not have strong score-reading skills, and the directors therefore employ approaches for teaching and conducting their choirs where the score is not the primary teaching tool. This research focuses on those choirs that are not auditioned and do not use the score as the primary teaching tool.

While Townsend (1996), Kennedy (2009), and Chadwick (2011) have provided interesting case studies of three choirs using an aural transmission approach, and I have contributed an Australian case study (Cooper 2013), I have not encountered a wider study that attempts to further definitions of aural transmission and strategies used by directors of non-auditioned choirs. Certainly no study of this kind has been conducted in Australia, where the choir culture continues to grow and diversify. This chapter therefore seeks to begin this discussion by drawing on my observation and interview of nine professional community choir directors working in Australia (mostly Sydney) in their regular practice with either non-auditioned community choirs or community singing workshop groups. It examines some of the strategies used by choir directors of Australian community choirs, which constitute "aural transmission." In doing so, it also suggests that "visual transmission" and "physical transmission" are two other key techniques used by community choir directors in their education practice, and examples of these will also be discussed. All three play an important role in teaching parts, rehearsing, vocal technique, pitch, rhythm, memorization, expression, articulation, feel, energy, and troubleshooting. There are several benefits associated with these approaches, including the capacity to create an inclusive and accessible learning environment where no prior musical or singing experience is required and the immediacy with which musical expression can be achieved. Though the focus of this study, and therefore this chapter, is on choirs where the score is not the primary teaching tool, many of these tools and techniques are also applicable to score-reading choirs.

Literature

Definitions of Aural Transmission

The term "aural transmission" has been applied by Townsend (1996, 9) to the teaching and learning practices of community choirs. He explained the term as meaning "that vocal parts were taught by a music leader through imitation" (10). Townsend observed music leaders at one African American Baptist church in Aurora, Illinois, United States, where aural transmission was the primary teaching approach, with scores only used occasionally. For these choirs, the aural transmission process included playing recordings of songs to the group and teaching a phrase or small section to each voice part by demonstrating and combining them additively. The imitation of a recording or leader facilitated the organic transmission of "other subtle nuances" (88) such as diction and vocal tone. While in one sense aural transmission appears very similar to rote learning, which is often criticized for its failure to embed deep understanding in singers (Brinson 1996; McGill and Volk 2007), Townsend identified the correlation between cultures that transmit their music orally and the aural transmission approach. Much of the African American repertoire, as well as the repertoire of many other cultures around the world including indigenous cultures of the Americas, sub-Saharan Africa, Polynesia, Australia, and Scottish Gaelic traditions (Nettl 1976; Sheridan, MacDonald, and Byrne 2011; Ross 1986), have been transmitted orally, with community members learning through immersion. Ethnomusicologists have suggested that adopting teaching approaches from the tradition of a particular song may be more appropriate than Western approaches, and in many cases this involves aural learning (Campbell 1991; Dunbar-Hall 2005). In the more structured context of a choir rehearsal, aural transmission honors the spirit of passing music on orally in a more formalized way. Aurally transmitted music from many cultures, especially African and African American music, formed a significant part of the repertoire of the Australian a cappella scene from the late 1980s (Rickwood 1997). Aural approaches have many other benefits, which will be discussed throughout the chapter.

A case study of the "Gettin' Higher Choir" in Victoria, British Columbia, Canada, reported "the teaching process is almost entirely by rote" (Kennedy 2009, 192) and noted that directors used a "call and response" approach to teach parts. Choristers were encouraged to acquire basic notational literacy in gentle ways, such as the inclusion of a section on basic theory in their choir folders and distribution of scores arranged specifically for the choir by their director. Participants spoke of the "chunking" method (Kennedy 2009, 193–194) where directors taught in manageable sections. This also referred to the pacing of the rehearsal so that material was not being taught too quickly (so that singers could keep up) or too slowly (so that singers would not get bored). Another important part of the choir's aural learning strategy was the "sourdough method" (193), which had an array of meanings deriving from a metaphor of "starter dough" (dough from a previous batch as the basis of a new batch), where old singers supported new singers to learn the singing techniques, repertoire, and culture of the choir. The choir's focus on "off-book" rehearsing and performing highlighted their aural focus (194). Kennedy's (2009) definition of aural transmission is derived from descriptions of music teaching and learning practices from various cultures around the world wherein listening forms the overarching method whether or not scores exist (Campbell 1991).

The University of Illinois Black Chorus (an African American choir) used aural transmission as its key approach for reasons of inclusion and so as to not intimidate singers, even though the director's preference is to use scores (Chadwick 2011). As with Townsend's study, the approach encouraged the "almost immediate possibility for nuance and expression. Even on the first hearing, the choir captures not just pitch and rhythm, but dynamics, intensity of tone, accents and aspects of the style. Musical expression is part of the music from the start, not something to be added on a week before the concert" (Chadwick 2011, 158–159).

In this study I have defined the aural transmission process to include anything the director did in a rehearsal that was audible. This included singing, speaking, playing an instrument, and body percussion. Verbal imagery has been used in vocal pedagogy for centuries, though there is contention regarding when and how it should be used. It is regularly employed when teaching vocal technique and for achieving different vocal tones (Freed 2000). Choir directors also use imagery for "phrasing, style and interpretation" (Bartle 2003, 42) as well as troubleshooting (Gonzo 1977). The power of a director's metaphor "as a vehicle to transfer perceptual, cognitive, emotional and experiential information from a thing that is understood (his metaphorical choice) to that which is less understood (the meaning of the music)" was articulated by Gonzo (1977, 10). He also identified the possibility of a metaphor failing if it is poorly chosen or not understood by the singers.

Beyond Aural Transmission: Visual and Physical Transmission

Although the term "aural transmission" embraces a wide range of strategies employed by directors in rehearsal, there are other dimensions to the transmission of the music that are not initially "aural." Directors use many visual strategies to assist with the teaching and learning processes of their choirs. I will refer to this usage as "visual transmission." It includes a set of visual strategies employed in the teaching of choral music in community choir settings but does not include traditional conducting gestures used in the conducting of a choral performance—for example, beat patterns, cues, and cutoffs. One example is the way directors use "hand levels to demonstrate the contour of song melodies" (Kennedy 2009, 192), and how "words of the song and choral cues were conducted instead of the standard beat patterns" in rehearsal (Townsend 1996, 76). Gesture is an important vocal pedagogical tool for technical, musical, physiological, and sensation-related principles (Nafisi 2010) and is used in conjunction with or instead of verbal imagery. Other visual modelling by the director such as mouth shape and eyebrow position has also been explored (Manternach 2012).

Musical notation has been used as a way of visually transmitting choir music for centuries. Gregorian chants were first learned from text and later had neumes written over the text. The earliest neumes were "used only as a general reminder to the singer of the course of a melody" (Parrish 1978, 8–9). Complete commercial arrangements for choir are now readily available.

In addition to aural and visual strategies, Backhouse (2010, 1995) placed a strong emphasis on the importance of movement and feeling rhythm in the body. I will refer to these kinesthetic/corporeal/movement dimensions of the teaching approach as "physical transmission." He believed that when teaching a song, starting with the rhythm helped everyone get the feel of the song in their bodies (2010, 32), and letting singers dance while singing or listening to a recording of the song gave them a new appreciation of the rhythmic feel or groove (2010, 30). Backhouse highlighted the importance of keeping singers aware of where the rhythm is in their bodies by using side-to-side–stepping groove and body percussion: claps, slapping thighs, and tapping shoulders (2010, 17–20). Wis referred to "physical metaphor" as "any gesture or movement that is able to get at the essence of the musical idea and involve singers in a concrete, bodily way" (1999, 25). She used this term to refer to gestures used by the director, as well as gestures executed by the singers themselves. A Dalcroze approach to the "philosophical, pedagogical and musical outcomes of choral pedagogy and practice" has been successfully applied to the teaching of vocal, aural, kinesthetic, ensemble, and music literacy skills as well as for nonmusical outcomes that enhance choral performance (Daley 2013, ii–iii). All of these authors highlight ways of teaching that do not focus on the score but instead utilize aural, visual, and physical strategies to facilitate choir experiences for singers.

Methodology and Participants

The methodology for this research involved the observation and interviewing of nine community choir directors, and analysis consisted of the coding of text data. As already noted, director participants were selected on the basis that their adult community choirs were not auditioned and the score was not used as the primary teaching tool. Survey data from the choirs demonstrated a wide range of ages and musical experience; however, that is not the focus of this chapter. Each director worked with a community choir on a weekly basis, and eight were observed in this context. The ninth director, who led choirs in Sydney for many years but has now moved away, was only observed in workshops in New South Wales. Three of the nine directors were observed in workshop and weekly rehearsal situations. I observed directors overtly, sitting in the rehearsal space, watching, listening, speaking with choristers, and taking notes (Gillham 2008) throughout 2013–2014. Each director was observed in at least two rehearsals and/or workshops. All nine were interviewed about their practice for between one to two and a half hours, and an additional experienced director, who sang in a number of community choirs and self-identified as an "expert helper," was also interviewed. All choir director participants had musical training. Nine had studied music at university (classical or jazz performance, composition or music education), though one did not complete the degree. The tenth trained in classical piano performance to Associate Diploma level. In spite of this, all directors said they learned their craft "on-the-job" rather than through training. Following a literature review, observation notes and interview transcripts were analyzed through the coding of text data. This analysis adopted Glaser's constant comparative method, whereby coding was compared "over and over again with codings and classifications that have already been made" (Flick 2002, 231).

Findings

Aural transmission was identified in the literature as a key theme, and from this I also identified visual and physical transmission as important associated themes. Other themes arising from the literature included blend, ensemble technique, pitch, expression, tone, troubleshooting, managing and organizing, director preparation, repertoire, and warming up. Additional themes from the observation and interview data included director histories, background information on songs, approaches to introducing a new song, the history of community choirs in Australia, composing and arranging for the choir, embodied singing, group formation, keeping a song going, showing singers the relationships between parts, rhythm and pulse, teaching songs in foreign languages, teaching parts, teaching vocal technique, women teaching men and men teaching women, use of gesture, the role of the conductor, maintaining interest in rehearsals, use of memory devices, teaching listening, working on transitions between sections of a song, teaching musicianship, demonstrating, use of imagery, and teaching approaches for workshops. Many of the identified themes overlap in some way with the themes of aural, visual, and physical transmission, and this chapter will therefore be structured around these three overarching themes.

Aural Transmission

All directors in the study used aural transmission as their main teaching approach. Singing, playing instruments, using body percussion, making recordings of voice parts, playing recordings of other artists, verbal direction, and imagery all constituted aural transmission strategies used.

The most obvious dimension to aural transmission is singing; however, directors used singing in a range of ways in the teaching process. All directors sang parts to teach the choir members, most using this as the primary method of teaching parts, though some used a keyboard or piano to demonstrate as well. For teaching parts, and at other times, directors used their voices to demonstrate all the required aspects of the music including pitch, rhythm, tone, dynamics, placement, register, vowel production, articulation, style, and groove. Singing was also used to cue entries and to keep a song going while navigating the different sections of a new song. For example, a director would start singing the chorus straight after the previous section at the moment when it was time to change into the chorus. Many directors switched between singing different voice parts in the middle of a section or phrase to help singers who were struggling in order to keep the song together. Vocal cues were often used to give starting notes, and instructions were sung on pitch and in time (such as singing "Let's do that again") to keep the flow of the rehearsal and avoid having to stop and start. Additive part-teaching was common, where some directors taught parts by singing one part, repeating it until the singers of that part were secure, then teaching a different voice part their line by singing over the top of the looping part that was taught first. This approach enabled singers to hear their part in relation to another part, and therefore in harmonic and rhythmic context from the first listening.

Most directors used an instrument at least some of the time for different purposes. Keyboards or pianos were popular for giving starting notes and playing parts. One director liked to do this because it is more "pitch accurate" than singing, "particularly if they've got a lot of vibrato," though another observed that "vocal tuning is different from piano tuning" and suggested that "people model better" from the voice. The keyboard was a useful tool when teaching members of the opposite gender, particularly women teaching basses, as the notes that basses are required to sing are outside the female vocal range. Male directors often had the option to use falsetto to sing women's parts at pitch, though at times parts were too high for their falsetto range. Some male directors used whistling to give pitches to women in these instances. One director described the way she used the piano as a reference point for pitch; for example, if a phrase started and finished on the same note, she was able to sustain that pitch on the piano as an aural reference. Some directors liked to use keyboard instruments for accompaniment, sometimes to support pitch and other times because it suited the song or style. Other directors, however, believed that demonstrating vocally was more effective than using an instrument to teach parts because singers could more easily copy the director's vocal nuances in terms of tone, ornamentation, articulation, and style.

For directors working a cappella, a pitch pipe or harmonica was used for pitch reference. One director used a ukulele to strum chords while teaching. This appeared to have several positive outcomes. It helped singers to understand the harmony as they were learning parts. This was useful because when working a cappella, while the director is teaching the first vocal line, it is not always easy to perceive the underlying harmony, particularly if it is an unusual chord progression. For a song the director had written and was teaching, there was an unusual chord progression of a series of chromatically ascending chords (mostly major, with one dissonant exception) and hearing the full harmony helped make sense of the parts as they were taught. The ukulele also helped maintain pitch, as the singers could hear it as a reference point at all times. Perhaps the high pitch of the ukulele was particularly helpful for female singers. The director made an aural and visual connection in the use of the ukulele: "it keeps the pitch and the feel of the song going in between . . . I use it as a conducting tool . . . [to] embody the feel of the song through the ukulele but I think it's more explicit because with my body movements [I'm not always facing them] . . . whereas with the uke, they can hear it even if they can't see me." In a similar way, another director often played the *djembe* in choir rehearsals, and the movements associated with playing it were indicative of rhythm, breath, phrasing, and feel–combining aural and physical approaches.

Body percussion was another aural strategy used by directors. Clapping, clicking, stamping, and slapping were common practices for keeping the beat or indicating tempo. Body percussion was also used to indicate rests (making a sound during a rest, particularly if it was on the first beat of the bar) or to maintain a sense of the pulse through sustained notes or passages. Clapping and tapping were used to indicate subdivisions of the beat or to communicate the feel of a song. Loud body percussion was used to build dynamics and also to elevate the energy of the group, whether for a song needing more energy or because the choir simply lacked energy that day. As with playing instruments, the visible dimension of body percussion was also helpful. Some directors used tapping gestures in a silent way to indicate the pulse without making a noise (which could have disrupted the atmosphere of a gentle song, for example). One director stated, "It's an accepted wisdom that once people have been working with me for a while, whatever I'm doing with my foot, that's where I want the beat to be." The foot movement varied from stomping to silently bouncing up and down in the air. As Backhouse pointed out: "When clapping, the work is not done solely when the hands meet. It's also what the arms do between claps" (2010, 18).

Many directors provided their singers with recordings of the vocal parts of their arrangements. Some recorded their own voices, and one woman found an octave-transposing tool that "makes me sound like a man." Other directors exported MIDI sound files from digital transcription software, often using a keyboard voice rather than a synthesized vocal sound, as it makes it easier to hear the pitch and rhythm. These recordings included individual parts, tracks with all vocal parts, and/or the whole arrangement if it is accompanied. Directors reported that they found playing recordings of other artists to be useful for communicating elements of the overall style or song to a group; however, one cautioned that recordings can "become authoritative" and was worried singers would simply copy the recording, which becomes problematic if arrangements vary slightly from those on the recording.

Speech was a very significant component of the aural transmission approach and related to all areas of the teaching. At times speech was used to give verbal directions, and at other times verbal imagery was used. Verbal directions were used for a wide range of reasons relating to all areas of the music. Directors often used speech to troubleshoot pitch, rhythm, vowel production, energy, vocal technique, and the feel of the song by describing and explaining what they wanted singers to do. Most made these instructions free of musical jargon so that all singers could understand and referred to lyrics to identify a section of a song rather than using bar numbers. Directors often described the pitch of notes in relation to each other, identifying whether the next note was going up or down from the previous one, when notes had the same pitch as the previous or an earlier note, and pitch relationships between phrases. They told singers when they were ahead of or behind the beat, and identified notes they were holding too long or too briefly. Words were used to describe the desired vowel sound and how to achieve it. Words of motivation and an enthusiastic vocal timbre were used to raise a group's energy.

Using the spoken word to communicate visual images relating to the overall feel or atmosphere of a song or individual vocal part, rhythmic feel, tone, or vocal technique proved effective. One choir director remarked on the strength of the "use of verbal language," saying of another choral director: "When he wants a group to do something that they're not doing, the words that he chooses, the way he expresses it is second to none. You see the value of it when they're able to do it immediately. . . . So they get that instant reward for effort which is not much of an effort at all, because it's been so lucidly and articulately put."

Some examples of imagery used to suggest the overall feel of the music included phrases such as "Sense of the end of the ocean, grandiose momentum"; "Aspiring upward, as if aspiring nobly toward the sea"; "You are like a rolling stone gathering moss, like a rolling snowball"; and "dirty bass line . . . lay down some filthy stuff, basses"; to individual words—"mellow," "plummy," "rich," and "warm." Imagery was also used to communicate the desired articulation: "Not pointy; smooth. Captain Legato, fighting the causes of boing"; "Accent and crispness with a nice kind of mellow center"; and "You know, one of those [acts out playing a synthesizer] on at first, then it fades."

Aspects of vocal technique were also addressed using imagery, including "Open up the back of your throat. Imagine there's a door here (back of the neck) and open it up"; "I recommend a more smiley kind of yodel"; "Get full voice for that top note. Be luminous and light. Just be a mock soprano for a moment"; and "I really want you to let that be spacious and luscious"—all encouraging an appropriate vocal tone for the song at hand.

The feel of the rhythm was often communicated through imagery with words such as "cruisey," "make it float a bit," or "Sopranos, don't rush through it, really savor it. Meander out. Don't push." Imagery was also used for troubleshooting, for example: "No, you're lazy. You're all hanging onto the bottom note, going 'Take me for a ride, note.' Find the note, harness the note, the note is your dog. At the moment the note is taking you for a walk. You're in charge of where the note goes." Comments used by directors ranged from being encouraging to jokingly chiding singers to help them achieve the desired effect, but were always made in good humor.

Visual Transmission

The musical score is the most common visual medium for communicating musical ideas. All of the community choirs in the study used scores at some point for learning and rehearsing, though for many singers aural learning was required to help them learn the music. The score provided a useful reference for the lyrics and pitch contour, and according to the directors, singers picked up more score-reading skills with increased familiarity. For some songs, choirs used lyric sheets instead of the full score. One director encouraged singers to draw reminders for the pitch contour onto their lyric sheet to make it more meaningful to them. The same director also used a large sheet of cardboard with the lyrics of shorter songs such as rounds written on it instead of distributing individual lyric sheets, as this meant the singers could look up rather than down at their sheets. Drawing markings on the cardboard lyric poster helped singers remember different aspects of the music. Phonetic transcriptions of songs in languages other than English were also used.

In addition to the regular gestures used by conductors in performance, such as beating time, cueing entries, and indicating dynamics, the choral directors used an array of gestures as part of the teaching process. Conducting the pitch contour in rhythm was an approach used by all directors in the study at least some of the time during the initial teaching of parts. This provided singers with a dynamic visual depiction of the music in terms of pitch and rhythm. Some directors used a two-handed pitch contour technique where two hands represented the pitch contour of two different voice parts simultaneously when combining the voice parts. Semitones often proved a difficult interval, and several directors used different gestures to indicate semitones to the group—on multiple occasions the semitone gesture involved a raised eyebrow. Gestures were used to communicate with the group without the need for verbal instructions. These could be to indicate which singers needed to be singing and when the director wanted to teach via call and response.

While some gestures used were common—such as conducting the pitch contour, finger to lips for a soft dynamic, cues, and cutoffs—many of the gestures were idiosyncratic, chosen to relate to a particular aspect of the song being taught. In one example, a director was combining two voice parts, the tenors singing on the beat with the sopranos singing off the beat. The director simultaneously kept the beat with one foot and indicated the syncopation with one hand, asking tenors to watch the foot and sopranos to watch the hand. Directors also used idiosyncratic gestures to remind singers of the lyrics by acting out words. Other examples of idiosyncratic gestures included fiercely eyeballing a voice section when it started to rush, and cutting off all voice parts except one by facing the voice part that kept singing and swiping hands to the side. Oftentimes, these gestures were probably unplanned and demonstrate the directors' capacities for spontaneous communication through gesture and nonverbal means.

The way in which a director moved while conducting communicated information to the singers. As mentioned above, the visible dimension of body percussion and instrument playing were indicative of the beat and tempo. One director used this movement to maintain the pulse in spite of the choir's rhythm getting slightly out of synchronization. In addition to this, movements associated with the body percussion or instrument, as well as movements in between these sounds, embodied the feel of the song and provided a visual model for how the singers might also feel, relate to, or respond to the song. Body movements and body language were effective in communicating dimensions such as breathing as well as dynamics and energy. For example, directors jumped or used their whole body to communicate an increase in dynamic or energy, not simply a hand gesture. Directors also moved towards and away from singers to achieve different effects in dynamics or, as they were teaching parts of a song, moving between voice parts. Teaching gestures often involved parts of the body apart from the hands, such as the head or shoulders, or leaning with the whole body.

Visual transmission worked particularly effectively for directors who encouraged or required singers to learn by ear rather than reading or following a music score or lyric sheet (whether or not a score was distributed). This meant that singers' eyes were not distracted by looking at a score and could focus their full attention on the director, thereby ensuring that the group was responsive to any gestures or movements the director made. That said, those directors were sparing with their gestures, so that every gesture communicated something important and there were no superfluous movements (for example, they did not cut off every phrase or beat time unnecessarily). In particular, a number of directors embodied the song as much as possible, expressing pulse, rhythm, groove, feel, pitch, dynamics, and expression physically with their bodies.

Physical Transmission

Physical transmission was not an approach used by all directors, but those who did use it in their teaching adopted a variety of concepts including rhythm, embodied singing, pitch, tone, and expression. One director described the importance of using physical transmission as a teaching method, saying: "I think possibly, that's what the issue is with a lot of people is that they're out of their body. You can't be." Another director expanded on this: "I just feel a lot of people are in their heads. We're often in our heads in our culture. We don't physicalize music very well." This director went on to discuss rhythm, which was the area most directors employed physical transmission approaches for, stating, "we don't have a physicality of it, many of us, in our bodies," and continued to describe the use of stepping in time to the beat to establish "the same internal beat" in the choir. The director believed "physicality is really the best way to do it, because we can't think it, we have to physicalize it. In a way, rhythm is a physical thing. We can't help but tap our toe. We can't help to tap our finger if we're feeling rhythm."

Another director utilized stepping extensively. In a workshop, the director worked on getting the singers to step in a way that embodied the groove of the song by saying, "Focus on your right foot . . . make it cool, you don't have to move your feet off the ground really" and demonstrated this by standing in the circle and stepping with the choir. The director described the way "the rhythm is more transparent to them, more obvious to them because sometimes some rhythms, syncopated things, they need some sort of reference point and so they know where that is." This allowed singers to feel the rhythm in relation to the pulse in their bodies. Stepping was also used to create focus and support other singers; for example, when the altos were singing a verse by themselves, the other singers were still performing the song by supporting them through moving with them. In a similar way to feeling the internal beat, this director found it useful to ensure that singers had a common feeling of the subdivisions of the beat or an awareness of the "smallest increment of the groove." The director was observed clapping the subdivision of the beat while stepping the pulse to cement the relationship between the two in a physical way.

Another director used physical transmission to teach a syncopated passage by getting singers to embody the rhythm before they sang it. The director asked them to do "a couple of rounds where we feel it but don't sing it"—that is, to feel the syncopation and encouraged singers to "feel it in your left shoulder." They followed the director's lead and lifted and dropped their left shoulders in time with the syncopated beat. This combination of physical transmission (feeling the rhythm in their bodies) and visual transmission (watching the director display the rhythm in his body) played an important role in establishing the feel of the song before they even started to sing it. Other context-specific strategies were used by directors in order to get singers to physicalize rhythms; for example, getting singers to stamp on a downbeat where they had a crotchet rest before the start of their phrase. Another example saw a director use a gesture to indicate the need to "lean" on a note (that is, to hold it slightly longer) and encouraged singers to use the same gesture to help them feel the rhythm.

When interviewed, several directors mentioned that a number of singers in their choirs were uncomfortable with movement and suggested that, for these individuals, movement did not benefit their singing. This perhaps serves the argument that many people are not experienced at physicalizing music, and that activities to develop these skills, in particular simple stepping exercises, would be beneficial. Embodied singing and teaching vocal technique in order to improve tone was another area in which several directors found physical transmission to be effective. A sense of grounding and feeling solid forms an important base to sing in an embodied way. The instruction to "sing like warriors" was used by one director to achieve this sensation. The director talked about the Māori Haka—an image that is very grounded and solid—to help singers to feel this way in their own bodies.

Another director talked a lot about the physical sensations in the body that are required for breath support. Singers were asked to feel different parts of the director's body as they demonstrated what to do with their bodies to support their sound. This included discussion of how to use the stomach muscles and diaphragm. The director said: "I talk physically a lot because there're just different sounds and I'll show them the difference. 'This is what it sounds like when your body's doing this. This is what it sounds like when you take this breath and you do a little bit of this.' There is a lot of that that I do and it creates an immediately different sound." In rehearsal, the director talked about the need to prepare the body to sing particular notes and asked singers, "Can you feel the difference?" The director then said, "Singing with your arsehole is what I'm asking you to do!"

Other directors worked with physical sensations to achieve a range of tonal colors in different ways. One director liked to use metaphor and spoke about a rehearsal where the bass section, as a group, were instructed to create the shape of the bow of a ship with their bodies as they sang part of a song:

> That's where all that choreography came from, was because I wanted them to sing with a lot of legato and a lot of sustain. But a metaphor is better than that because you can say to them, "sing with legato," "sing with sustain," and that conveys the technical aspects of what you're wanting. But if you're successfully able to say, "you're a fucking ocean liner, you're the QE2 sailing through the Atlantic evening." They can feel that. To me that's a much more powerful way of working with them, sort of visual imagery and imagination. It's like it conveys all of the necessary information if the metaphor you get is good enough. I'll often say to people you've got to be like a sort of a, you're singing a slow song, so it's like a tai chi master. You're doing your sort of super slow movements and if danger approaches, you're just there. So it's like this notion of being very still and slow and present, but at the same time attuned to the environment, so you're aware of the need to change quickly.

In a similar way, another director sometimes used hand gestures to help singers embody a particular tone, such as clasping their hands together in front of their body when aiming for a sweet, pure, church-style sound.

Physical transmission was also useful in the teaching of an understanding of pitch. One example was communicating to singers which part of their tessitura they should be using at any particular time—singing in the high part or low part of their vocal range. This was particularly useful for directors teaching the opposite gender. One director found it important to get singers to feel the resonance of their own voices in their bodies to help them understand pitch: "I find that if I can actually get them to put their hand on the part of their body that should be resonating, in their chest or their head, and we try to physicalize the sound, so they can feel it in their body as a resonance as much as possible. And that's helped some men, because otherwise, they're just grabbing in the air. They don't really understand what that note should feel like in their body."

In a similar way, another director spoke of understanding this resonance in relation to the tonal center. The director talked to singers about using the tonal center to find their note if they got lost by trusting their body in knowing where a note should resonate in their body. In the director's words: "I'm trying to explain to them that it's of the body. You're the instrument and where is it vibrating, where do you feel it? It's valid. I said you don't have anywhere to put your fingers on buttons, you're not a saxophone. . . . You know where that feels and choirs are fantastic that way." This director believed it helps to "actually assign those notes to a certain feeling that's muscular." This penetrates beyond an understanding of the pitch to the overall feel of the song:

> I like them to locate the sound. I find that people that can't locate the sound physically get really lost and even if they're contemporary-classical readers they get really lost because they can't stitch it to a score. They don't even think physically. For me the physical is the feel of a song. So you put it into your hips. I think women are very sensual beasts and they worry a lot about their bodies, so I ask them to actually kind of put the feel of a song into where they think they have their weight, so their hips, or their boobs, put it into your body because that's the feel of you and that's the feel of the song.

Physical transmission was also used for vocal placement and technique, encouraging singers to feel their voices in their bodies. Statements such as "many of you will find it easier to flip over to your lighter voice. Rather than pushing your loud voice, use your lighter voice" allowed alto singers to feel and understand the sensations of different placements and techniques. Similarly, for helping inexperienced male singers to sing in the correct octave, one director said: "Tenors, get together so you know what octave you're in. I'm assuming you're in your high one, not your low one." Another director used humor to encourage the physical transmission of basses singing in their higher octave: "Get up there! Someone's down there. If someone next to you is down there, look at them like they've farted." It is clear from these statements and observations that directors refer to all parts of the body as part of the physical transmission approach in order to achieve the desired sound from their singers, and that in this regard nothing is sacred.

Various researches have highlighted an array of aural, visual, and physical approaches used by choir directors; however, discussion of the holistic integration of these three in the context of community choirs where scores are not the primary teaching tool is scarce. The following table seeks to integrate the wide range of aural, visual, and physical tools and techniques directors used to teach their community choir members, with examples from the literature (table 17.1).

Table 17.1. Aural, visual, and physical approaches used by directors in the study, with examples from the literature in italics

Aural	*Visual*	*Physical*
Singing	Visual reference	Stepping
Call and response teaching	Score	Feeling a common beat
Correlation with oral traditions	Lyric sheet	Embodying the feel and groove of a song
Singing parts	Large cardboard sheet	Making the rhythm more transparent by feeling the rhythm in relation to the pulse
Additive part-teaching	Phonetic transcription of lyrics in foreign languages	Feeling the subdivisions of the beat in relation to the pulse
Demonstrating pitch, rhythm, vocal tone, articulation, vowel production, registration, style, and groove	Gesture	Creating focus and support
Cueing entries	Conducting pitch contour in time	Rhythm
Keeping a song going	Difficult intervals, especially semitones	Context-specific teaching strategies involving physicalizing rhythm
Singing instructions	Nonverbal instructions	Embodying the rhythm while teaching parts
Singing starting notes	Reminding singers of the lyrics	Embodied singing
Instrument	Idiosyncratic gestures for parts of particular songs	Sense of grounding in the body
Playing starting notes	*Technical, musical, physiological, and sensation-related dimensions of vocal pedagogy*	Vocal technique
Playing parts	*Physical metaphor in the form of conducting gestures*	Physical sensations required for breath support
Accompaniment	Visual modelling	Physical sensations required for various vocal tones, techniques, and placements
Pitch reference (especially for a cappella)	*Modelling mouth shape, eyebrow position, posture, etc.*	
Helping singers understand the harmony when teaching parts	Movement	
Visual dimension of playing instrument conveys the feel of a song	Communicating the beat	
Body percussion		
Keeping the beat		

Table 17.1. *(Continued)*

Aural	*Visual*	*Physical*
Indicating rests	Communicating the feel	Movement
Building dynamics and energy	Dynamics	Movements associated with visual images to achieve vocal or musical effects
Visual dimension of body percussion conveys the pulse and feel	Energy	*Physical metaphor in the form of singers executing movements*
Recordings	Embodying the song	*Dalcroze approach*
Individual or combined voice parts		Pitch
Other artists		Understanding tessitura
Speech		Feeling resonance in the body in relation to the tonal center
Verbal direction: troubleshooting pitch, rhythm, vowel production, energy, and vocal technique		Muscular sensations of pitch
Verbal imagery—for the overall feel of the song, vocal technique, rhythm, troubleshooting, *phrasing, style, and interpretation*		Feel
Rehearsing		Feeling the song in the body
"Chunking"		
"Sourdough" method		
Off-book rehearsal		

References

ANCA. 2014. "Australian National Choral Association." Retrieved from: http://anca.org.au/find-choir.

Backhouse, Tony. 1995. *A Cappella: Rehearsing for Heaven: An A Cappella Choral Workbook.* Chatswood, NSW: Redback Press.

———. 2010. *Freeing the Song: An Approach to Directing Vocal Groups.* Bondi, NSW: École de Fromage.

Bartle, Jean Ashworth. 2003. *Sound Advice: Becoming a Better Children's Choir Conductor.* Oxford: Oxford University Press.

Brinson, Barbara A. 1996. *Choral Music Methods and Materials: Developing Successful Choral Programs (Grades 5 to 12).* New York: Schirmer Books.

Campbell, Patricia Shehan. 1991. *Lessons from the World: A Cross-cultural Guide to Music Teaching and Learning.* New York: Schirmer Books.

Chadwick, Sheelagh. 2011. "Lift every voice and sing: Constructing community through culturally relevant pedagogy in the University of Illinois Black Chorus." *International Journal of Community Music* 4 (2): 147–162. doi:10.1386/ijcm.4.2.147_1.

Cooper, Naomi. 2013. "Impacting communities: Tools and techniques for empowering untrained singers to sing in a group." *Proceedings of the Nineteenth Australian Society for Music Education National Conference: Redefining the Musical Landscape: Inspired Learning and Innovation in Music Education, September 28–29.* Parkville, Vic.: Australian Society for Music Education.

———. 2014. "Seeking a 'True' Approach for Directing Non-Notation Reading Choirs: A Literature Review." In *The Truth Is Out There,* edited by Julie Lunn and Stephanie Bizjak. Perth, WA: Black Swan Press, Curtin University.

Daley, Caron. 2013. "Moved to Learn: Dalcroze Applications to Choral Pedagogy and Practice." DMA diss., University of Toronto.

Dunbar-Hall, Peter. 2005. "Colliding Perspectives? Music Curriculum as Cultural Studies." *Music Educators Journal* 91 (4): 33–37. doi:10.2307/3400156.

Flick, Uwe. 2002. *An Introduction to Qualitative Research.* 2nd ed. London: SAGE.

Freed, Donald Calleen. 2000. "Imagery in Early Twentieth-Century American Vocal Pedagogy." *Journal of Singing* 56 (4): 5–12.

Gillham, Bill. 2008. *Observation Techniques: Structured to Unstructured.* London, New York: Continuum International Publishing Group.

Gonzo, Carroll L. 1977. "Metaphoric Behavior in Choral Conducting." *Choral Journal* 17 (7): 8.

Kennedy, Mary Copland. 2009. "The Gettin' Higher Choir: Exploring culture, teaching and learning in a community chorus." *International Journal of Community Music* 2 (2–3): 183–200. doi:10.1386/ijcm.2.2&3.183/1.

Manternach, Jeremy N. 2012. "The effect of nonverbal conductor lip rounding and eyebrow lifting on singers' lip and eyebrow postures: A motion capture study." *International Journal of Research in Choral Singing* 4 (1): 36–46.

McGill, Stan, and Elizabeth Volk. 2007. *Beyond Singing: Blueprint for the Exceptional Choral Program.* 1st ed. Milwaukee, WI: Hal Leonard.

Nafisi, Julia. 2010. "Gesture as a tool of communication in the teaching of singing." *Australian Journal of Music Education* (2): 103–116.

Nettl, Bruno. 1976. *Folk Music in the United States: An Introduction.* 3rd ed. Edited by Helen Myers. Detroit, MI: Wayne State University Press.

Parrish, Carl. 1978. *The Notation of Medieval Music, Vol. 1.* Hillsdale, NY: Pendragon Press.

Rickwood, Julie. 1997. "Liberating Voices: Towards an Ethnography of Women's Community A Cappella Choirs in Australia." MA thesis, Australian National University.

———. 2010. "Singing in between: Re-visioning intercultural community singing." *Re-Visions: Proceedings of the New Zealand Musicological Society and the Musicological Society of Australia Joint Conference, Dunedin, New Zealand, December 2–4,* edited by M. Poole, 218–229. Dunedin: New Zealand Music Industry Centre.

Ross, Margaret Clunies. 1986. "Australian Aboriginal oral traditions." *Oral Tradition* 1 (2): 231–271.

Sheridan, Mark, Iona MacDonald, and Charles G. Byrne. 2011. "Gaelic singing and oral tradition." *International Journal of Music Education* 29 (2): 172–190. doi:10.1177/0255761410396960.

Townsend, Robert Toussaint. 1996. "The Music Teaching and Learning Process in an African-American Baptist Church." PhD diss., University of Illinois at Urbana-Champaign.

Wis, Ramona M. 1999. "Physical metaphor in the choral rehearsal: A gesture-based approach to developing vocal skill and musical understanding." *Choral Journal* 40 (3): 25–33.

CHAPTER 18

Engaging with Sax beyond Conservatoire Walls

The Community Activities of the Queensland Conservatorium Saxophone Orchestra

Diana Tolmie

Currently the large ensemble course at Brisbane, Australia's Queensland Conservatorium Griffith University (QCGU) is pass/fail "compulsory-for-credit"—that is, part of the bachelor of music program for first- and second-year students. Performing ensemble options include the Queensland Conservatorium Symphony Orchestra, Queensland Conservatorium Chamber Orchestra (QCCO), Queensland Conservatorium Wind Symphony (QCWS), the Con Artists (CA), Queensland Conservatorium Big Band (QCBB), and the Queensland Conservatorium Saxophone Orchestra (QCSO). The first four ensembles apply a model rotating personnel per project (one to two concerts per semester), with activities held within the semester timetable. There is no room for event planning beyond the students' three-to-four-year degree owing to the interruptive turnover of graduating students and minimal alumni participation. For the classical saxophone students, enrollment possibilities are with the QCWS, CA, QCBB, and QCSO.

Usually, engagement with the community is limited to university-site ticketed or free concert performances. Outreach for the symphony orchestra has experimented with offsite venues such as an inner-city church and has enjoyed enthusiastic audience outcomes and heightened operational challenges. Another event performing in a local music festival coincided with the students' mid-semester vacation. Personal observation understood this to have been met with contention from some staff and students who perceived "out-of-hours" commitment as conflicting with past practices. The QCWS does have a tradition of community outreach with pre-tertiary schools in addition to onsite conservatoire concerts. However, these events take place only once or twice per year owing to the size of the group (sixty plus members) and the consequent cost and logistics of driving the required long distances.

In contrast, the Con Artists is a big band of roughly twenty-two jazz and classical students who perform in-house concerts, plus external "gigs" in jazz festivals and at metro/regional venues, for example, the Brisbane Jazz Club and the Byron Bay Beach Hotel. Some of these activities are "for fee," whereby earned money is contributed towards CD recordings of the group collaborating with guest artists performing traditional as well as new inter/nationally composed music.

The QCSO is considered one of the more recent and proactive ensembles at its institution. In order to consider the community activities and perceptions of the students, the evolution and ethos of the ensemble needs first to be explored in depth.

About the QCSO

Founded in 2008, the QCSO was formed initially as a biannual event to give the saxophone students of the QCGU additional performing experience otherwise not possible considering the nominal opportunities for classical saxophonists in traditional mediums. This evolved into weekly three-hour rehearsals plus tutorials in 2010 supporting the volume of activities the group undertook. Directed with an entrepreneurial mind-set, the ongoing overarching aim is to allow students the opportunity to practically exercise and experience music industry realities otherwise not present within the degree environment. By assigning those in the group various roles such as librarian, treasurer, composer, arranger, tutorials organizer, website manager, and so on, all students have "ownership" of the ensemble and develop "real world" skills beyond performance.

Community engagement and networking are key priorities, and although enterprising behavior is encouraged, a primary learning outcome is to foster "can-do" confidence to complete self-directed and promoted artistic projects. Rehearsals and "in-house" performances are conducted at the QCGU with all students possessing their own instruments except for the bass saxophone provided by the institution. The group store their music on a bespoke online library governed by OurDisk (Hawkins 2014), one of the group's corporate sponsors.

Since 2010, the QCSO has engaged between ten to twenty schools concerts, master classes, and workshops per year throughout the rural, regional, and metropolitan community, where fees charged are reserved for the ensemble's touring. As of 2011, the QCSO began an aggressive curriculum vitae–building regime by performing at national and international conferences, festivals, and educational music camps. In order to maintain a high calibre of performance and inter/national benchmarking, guest saxophone lecturers/performers network and perform with the students throughout the academic year.

The years 2011 and 2012 were the QCSO's period of fund-raising for the twenty-day European tour. During this process the group continued their schools activities; performed at events and venues such as the Fête de la Musique, retirement villages, and collaboratives with other community music institutions; conducted a Pozible crowd funding campaign; developed a logo, website, and social media page; performed live on ABC radio; and enjoyed a sell-out crowd at the Brisbane Jazz Club titled "Sax to the Max" with invited community groups and guest professional musicians. Local music and non-music businesses were approached and donated in-kind and financial support. These included a Returned Services Leagues Club (RSL), a woodwind repairer/instrument retailer, and a law firm.

Music performed on the international tour was composed and arranged by QCSO members, other QCGU composition students, and Brisbane professional composers. At the end of the year the group recorded a CD of these commissions to formulate *Australian Made 2012,* commercially available on CD Baby and iTunes. QCGU provided the recording venue, and three bachelor of music technology students volunteered their services for sound recording and engineering.

For four years the QCSO has enjoyed a relationship with the Queensland Symphony Orchestra (QSO), performing in their education series concerts twice yearly. This has been a tremendous experience for the students, who would otherwise not enjoy the professional orchestral environment so early in their training. From this, the students have been exposed to the power of "branding" as a valuable tool towards generating large-scale interest in the group and classical saxophone awareness. The QSO education concerts enjoy audience attendance from five hundred to two thousand school-aged students and teachers per concert.

Activities of this extent were reliant on creating a student awareness of community dynamics—that is, their understanding the importance of collegiality to the group itself and the sustainability of professional practices that result in long-term relationships. In addition, the people who trusted the quality of the QCSO and interacted with our efforts so positively were incredibly valuable in creating this collective music appreciation experience. Although activities were carefully planned with sincere consideration of all stakeholders, there had not been any reference or comparison to the written literature of other university ensembles regarding community interaction, primarily because, to our knowledge, none had existed at the time.

On considering the definition of community music, Brydie-Leigh Bartleet acknowledges the broad debate among scholars yet summarizes: "it is a group activity where people join together to actively participate in the music-making process. It encompasses a wide and diverse range of musics, which reflect and enrich the cultural life of the participants and their broader community" (2008, 3). This statement invites scrutiny of the cultural life of the QCSO students in the sense that the term "culture" can be considered as the "ideas, customs, and social behavior of a particular people or society" (n.a 2015). Furthermore, this can include their education environment and opinions regarding interaction with their community subsets—in this case school-aged students, schoolteachers, venue management, visiting artists, and the broader community. Mutually so, the community's opinions and cultural experiences of QCSO are equally as valued in defining the future music-making choices of the QCSO, directly impacting learning outcomes.

From an education perspective, there is a growing amount of literature regarding pre- and non-tertiary groups engaging with the broader community, in addition to community music education programs centered on aspects of cultural development or traditional practice sustainability. These programs very often extend to those considered minority groups, such as the prominent Melbourne's Choir of Hard Knocks for the homeless and disadvantaged (n.a 2007), or the more recycle-friendly Landfill Harmonic, conducted by Favio Chávez in Cateura, Paraguay (n.a. 2012). Relating to the single-reed wind instrument community, a colleague runs a group titled Clarinets for Conservation wherein American teachers travel to Tanzania for six weeks per year to meet with a regional community and offering performances, instruments, accessories, and clarinet lessons to local schoolchildren and teachers (Haug 2013). They also plant slow-growing Grenadilla trees, which are a declining population owing to unsustainable clarinet manufacturing practices—in short, holistically engaging with the educational, cultural, and agricultural development of the community. These are but a small sample of the depth of community music engagement that is available in the world, and it is no wonder that defining the terminology has enjoyed such robust discussion.

The literature regarding tertiary ensembles engaging with community is currently minimal. Dimitra Kokotsaki and Susan Hallam have presented UK studies exploring higher education music and non-music students' understanding of the virtues and salient attributes of participative music making (2007, 2011). While these are useful to aid comprehension of student cultures of large and small tertiary ensembles, there is no discussion that develops the understanding of students' perceived value of interaction with the broader community. An Australian study identified varying styles of tertiary ensemble direction, noting an approach of one research participant who valued community engagement and networking (Harrison, O'Bryan, and Lebler 2013). In this publication, neither the students nor the community was referenced to corroborate the participant's understanding. Yet Stephanie Pitts concurs with the crux of Harrison and colleague's message that "the lecture room walls are highly permeable in a music department, and arguably more learning (or at least as much) takes place outside them than within" (2013, 195) and promotes ensemble participation as beneficial. She also criticizes traditional curricula, warning that the "focus on results and success risks stifl[ing] the creative opportunities of performing arts departments and their students" (Pitts 2013, 199). Rather, an educator needs to look bravely beyond the four walls of the conservatoire. The pre/non-tertiary music education sector offers some insight into this opinion.

A two-year study of community music in Australia titled *Sound Links* revealed the need for more school–community interactivity, stating:

> By participation in community music ensembles, students can access repertoire, styles of music, and examples of pieces of music for analysis beyond the music that is studied in classrooms. Community music activities can also provide teachers and students with access to music with cultural specificity, to instruments and performers. Performing groups that specialize in the music of a specific cultural background could provide resources for classroom use in the form of notation and recordings; members of these

> groups could become interviewees in student assignments. Performances that integrate local community music groups and school performing groups provide a means for linking school music studies with local music activity. (Bartleet et al. 2009, 150)

Although this is suggesting that school-age students partake in external community music programs to supplement their education, tertiary institutions need not rule themselves out of this discussion. In particular, accessing the community for alternate venues/audiences encouraging repertoire diversity creates an opportunity to discover symbiotic relationships that transcend the traditional stereotypes of audience-as-listener and musician-as-performer.

It could be argued that the QCSO cannot be categorized within the community music genre, as it is perhaps not as immersive, reciprocal, or permanently fixed within the broader community as the previous examples. Certainly, a brief glance will show an enterprising ensemble that gains financial reimbursement for realistic self-benefit. Further observation will reveal a life cycle of sharing education and experiences that aligns with the identified nine key domains of community music of the *Sound Links* study: (1) infrastructure; (2) organization; (3) visibility and public relations; (4) relationship to place; (5) social engagement; (6) support and networking; (7) dynamic music making; (8) engaging pedagogy and facilitation; and (9) links to school. The most important characteristics of almost any community music project can be described under these headings (Bartleet 2009, 28).

Methodology

The following research was based on case-study analysis typically sourcing published documentation, client/student feedback, direct observation, and participant-observation evidence (Yin 2003). Documentation predominantly consists of newspaper articles, e-mail correspondence, and concert reviewer reports as an outcome of engagement with the students, director, and clients of the QCSO over a four-year period. The e-mail correspondence has been de-identified in accordance with ethical considerations, as have those conversations recalled by the director. The mostly unknown biases of these authors aside, the diversity of data is useful in validating observation claims from the researcher. It must be mentioned that the chapter author is both researcher and director of the ensemble whose autoethnographic account will pervade this case-study analysis. This choice of method aims to "gain a cultural understanding of self and others" (Chang 2008, 5). As the author is an active participant in the community of the QCSO, her account will constitute an insider viewpoint on the ensemble's planning and interaction within the broader communities. Thus, to add a less-biased perspective, a closed Likert and open-ended online questionnaire was administered via Survey Monkey and distributed to current and past members of the QCSO.

This online survey consisted of twelve questions investigating the students' perceptions of learning outcomes and the value of QCSO experiences. Not all alumni were contacted owing to out-of-date e-mail addresses or lack of contact by the director and group members. Of the twenty-eight students e-mailed participant invitations (roughly 80 percent of the total population of past/current members), twenty-four responded, producing an acceptable 85.71 percent response rate (Nulty 2008). The choice of online survey was to ensure time and cost convenience with respect to implementation, use of the survey tool, and reminder updates. The initial aim of the survey was to identify the effect of enterprise activities within their bachelor of music curriculum. What became apparent was the students' perspective of engagement within a community beyond their institution.

The demographic of the survey respondents ranged from first year undergraduate through to third year graduated (see table 18.1) with a seventeen to seven undergraduate to graduate ratio (see table 18.2), and the reverse ratio in male to female respondents (see table 18.3). This age range translates to seventeen to twenty-three years old.

The high ratio of females in all categories reflects the saxophone gender trend at the QCGU. It is what I consider the result of the "Lisa Simpson effect" whereby the saxophone has shifted from a gender-neutral instrument to one more associated with feminine role models such as the infamous baritone saxophone–playing Lisa Simpson animated cartoon. This observation

Table 18.1. Year level of QCSO respondents

Year Classification	*Number*
1st year undergraduate	5
2nd year undergraduate	6
3rd year undergraduate	5
4th year undergraduate	1
1st year after undergraduate degree graduation	4
2nd year after undergraduate degree graduation	2
3rd year after undergraduate degree graduation	1
Total	**24**

Table 18.2. Undergraduate to graduate ratio of QCSO

Student Classification	*Number*	*Percent*
Undergraduates	17	70.83
Graduates	7	29.17
Total	**24**	**100.00**

is confirmed in a 2003 study on musical participation of Brisbane school-age boys who considered the saxophone a feminine instrument (Harrison 2003). Conversely, this is not reflected so strongly in the professional classical saxophone performance arena. It is generally observed that males maintain a majority high-profile presence at World Saxophone Congresses and similar events in addition to tertiary-level staff appointments.

The QCSO Director's Perspective

Reflecting on my own undergraduate days as a classical clarinet student at the Queensland Conservatorium, the classical saxophone had always been deemed the "poor cousin" of the clarinet. Weekly single-reed workshops were directed by our clarinet lecturer; the saxophone students were largely outnumbered four to one and rarely performed, let alone offered critique. The saxophone repertoire was comparatively contemporary, mostly attributable to its development a number of centuries later than all its wind family members. As a conservatoire wind lecturer I noticed that this had not changed: the saxophone students appeared less motivated and lacking a sense of purpose towards their education in comparison to the linear career dreams of their "wealthier"

Table 18.3. Gender ratio of total vs. undergraduate vs. graduates of QCSO

Gender	*N = 24*	*Of 100%*
Males	7	29.17
Females	17	70.83
Gender—Undergraduates	*N = 17*	*Of 100%*
Males	5	29.41
Females	12	70.59
Gender—Graduates	*N = 7*	*Of 100%*
Males	2	28.57
Females	5	71.43

cousins. Upon an abnormal influx of saxophones one year I recognized an opportunity to change this pattern, and so the QCSO activities began.

As a freelance woodwind specialist of twenty-five years I understand the value of networking and creating contacts with the community. As a tertiary instrumental lecturer of fifteen years I also acknowledge the intensely elite environment a conservatoire can foster, creating a heightened egocentric perspective on one's degree to the detriment of future employment opportunities. Graduation, which should be considered an exciting milestone, is viewed rather traumatically. As one saxophone student wrote on Facebook: "I have a degree in classical saxophone. Great! Now what do I do with it?!" (De-identified, 2010). I wanted to offer the students the opportunity to have a smoother transition, to be inspired by the value of their music making through the responses of unknown listeners who were perhaps either not as privileged or talented as they—or rather, not as musically developed. I was also determined to change the exclusive culture not only of the saxophones within the wind department, but also of the conservatoire within the broader community. In addition, I aimed to give students the opportunity to take pride in their diverse capabilities; understand the power and impact their music making could have via performance, recordings, Web presence, social media, and reputation; as well as implement and achieve long-term goals.

It has been quite the journey so far, one that has required a tremendous amount of energy, personal finances, exhaustion of my professional networks, forward planning, and an intense dislike for the word "no." At times I have been ridiculed for developing such a genre so publicly (a saxophone orchestra is not as common as a string orchestra). One colleague called it a "stupid idea," and others criticized me as an imposter considering clarinet initially had been my primary instrument and I had worked in the orchestral medium for so long. I marveled that aspiring classical saxophonists were brave enough even to attend a conservatoire in light of this prevailing traditional mind-set.

If their willingness to participate in my adventures is any proof, the student response was overall positive. I would like to think they viewed my proactivity as support they had otherwise not had and responded in kind with a mostly jolly approach to everything, including new music exploration, diverse forms of fund-raising, or gig locations. However, I am inherently aware that longevity in the music industry affords one a dogmatic perspective of what is required for vocational preparation. I am also aware that a veteran approach can blindside one into thinking that students are mindful of these educational values and will act sincerely. I recall one of the first students of the QCSO adopting a "strategic approach" to her learning, that is, focusing on her grades more than the bigger employability picture (Entwistle and Peterson 2004, 415), quipping to her younger colleagues, "Just don't forget who is on your performance exam panel at the end of the year!" It would appear that my "position of power" had influenced her consideration to resist QCSO activities. She had also declared that the QCSO was a good "GPA-booster" during the short time it was a graded course. Such dispiriting words were not welcome, as they indicated a self-serving and therefore non-altruistic attitude—the opposite of what I was hoping the students would develop. However, these were the outspoken musings of only one, and it was not until conducting this survey that I fully learned the collective student opinion.

Student Perspectives

When asked, "What were the benefits you experienced being a part of the QCSO?" students were given an option of musically technical, community, and business skill categories (see table 18.4). Technique, tone awareness, repertoire, intonation, and rhythm ranked highly, demonstrating that the ensemble maintained an intrinsic focus on developing a good "product" that espoused the fundamentals of their own one-to-one music education. This was closely followed by networking with visiting artists, music business skills, sharing

Table 18.4. Perceived benefits by students

What were the benefits you experienced being a part of the QCSO? (multiple response)	*Response*
Performance music education—intonation	24
Performance music education—tone awareness	23
Performance music education—rhythm	21
Networking with visiting artists	21
Performance music education—repertoire	20
Sharing music with school-aged students	20
Performance music education—technique	18
Sharing music with community members	16
Music industry awareness	16
Networking with school education specialists outside the Queensland Conservatorium	15
Collegiality	14
Leadership skills	11
Music arrangement experience	9
Composition experience	5

music with school-age students and community members, and then collegiality. More music-specific skills such as composition, arranging, and leadership were not as predominantly ranked. This was expected, as not all participants had partaken of these activities.

When asked, "Overall, how would you rate the QCSO as valuable to your music experiences?" the summary response was 4.7, with five ranked highest on the Likert question. Although invited to make a comment about their choice, most early in their degree opted not to; commentary was more common from those enrolled later in their degree or graduated. For some of these older undergraduate students, the choice of the word "we" indicates the development of ownership and collective "commitment": for example, "I enjoy being part of this ensemble very much as it provides such a broad range of experiences and gigs. Out of every ensemble in the university *we* are surely the one that has the most performance opportunities" (Participant no. 7, third year).

Yet some from this subset were firmly entrenched in considering personal benefit of musical development. For example, "Wide range of styles and ensemble experience. Good place to develop tone, technique and intonation in a year-long regular commitment" (Participant no. 3, third year).

To those who are graduated and employed in education, the consideration for the QCSO activities reveals an appreciation and confidence to apply and share the knowledge taught, understood, and demonstrated within the QCSO activities.

> My involvement with QCSO has allowed me to grow both professionally, and personally as a musician and inter/intrapersonally, being able to not only perform publicly, but also plan, market and publicise performances. The valuable pedagogical experiences I gained from my time with QCSO has [*sic*] also allowed me to extend my music educational ability to aide my students as they aspire to achieve their own personal musical goals. (Participant no. 2, first year graduated)

Some responses possessed even more altruistic qualities: "It taught me more about the Saxophone and has inspired me to set up Sax Orchestras for schools in the future" (Participant no. 6, first year graduated).

Student Opinions of Schools and Community Events

The research revealed that the students enjoyed travelling to the schools or music camps and playing "gigs" where the school audience represented diverse socioeconomies and numbered anywhere from twenty to two thousand people. In particular, 100 percent of the respondents related it as either valuable or most valuable to their understanding of music education and pedagogy (see table 18.5).

QCSO students appreciated the interactive nature of the tutorials and workshops with school students and generally labelled the engagements that only performed as "weird." As one student stated, "For most, they were only valuable if we had more engagement with the kids" (Participant no. 20, third year). In the same manner, their performance of a forty-minute contemporary soundscape for a local music festival was not nearly as highly relevant to their personal musicianship or pedagogical understanding. They reported to their director that they found it and the audience too esoteric for their musical tastes. One student's parent advised her, "It's like a Picasso—you don't question it, it just *is*" (Personal communication, July 2011).

Table 18.5. Some sample results to the question: "How would you rate the value of these experiences towards understanding music education and pedagogy?"

Category	*Not at all valuable*	*Not very valuable*	*No opinion*	*Valuable*	*Most Valuable*	*N/A*
Schools concerts and workshops, Brisbane Metropolitan Areas	0	0	0	17 (70.83%)	7 (29.17%)	0
Schools concerts and workshops, Queensland Regional	0	0	0	16 (69.57%)	7 (30.43%)	1
Schools concerts and workshops, Queensland Rural	0	0	0	14 (73.68%)	5 (26.32%)	5
Queensland Symphony Orchestra Schools Concerts, QSO 2013	0	0	2 (11.76%)	11 (64.71%)	4 (23.23%)	7
Contemporary soundscape performance	2 (16.67%)	4 (33.33%)	4 (33.33%)	2 (16.67%)	0	12
MOST Music Camp performance	0	0	4 (23.53%)	9 (52.94%)	4 (23.53%)	7

Regardless, the response to "I feel the QCSO activities that involve communities and venues outside of my tertiary institution have helped my overall progress as an undergraduate student" rated 4.26 out of a possible overall 5. Aside from citing exposure to career realities, they realized the value of networking within the community and the reliance on these people for future mutual working relationships: "It also exposes us to a broader demographic and, who knows, some of us may end up teaching at some the schools that have been visited" (Participant no. 7, third year); while those earlier in their degree retained their more introspective view: "Most musicians will teach therefore school concerts provide an insight into what teaching will be like. Performance experience in general is valuable—community and school concerts help provide this experience" (Participant no. 3, first year).

Some students expressed surprise that the community would embrace their music making: "Before doing schools concerts I didn't realise how much schools actually want us to play at their schools. I would certainly feel more confident planning a concert knowing that it will be well received" (Participant no. 15, first year).

As these questions were initially worded to discover the effect of extracurricular enterprise activities on tertiary music education, an opportunity still exists to explore the students' impression of community engagement in further depth. The community's response is perhaps even more encouraging for the students to continue this activity.

The Professional Community Perspective

From my experience, school communities always express gratitude for the time Conservatorium students take to be with their own. They appreciate their advanced musical inspiration, the close-to-school-age group, and their personal conduct. One music teacher commented that the students were not "up themselves" (an Australian slang terminology for "arrogant"; n.a. 2011). This is telling, as it reveals an elitist astigmatism and a commonly voiced concern when seeking performance opportunities for the students. By paying for the students' services, the schools also feel as though they are contributing back to the students' education, understanding that all funds go towards our touring and future teachers: "I hear you guys are going on tour? Well that is a very well-deserving cause because it benefits us in the end" (personal communication with a de-identified secondary private school instrumental teacher, March 2012). Rural communities are most enthusiastic that a group of undergraduates can be bothered to travel the distance to share music making with them.

In general, the fact that the QCSO is allowed repeat business at the schools year after year is a genuine compliment and evidence that relationships with this aspect of the community are strong and include mutual respect.

The QCSO collaboration with the Queensland Symphony Orchestra (QSO) education performances is very welcomed by their management and performing members. They communicated that the orchestral medium requires more connection with many facets of the community. In particular, they do not wish to be viewed as "out-of-date" by their potential future subscribers. As the saxophone is not considered a full-time orchestral instrument, both parties realize the opportunity to capitalize on each other's strengths. One student described it as "the QSO's kudos versus the QCSO's 'coolness.'" One QSO member exclaimed her amazement that the projects happened at all: "It is something we NEVER do! It is great for the kids in the audience and for us too!" (personal communication with de-identified QSO performer, October 5, 2013). Perhaps the most telling form of feedback from joining these communities is via word-of-mouth evidenced in the auditioning room when students are asked, "Why do you want to attend the Queensland Conservatorium?"; the answer: "To join the saxophone orchestra—I heard them play with the QSO and I loved it!" (personal communication, October 2012).

Inter/national artists' suggest they feel comfortable contacting the QCSO for joint venture proposals owing to their website, sound cloud, social media, and subsequent demonstrated professionalism. Feedback consistently describes the ensemble as an open-minded "bunch of students" with a lot of potential, a cohesive group, and a pleasure to be a part of. Their obligatory politeness aside, it is my observation that this frequency of visiting artists has helped develop a stronger saxophone community in Australia, creating networks between teaching professionals as well as students.

The Nonprofessional Community Perspective

Given the need for tour funds, as well as desire for classical students to be exposed to the jazz style useful for future employment, I sought the assistance of the Brisbane Jazz Club (BJC) to host our "Sax to the Max" event. The BJC is a restaurant venue by the Brisbane river that has cabaret seating with the opportunity to purchase drinks and food. The evening involved Stax of Sax: a metropolitan community band, a local school saxophone quartet, current Conservatorium staff, and lead professional Brisbane saxophonists. Big band charts were arranged by me and the students, and a rhythm section plus vocalist from the Conservatorium donated their services to the QCSO performances. One piece titled "Counting to Infinity," written by Grammy nominated ex-Brisbane composer Tim Davies, required a *didgeridoo* performer. Wanting to honor and include the original custodians of the land, one of the students recommended a high school student, a descendant of the Djabera Djabera tribe of the Western Australia Kimberleys, to perform with us.

The general response of those who govern the Brisbane Jazz Club (managers and volunteers) was that they were thrilled that jazz saxophone is still well received and considered such an important part of the community, particularly by classical and jazz students of the Queensland Conservatorium. As a BJC volunteer wrote in his show report:

> This all goes to prove that jazz in Brisbane is swingingly healthy and that the saxophone is way up there as one of its favourite instruments. In all we were treated to the sounds of around thirty saxophone players and at 152 people through the door it was a busy night with only one volunteer doing a great job. I'm sure that this will continue to be a great attraction and we will eagerly look forward to the next occasion. (Review: Queensland Conservatorium Saxophone Orchestra, Thursday, May 24, 2012)

The audience was comprised of all students' immediate networks in addition to those curious as to what the group could do in this medium. All remarked that it was a wonderful idea to bring the greater saxophone community together, for the younger members to aspire to the older music generation and hoped it would happen again soon. The fact that the venue was more than sold out was an additional bonus.

The Pozible crowd-funding campaign was an interesting experiment for all of us. Crowd funding can be summarized as an online rewards-based donation program where one uploads the cause description in form of a video, sets donation amounts, and attaches optional rewards to be received once the target is met. We had pitched for $10,000. Initially the students strongly resisted this idea, stating that their friends would probably like to donate but did not have any money to do so. They were not entirely convinced when I suggested that their parents do, their parents' friends do, their students' parents do, and that there was a larger community out there that might value what it was they did and recognize the educational value to all concerned. I remember that conversation very well, with me stating, "I am not liking you all for this hour" and feeling very deflated that the students were not as enthusiastic about the plan as I was.

With a well-planned campaign, to their surprise donations trickled through the site up to $7,500. Then it just stopped. With ten days to go I was concerned that we had bid too high. Pozible will only award the money if the target has been achieved within the suggested time line. An anonymous donor, a family friend of one of the students, dropped $5,000 into the site at the same time as a student's parent had deposited $50. After the parent recovered from the heart attack at mistakenly thinking that $5,000 would be charged to her Visa card, there was much celebration for all. We were going on tour to explore our international community!

As one of the crowd funding Pozible rewards we performed at the Halcyon Waters Retirement Village, situated forty-five minutes from Brisbane. The students performed two sets, with each piece introduced by a student who also talked about her/himself and their music aspirations. Here is the feedback from one enthusiastic listener:

> The concert by the kids from the Con. on Sunday was just SUPERB, SUPERB, SUPERB. We took along, as our guest, a Saxophonist who had performed both in Aust and the U.K. and this gent was able to share his wealth of knowledge with the lead alto-sax player. It also seems as if Geoffrey will find a spot in his fifteen-piece band for one of the young lads who not only had the talent but had expressed interest in joining. Please, could you give another donation to them next year so they may return! (E-mail forwarded by an audience member from the managing director of the retirement village, 2012)

During the break, the students were encouraged not just to talk among themselves but rather to go out and engage with some of the one hundred plus audience members and ask them about their interests (musical and otherwise). I had suggested that old people not only don't like being old, they don't like being made to *feel* old, so to try to connect with them as much as possible. The feedback from the concertgoers was heartening, for the head of the social club made a point of saying, "You have restored our faith in the youth of today!"

A few months after the tour the QCSO recorded a CD of all the Australian-composed works performed at the various festivals and conferences throughout the year. If anything, it was great to have a record of our hard work as well as give something back to those who had supported us, particularly the composers. One fourth-year student marveled at the development of the cohesive culture of the saxophone students: "It was pretty amazing to see everyone listening really critically and intently on the takes by the end of the sessions. No one seemed bored or disinterested—they were really wanting the best recording for everyone" (Personal communication, October 28, 2012).

The Pros and Cons of the QCSO

For a "large ensemble" the QCSO is reasonably small by comparison. The organizational planning of similar activities for a large group of eighty plus players would be heavily resource dependent not only for just those within the group but also for the interested community groups. The larger the group, the less likelihood for cohesion because of subgroups within it and the greater need for an autocratic approach by the director. As one student commented in the survey:

> The small nature of the ensemble was great for camaraderie and group togetherness. It also meant that individual opinions and ideas could be considered by the rest of the group. It was a great environment for collaboration. This was different from experiences in, say, the wind orchestra, which was larger and more traditional about the prevailing opinions always being the conductor's. (Participant no. 23, second year graduated)

This sentiment is further supported by "[the QCSO] was very open and supportive and we were like a family! Everyone pitched in and helped" (Participant no. 6, first year graduated).

However, there was a perceived downside to being such a community active ensemble: "QCSO definitely is one of the hardest working groups I have played in. We also have the most concerts and things on each semester. Mostly I enjoy how busy the group is, but it can sometimes be difficult when we have events scheduled in study week, exam week, and holidays" (Participant no. 5, third year student).

Sadly, the community, nor life as a musician, does not operate according to a university timetable. One of the oldest participants summed up her impression of the development of the group:

> I was a member when the ensemble first started and it is mind blowing to see just how far the group has come. Playing in the ensemble was a real

> life experience—from organising our own rehearsals to playing students' compositions and finding performance opportunities. It also increased a lot of students' commitment levels to their instrument and university life. Thinking back to my first year at the Con I can only recall about three [*sic*] saxophone players in total (there were more but they never showed up [to workshop]). When the saxophone orchestra started I am certain attendance increased and the saxophone community at the Conservatorium began to thrive. (Participant no. 16, third year graduated)

Discussion

Bartleet mentions "Huib Schippers' notion that behind every vibrant community music program is a 'mad' person; someone who defies all odds and madly devotes their lives to the needs of their community music group" (Bartleet 2008, 11). As mentioned in the director's autoethnographic account, if she did not consider herself a "madwoman" certainly others did. Traversing unchartered territory for QCGU ensembles such as crowd funding, QSO engagement, development of a rare genre, an all-saxophone big band, and so on for the sake of music experience and community engagement indicates, at the very least, a driven person.

However, it would appear that the students' notion of "community," the value of such, and the necessity to develop a more selfless outlook are not as universally grasped. Rather, they are based on personal development, reflection, and time spent away from the Conservatorium, as was evidenced by the older students wishing to replicate these experiences within their immediate music communities—namely schools. Indeed, the fact that the younger students chose not to comment in spite of the high personal ranking of the QCSO experiences indicates that it takes some time for them to synthesize the knowledge, comprehension, and application of these activities. This is not entirely unexpected, as Bloom's Taxonomy for Learning does suggest that the higher-order cognitive skills will stem only from a solid grounding of the lower-order cognitive skills (Anderson et al. 2001), and varying student approaches to education must be taken into consideration (Biggs and Tang 2011) when analyzing outcomes.

This also may explain why the fundamentals of music making such as "intonation," "tone," and "rhythm" ranked so highly, as these are primary concepts of focus for students preparing recital pieces, although networking with visiting artists and sharing music with school-age students did honor a higher than 83 percent response, with "sharing music with community members" ranking above "collegiality" (see table 18.4). It would appear that connecting with externals was valued slightly more highly than connecting with each other; however, this could be a result of the undergraduates outweighing the graduates and therefore skewing the results with their "youthful" outlook on such processes. This is more likely given the older students' inclusive commentary, ever-present use of the word "we" as opposed to "I," relating the group to a "family," and commenting on its ideal size for collaboration. As Kokotsaki and Hallam citing Blank and Davidson suggest: "the smaller the group the more important personal friendship seems to be" (2007, 95), such as in string quartets.

Student awareness of a community outside conservatoire walls appears to lie on a spectrum ranging from the community providing performance experience to a window into possible career futures. The latter is an example of debunking feared "possible self" (Markus and Nurius 1986) conservatoire students' perceptions of reduced music employment. As Dawn Bennett succinctly explains, "the possible selves framework holds that individuals develop both positive conceptions of hoped-for future selves as well as negative images of feared future selves" (Bennett and Freer 2012, 277). In relation to this instance, one QCSO student had not considered the possibility of becoming a community musician owing to her perception that her efforts would not be required. As her teacher, I understand that this student has since not only approached her alma mater to hire her saxophone quartet but now teaches there. Her commentary, schoolteacher, and audience feedback opens the discussion that there is an inbuilt/early understanding that strong barriers exist between conservatoires and the greater community—from feared arrogance to stereotyping "old people" to surprise that classical students can perform jazz and attract a sellout crowd. Conversely, the students' lack of faith in their community to respond to their fund-raising efforts undermines the students' confidence, demonstrating a lack of arrogance. A conservatoire elite institution appearance is by default to blame, but it can be speculated that its lack of community engagement on a greater scale helps to perpetuate it. In a Western society where music and knowledge are virtually ubiquitous and contributed by many regardless of qualifications, it makes sense that shared music-making experiences should follow suit, engaging with the energy and proactivity of up-and-coming musicians. Isolating the training of these musicians for three to four years where observation of their progress can be visited onsite may be traditional but does not reflect the current methods of music consumerism or education (Hallam and Gaunt 2012; Myles-Beeching 2010; Cutler 2010). At the very least it is reinforcing the same patronage challenges that professional orchestras are nationally experiencing (n.a. 2013).

This argument for learning beyond the curriculum and conservatoire as a community-active "student musician" versus satisfying curriculum requirements as a "music student" is reflected in another study where confusing ensemble assessment leads directors to form their own agendas of teaching music. The authors concur that it is conservatoires' broader image problem that contributes to this: "This subversion is emblematic of the current perception of Conservatoria amongst disenfranchised and frustrated musicians and academics, many of whom see the institution as either irrelevant to the current crop of media-savvy students (see Schippers 2004), or conversely, disrupting hundreds of years of conservatorium tradition through the addition of courses in popular music or business" (Harrison, O'Bryan, and Lebler 2012, 12).

As the QCSO has demonstrated, there is an opportunity to interact with a variety of community groups, enriching the student experience while supporting the Griffith University's proposed graduate attribute degree outcomes, namely, the creation of musicians who are

- knowledgeable and skilled in their disciplines;
- effective communicators and team members;
- innovative and creative, with critical judgement;
- socially responsible and engaged with their communities;
- competent in culturally diverse and international environments (n.a. 2014).

Implications

The transferability of the QCSO concept is dependent on (a) the size of the group, (b) the experience and networks of the director, and (c) the leadership capabilities within. As mentioned, the costs and logistics make it cumbersome for larger ensembles to achieve a similar model. Considering slashed education budgets and bloated curricula, programs such as these are more reliant on the industry networks of the director, plus the perceived value of the time, energy, and commitment of all participants. In addition, not all ensemble directors may have the diverse industry experience or connections that are required to create links to the community. That stated, it is not to suggest that staff and students cannot pool resources and share contacts. From experience, leadership within the group is largely understated as a productive conduit between the student and the ensemble director. As previously acknowledged, a generation gap, greater industry experience, and outlook on employment trends can create an opposing set of values between teacher and student. A higher population of "student musicians" than "music students" can create a more functional, and therefore viable, group.

Regardless, a model such as this does require a "mad person" possessing a strong vision. But the question remains, what if that mad person leaves? Could the ensemble sustain itself independently? Aside from community engagement, the enthusiasm and commitment engendered by the saxophone students has largely resulted from setting long-term, high-level goals such as inter/national conferences. Motivation tends to run high in the international touring years, with leadership from all parties, director and students, increasing. It is no coincidence that the present standard of performance exceeds those of previous years. Without this underlying motivation, the overarching message of the group's sense of existence would be unclear.

One might suggest unleashing the bachelor of music chamber music program out into the field. However, the observed differences between the educational approaches, career motivations, and stages of experiential synthesis of all participants must be taken into consideration. So long as the saxophones are in a directed and mentored environment, the formation of undirected ad hoc groups in the early stages of valuing community as relevant to their future employment, let alone education or a sense of altruism, would be risky at best. Ramifications could include negative experiences for both parties and sullying the institution's reputation, prolonging the "up itself" illusion. Further investigation into a suitable model is required.

The activities of the QCSO demonstrate a keen appreciation of connectivity with the community in the music education, entertainment, and international spheres. One observation is that this kind of activity, while mutually valuable, may be construed as more beneficial to the Conservatorium students. Indeed, it was observed that they do not fully recognize the inherent value of their activities until later years. That stated, it can be surmised that well-directed ensembles within bachelor of music curricula can enrich the lives not only of the young tertiary student musicians involved but also of those who engage with them. Further research into this area would reveal more definable outcomes.

It can be suggested that the model QCSO represents is best reserved for smaller groups that are flexible, are community focused (internally and externally), possess strong leadership from the director, and have industry connections. The short-term benefits include: (1) a creative form of music education and entertainment for all; (2) increased collegiality and cohesive tertiary departmental behavior; and (3) strengthening conservatorium–community engagement. Long-term benefits include: (1) strengthening graduate employment capabilities; (2) linkage to prospective graduate employment; (3) minimizing the "ivory tower" perception the community has of the conservatoire education system; (4) creating a healthy pro–education/community lifecycle among graduates and future conservatoire students; and (5) ensuring differentiation to other tertiary music education providers.

As tertiary music institutions become more competitive for students, and students more discerning, community engagement, support, and appreciation will be crucial if these institutions wish to sustain their core practices. Likewise, as the community identifies with the efforts these students make, the four walls of the conservatoire will become increasingly transparent.

References

Anderson, Lorin W., David R. Krathwohl, P. W. Airasian, K. A. Cruikshank, R. E. Mayer, P. R. Pintrich, Benjamin Samuel Bloom, and M. Wittrock. 2001. *A Taxonomy for Learning, Teaching, and Assessing: A Revision of Bloom's Taxonomy of Educational oObjectives, Abridged Edition.* White Plains, NY: Pearson Longman.

Bartleet, Brydie-Leigh. 2008. "Sound links: Exploring the social, cultural and educational dynamics of musical communities in Australia." *International Journal of Community Music* 1 (3): 335–356. doi:10.1386/ijcm.1.3.335_1.

———. 2009. "Community music: Australia's 'unsung hero.'" *Music Forum* 15 (4): 26–29.

Bartleet, Brydie-Leigh, Peter Dunbar-Hall, Richard Letts, and Huib Schippers. 2009. *Sound Links: Community Music in Australia.* Brisbane: Griffith University.

Bennett, Dawn, and Patrick Freer. 2012. "Developing musical and educational identities in university music students." *Music Education Research* 14 (3): 265–284. doi:10.1080/14613808.2012.712507.

Biggs, John, and Catherine Tang. 2011. *Teaching for Quality Learning at University.* 4th edition. Maidenhead, Berkshire, UK: McGraw Hill.

Chang, Heewon. 2008. *Autoethnography as Method.* Walnut Creek, CA: Left Coast Press.

Cutler, David. 2010. *The Savvy Musician: Building a Career, Earning a Living, and Making a Difference.* Pittsburgh, PA: Helius Press.

Entwistle, Noel J., and Elizabeth R. Peterson. 2004. "Conceptions of learning and knowledge in higher education: Relationships with study behaviour and influences of learning environments." *International Journal of Educational Research* 41: 407–428. doi:10.1016/j.ijer.2005.08.009.

Hallam, Susan, and Helena Gaunt. 2012. *Preparing for Success: A Practical Guide for Young Musicians.* London: Institute of Education, University of London.

Harrison, Scott. 2003. "Musical Participation by Boys: The Role of Gender in the Choice of Musical Activities by Males in Australian Schools." PhD diss., Queensland Conservatorium Griffith University.

Harrison, Scott D., Don Lebler, Gemma Carey, Matt Hitchcock, and Jessica O'Bryan. 2012. "Making music or gaining grades? Assessment practices in tertiary music ensembles." *British Journal of Music Education* 30 (1): 27–42. doi:10.1017/s0265051712000253.

Harrison, Scott, Jessica O'Bryan, and Don Lebler. 2013. "'Playing it like a professional': Approaches to ensemble direction in tertiary institutions." *International Journal of Music Education* 31 (2): 173–189. doi:10.1177/0255761413489791.

Haug, Michele Von. 2013. "Clarinets for Conservation." Retrieved from: http://www.clarinetsforconservation.org/about-us.html.

Hawkins, Jason. 2014. "OurDisk." KND Digital. Retrieved from: http://www.ourdisk.com/.

Kokotsaki, Dimitra, and Susan Hallam. 2007. "Higher education music students' perceptions of the benefits of participative music making." *Music Education Research* 9 (1): 93–109. doi:10.1080/14613800601127577.

———. 2011. "The perceived benefits of participative music making for non-music university students: A comparison with music students." *Music Education Research* 13 (2): 149–172. doi:10.1080/14613808.2011.577768.

Markus, Hazel, and Paula Nurius. 1986. "Possible selves." *American Psychologist* 41 (9): 954–969. doi:10.1037/0003-066x.41.9.954.

Myles-Beeching, Angela. 2010. *Beyond Talent, Creating a Successful Career in Music.* New York: Oxford University Press.

n.a. 2007. "Choir of hard knocks." Australian Broadcasting Commission. Retrieved from: http://www.abc.net.au/tv/hardknocks/meet/default.htm.

n.a. 2011. "Koala Net." Retrieved from: http://www.koalanet.com.au/australian-slang.html.

n.a. 2012. "Landfill Harmonic: Paraguay recycled orchestra plays instruments made out of rubbish." *The Daily Telegraph,* December 13, 2012. Retrieved from: http://www.telegraph.co.uk/news/earth/earthvideo/9742488/Landfill-Harmonic-Paraguay-recycled-orchestra-plays-instruments-made-out-of-rubbish.html.

n.a. 2013. "TSO ticket sales slump." Australian Broadcasting Commission. May 27, 2013. Retrieved from: http://www.abc.net.au/news/2013-05-27/tso-ticket-sales-down/4714286.

n.a. 2014. "Griffith Graduate Attributes." Griffith University. Retrieved from: http://www.griffith.edu.au/learning-teaching/student-success/graduate-attributes.

n.a. 2015. "Culture." Oxford University Press. Retrieved from: http://www.oxforddictionaries.com/definition/english/culture.

Nulty, Duncan D. 2008. "The adequacy of response rates to online and paper surveys: What can be done?" *Assessment & Evaluation in Higher Education* 33 (3): 301–314. doi:10.1080/02602930701293231.

Pitts, Stephanie E. 2013. "Would you credit it? Navigating the transitions between curricular and extra-curricular learning in university music departments." *Arts & Humanities in Higher Education* 12 (2–3): 194–203. doi:10.1177/1474022212473531.

Yin, Robert K. 2003. *Case study research, design and methods.* 3rd ed. Thousand Oaks, CA: Sage Publishing.

About the Contributors

Editors

Brydie-Leigh Bartleet is director of the Queensland Conservatorium Research Centre and deputy director (of research) at the Queensland Conservatorium Griffith University, Australia. She has worked on a range of national and international projects in community music, arts-based service learning with Australian First Peoples, intercultural community arts, and arts programs in prison.

Melissa Cain is an educator and musician with a passion for South East Asian and Pacific musics. She has qualifications in music, education, Indonesian, and ethnomusicology, and studied Javanese and Sundanese *gamelan* while resident in Singapore for twenty years.

Anne Power is a music curriculum expert at the University of Western Sydney. She is known for leadership in the field of professional practice and is a member of the Centre for Educational Research there.

Mari Shiobara is a professor of music education and head of the Department of Music Education and Early Childhood Education at Kunitachi College of Music in Tokyo, Japan. Educated in both Japan and the United Kingdom, she studied piano performance at the Royal Academy of Music and received both her MA and PhD in music education from the University of London Institute of Education.

Diana Tolmie has so far experienced an exciting career instigated by a Churchill Fellowship and Queen Elizabeth Trust Award. She is currently exploring academia as an associate lecturer of music studies and professional practice, and as clarinet and saxophone lecturer at the Queensland Conservatorium Griffith University.

Authors

Dawn Bennett is a Distinguished Research Fellow and director of the Creative Workforce initiative at Curtin University, Australia. Her research interests include creative labor markets, identity development, music education, and research frameworks.

Jennifer Cattermole currently lectures in ethnomusicology at the University of Otago, Dunedin, New Zealand. She is interested in researching music's role in maintaining and transforming relationships between people and between people and places.

Naomi Cooper completed her bachelor of music at the University of Western Sydney. She is now pursuing her aspirations to become a choral director.

Eugene Dairianathan is an associate professor and head of the Visual and Performing Arts Academic Group at the Singapore National Institute of Education (NIE). He was the first graduate to be awarded a PhD in music by Nanyang Technological University, Singapore.

Gillian Howell is a musician, educator, and researcher who designs and leads composition workshops, improvisation projects, and large-scale participatory events for orchestras, festivals, and schools, with newly arrived refugee and immigrant children, and in post-conflict and developing countries.

David Lines is the associate head of music and coordinator of music education at the School of Music, University of Auckland. His teaching includes a variety of music education and postgraduate research contexts across the school.

Lum Chee Hoo is the head of UNESCO-NIE Centre for Arts Research in Education (CARE), part of a region-wide network of Observatories stemming from the UNESCO Asia-Pacific Action Plan. He also coordinates the master in education (music) program and teaches courses primarily related to research in music education and primary music education in the Visual & Performing Arts Academic Group at the National Institute of Education (NIE-NTU), Singapore.

Christian Mau is a certified master and teacher of the Myōan style of *shakuhachi,* a Japanese bamboo flute. He received his master of music degree in ethnomusicology and went on to earn a PhD, both from the School of Oriental and African Studies, University of London. He is one of the founding members of the Asia Pacific Community Network (APCMN), which has held seminars in Brisbane, Australia (2013), and Tokyo, Japan (2015).

Phil Mullen is one of the world's leading community music trainers. He developed community music training at Goldsmiths College, University of London, which is the world's longest-running accredited community music training program.

Karyn Paringatai is a lecturer in Te Tumu: School of Māori, Pacific, and Indigenous Studies at the University of Otago, where she teaches Māori language and Māori performing arts.

Te Oti Rakena trained as a classical singer in the United States at New England Conservatory in Boston and received his doctorate from the University of Texas at Austin before commencing postdoctoral studies in Europe. Currently he is the associate dean Māori and Pasifika for the Faculty of Creative Arts and Industries and associate head of performance (classical) and the coordinator of vocal studies in the School of Music at the University of Auckland.

Julie Rickwood is a music and performance researcher and practitioner based in Canberra, Australia. She is currently a visiting fellow at the School of Music, Australian National University. Her research has previously concentrated on the Australian a cappella scene and the community singing movement.

Kirstin Robertson-Gillam is a registered music therapist, a social researcher, a registered nurse (general and midwifery), a registered psychotherapist/counsellor, a Tier 1 WorkCover provider, and an Employee Assistance Program counsellor.

Joanne Ruksenas is a PhD candidate at the Queensland Conservatorium Griffith University and School of Public Health at Griffith University. Her research examines the effect of active engagement in music lessons on the development of resilience in preschool children.

Leonard Tan is an assistant professor of Music at the National Institute of Education (NIE-NTU) in Singapore, where he teaches courses in music education and conducting and directs the NIE Winds.

Jennifer Walden has recently completed a doctorate at the Queensland Conservatorium Griffith University on how best to transmit diverse musics in today's classrooms.

Index